Caresse CROSBY

From Black Sun to Roccasinibalda

ANNE CONOVER

CAPRA PRESS
SANTA BARBARA

1989

Foreword by William F. Claire is reprinted with permission of Horizon Publishers, Inc.,
June 1986.

Chapter VII, in somewhat different form, first appeared in An International Journal, Vol 4,
1986, ed. Gunther Stuhlmann.

Letters from Caresse Crosby to Ezra Pound are from the Ezra Pound Archive, Collection of
American Literature, Beinecke Rare Book and Manuscript Library, Yale University.

Excerpts from *Black Sun: The Brief Transit and Violent Eclipse of Harry Crosby*, (c) 1976 by
Goeffrey Wolff, are reprinted by permission of Random House, Inc.

Typesetting by the TypeStudio, Santa Barbara.
Cover design by Graficus, Santa Barbara.

LIBRARY OF CONGRESS CATALOGING-IN-PUBLICATION DATA

Carson, Ann Conover, 1937-
Caresse Crosby : from Black Sun to Roccasinibalda.

1. Crosby, Caresse, 1892- --Biography. 2. Poets,
American--20th century--Biography. 3. Publishers and
publishing--France--Biography. 4. Americans--France--
Paris--History--20th century. I. Title.
PS3505.R865Z4 1989   811'.52 [B]   89-22054
ISBN 0-88496-302-0

CAPRA PRESS
Post Office Box 2068, Santa Barbara, California 93120

CONTENTS

FOREWORD

The name Caresse Crosby is almost unknown today. Yet Crosby was a significant figure in the fertile world of Paris publishing in the 1920s, instrumental in bringing to fruition many important works under the imprint of the Black Sun Press, and a coruscating personality in the colorful pantheon of those who came to international prominence as the so-called "Lost Generation."

In the literature, she is often overshadowed by her then-husband, Harry Crosby. The life of Harry Crosby has been well documented, most recently by Geoffrey Wolff, in his *Black Sun: The Brief Transit and Violent Eclipse of Harry Crosby*, published by Random House in 1976. Indeed Harry Crosby's life was violent, brief and, apparently, insane. But it was the question, "What happened to Caresse after Harry?" that intrigued Anne Conover. She began dedicated research into Caresse Crosby's life and times, and uncovered a fascinating woman who has received insufficient acclaim for her many contributions. Even Geoffrey Wolff, in his study of Crosby, dismissing the fascinating period of Caresse Crosby's later years in two paragraphs of his Postscript to *Black Sun*, described her as an "odd mixture of shrewdness and goofiness."

George Bernard Shaw once said, "The greatest sin is not to love or hate someone, but to be indifferent to them." And it is this indifference to Caresse Crosby that author Anne Conover has attempted to address and redress, through a study of Crosby's papers at the Morris Library, Southern Illinois University, and through in-depth interviews with leading figures all over the world who have had some association with Caresse Crosby. Her discoveries, I believe, right a serious wrong. She has rediscovered a woman ahead of her times, influential to writers and artists beyond the dreams of those who would like to influence writers and artists, and a woman who endured — often spectacularly so. Her life was filled with accomplishments of some magnitude, all carried out with a remarkable *joie de vivre*.

—William F. Claire, Poet and Publisher, *Voyages*

ACKNOWLEDGEMENTS

This book would not have been possible without the enthusiastic support of the Bennington Writing Workshops (Brian Swann, director), and especially of my mentor in the writing of Creative Non-Fiction, Scott R. Sanders, who found merit in the project and suggested a publisher. In Scott's words: "Writing is a lonely business, the most isolating of all art forms. We need to gather once in a while to share our work . . . to hear other human voices."

I am also deeply indebted to the staff of the Morris Library, Southern Illinois University at Carbondale, who were unfailingly helpful: Dr. David V. Koch, curator of Special Collections; Sheila Ryan, curator of manuscripts (for the photo research); and Shelley Cox. Beatrice Moore of Carterville, widow of Harry T. Moore, also gave freely of her time and intelligence in assisting my research.

Of the many others who gave abundantly of their efforts, I wish to thank:

Polleen Peabody Drysdale of London, Caresse's only daughter, who graciously received me and gave generously of her memories and permission to quote from her unpublished memoir;

Richard Peabody, editor of Gargoyle and D.C. Magazines: A Literary Retrospective, who put me in touch with many valuable resources (when I first contacted Rick, I assumed he was a descendant of Caresse's first husband, which he is not);

Evelyn Lazzari, widow of Pietro, who offered memories and tea and sympathy and started me off on my path of discovery;

Allegra Fuller Snyder, Buckminster Fuller's daughter, and her husband, Robert Snyder, who contributed the narration of the film, Always Yes! Caresse; Selden Rodman, for permission to quote from his unpublished diaries; Kay Boyle, Caresse's closest and only remaining friend of "the passionate years," who reviewed that portion of the manuscript;

In Paris: Henri Cartier-Bresson and Josef Erhardy;

In New York: Helen-Louise Simpson Seggerman, who contributed memories of the brownstone on East 91st Street and of her parents, the Kenneth Simpsons; Andreas Brown of the Gotham Book Mart, and the late Frances Steloff, whose memory remained extraordinarily clear and faithful into her 90s; Buffie Johnson, Bertha Klausner, Priscilla Morgan, David Porter, Sam Rosenberg, George Stillwaggon, and Dorothea Tanning Ernst;

Of the Washington years: Ellen Barry, Garry Davis, the late Major Howard "Pete" Powel, Mrs. Raymond Piland of Bowling Green, Va. (owner of Hampton Manor); and Lucy Keith Tittman (of Concord, Mass.), who lived at 2008 Q Street in the '50s and shared her letters and memories.

In Italy: the late Roloff Beny and Robert Mann; Giuseppi Picchi, mayor of the Commune of Roccasinibalda; Giuseppi de Stefani, owner of the

Castello; and Dr. Luigi Ceccarelli, the accommodating friend who put me in touch;

Also special thanks to Desmond O'Grady of Kinsale, County Cork, Ireland, and Professor Sy M. Kahn of the University of the Pacific, who filled in the gaps on Caresse's life at the Italian "Center for Creative Arts and Humanist Living";

Walter Phelps Jacob of Cape Elizabeth, Maine, Caresse's only surviving brother, who despite "the considerable age differential" and the "very different worlds lived in by Sister Poll and myself," received me and reminisced about the Jacob family; and Josette Spiero, Caresse's daughter-in-law, for memories of "Billy" Peabody.

Others who were contacted for briefer interviews, in person, by mail, or by telephone, were: Malcolm Cowley, Larry Allen (childhood friend of Romare Bearden), Catherine Hios (sister of Michael Lekakis), the late Sarah Hunter Kelly, Robert Payne, Ted Peckham, Florence Tamburro, Arthur Wagmann, Volkmar Kurt Wentzel, Billie Wills, and Mrs. Theodore Watson (Leonard Jacob's widow). Of those who died almost on the eve of an interview — most recently Isamu Noguchi and Edward Weeks — Romare Bearden, Salvador Dali, Archibald MacLeish, Harry T. Moore, and Helen Simpson: their loss is felt on these pages.

With grateful appreciation to George Robert Minkoff for providing a rare copy of the Bibliography of the Black Sun Press; the late George Butterick of the University of Connecticut, Storrs, who provided access to the Charles Olson letters (and to Charles Boer, who catalogued them); to Edith Wynner, who introduced me to the Schwimmer-Lloyd Colllection on World Peace at the New York Public Library; to Marc Pachter, assistant director of the National Portrait Gallery (author of Telling Lives) for his helpful suggestions and for the support of the members of the Washington biographers' group.

To Derek W. Marlow, who visited Roccasinibalda in the '60s and suggested Caresse as a subject;

To Dr. Karen Shanor, who helped to explore Caresse's psyche, and who encouraged me through the birthing process;

To Veronica Wilding-White, who began the word processing of the manuscript; and to Mary W. Matthews, who finished it, without whose intelligence, skill, good humor, and long hours at the computer we could not have gone to press on schedule;

To Noel and Judith Young and Lynn Maginnis of Capra Press, who shared my enthusiasm and were the "wind at my back" in seeing the manuscript through to hard cover;

To Hugh M. Pinkerton, William Paul Pinkerton, and "Polly" Parsons Pinkerton, who taught me the beauty of the English language; and to my mother, Louise Pinkerton Conover, who inspired me to write it;

To my daughter, Natalie Ambrose, and to my husband, Thomas B. Carson, neglected during the many months from prologue to finis, but without whose cooperation and love I could not have stayed the course.

PROLOGUE

Her name was Mary, but they called her Caresse. In the Romance languages, Cara, Caresse, Caressissima all mean "a giver of love." Her friend Anaïs Nin described her as "a pollen carrier," one who "mixed, stirred, brewed and concocted friendships together, who encouraged artistic and creative copulation in all its forms and expressions, who trailed behind her, like the plume of peacocks, a colorful and fabulous legend."

And the way she walked! Aging Don Juans, savoring the conquests of some 50 years before, still remember the feline grace of those racy legs, the well-rounded derrière. She was petite, but she carried herself well, with a touch of class, of character, of Back Bay Boston. From whatever perspective one viewed her, Caresse sailed into a room, and if there wasn't excitement in it, she created it.

She had classic cheekbones and beautiful, translucent skin. A mass of dark waves, cropped short, framed a pert face with a fringe of bangs. Her eyes — which bewitched lovers described as "wayward" — were a fathomless seablue-green. She focussed them directly on her victims with curiosity and delight and a hint of mockery, the frequent façade of a "flapper" peering over a *coupe* champagne glass saying, "Here's looking at you!" Whatever "It" was, Caresse had it.

She dressed — sometimes outrageously — in bright-colored "costumes," always with flair. In the frontispiece of one of her slim volumes of poetry, Caresse is reclining on a chaise longue like the Empress Eugenie, swathed in a Roman toga. She appears strikingly contemporary in fading photographs wearing a chic cloth-of-gold evening suit by Vionnet, a man-tailored dinner jacket accented by a large lace jabot, an above-the-knee skirt. She walked, cat-like, into a Faubourg St. Germain drawing room leading Narcisse Noir, the black whippet, whose gold-lacquered toenails matched his gold necklace. As an American expatriate in Paris, Caresse provided titillation, excitement, and innovation to moribund Proustian characters in their ancestral homes.

In the '20s, Caresse led the procession of atelier students to the Quatre Arts balls, stripped to the waist as an Inca princess. Even her then-husband Harry did not recognize the exquisite *nichons* in the passing throng on the Boul' St. Germain. She picked a fight with Picasso. She dreamed up a Surrealist Ball for Dali. A Paris press report announced, "*Caresse Crosby à l'inventé le soutien-gorge — et Hemingway.*" And if she did not quite *invent* Hemingway, she founded an avant-garde Left Bank publishing house that printed Ernest and Scott, and many other titans of her time — Lawrence, Pound, and Joyce.

She consorted with counts and lords and the Maharanee of Cooch Behar and Mahatma Gandhi. And when Harry shot himself in a suicide pact with the Other Woman — a "Fire Princess" — Caresse retaliated by saying "Yes!" to life and to some 200 lovers, and all of them *special*. She never looked back. She never turned to stone.

In the spring of Holy Year, 1950, Caresse was traveling some 40 miles northeast of Rome on the Via Salaria, the ancient route since the time of Caesar, by which salt gathered along the seacoast was carried to the capital. (A good worker was "worth his salt" in Rome's heyday.) Her destination was a massive eagle-shaped fortress spreading its wings above the Turano River that winds like a ribbon through the Sabine Hills. Every peak is topped by a legend — Farro Sabina (where the Sabine women were raped), Farro Nerola (where Nero was born), Farro Ornaro (where Beatrice Cenci was held prisoner by her lord and master). The villagers say the Castello is haunted by a genuine ghost, "La Donna Bianca," whose eerie cries can be heard as she paces the battlements lamenting her lost lover. And across the valley that first night, Caresse swore that she saw a white, luminous form on the highest turret, vague and indistinct, but surely *there*.

Caresse still qualifies as an interesting woman. Her short, softly-waved hair is sprinkled with white, but her eyes still bewitch. She walks with a quick step, impulsively. Even after the long journey, she appears fresher than anyone else. It was not lost on Caresse that this was "the summit" of her life, that the Castello — and the title of Principessa that goes with the territory — was a spectacular *finis* to a fascinating life story. The feudal estate of Roccasinibalda and its titles passed through the hands of Popes Clement VII and Paul IV and a number of noble families, but despite wars, plagues, neglect, and time, the Castello endures.

By what circuitous route did this "chargée d'affairs of the heart of the world" (to quote Anaïs) arrive in the Sabine Hills? For the moment we shall leave her there. . .

"Those who restrain desire do so because it is weak enough to be restrained."

— WILLIAM BLAKE

Chapter I

THE PASSIONATE YEARS

Mary Peabody first noticed Harry Crosby emerging from the subway station in Copley Square. At first glance, he was a slight man, of middle height, almost ungainly in an American Field Service uniform. But she "caught a look so completely *right* that from that moment, I sensed my destiny . . . ." ("He didn't look like anybody else on the street . . . or anywhere. He was just *different*.")

Mary wasn't sure he had noticed *her*. Yet the next morning, Harry's mother, Henrietta, telephoned to ask if Mary might chaperone her 21-year-old son, a Harvard undergraduate, and a dozen or so of his friends on an Independence Day outing at Nantasket Beach. Everyone in Boston knew about Mary's sad plight. They considered her husband, Richard Peabody, yet another casualty of the Great War. He had returned with body intact, but mind out of focus. He tried to replace the close calls and life-threatening thrills of war by chasing fire trucks; to erase the nightmare of mangled bodies by drinking himself to oblivion.

With Dick away at a sanitarium, Mary's social life suffered. Henrietta Crosby felt sorry for the attractive young woman kept tightly at home with her parents-in-law and two small children. That night, she seated Mary on Harry's right at dinner. He never spoke once to the girl on the left. Afterwards, at Nantasket's amusement park, they cuddled in a small boat through the Tunnel of Love, and Harry first said, "*I love you.*"

In Harry's observations on the dynamics of love, he wrote that "a love affair should be as delicate and as swift as a modern pursuit plane." For almost three years he pursued Mary. The fact that she was seven years older and married, to a member of their same social set, with two small babies, never deterred him. He first tried persuasion and vowed a life of good deeds. When that failed, he threatened to kill himself.

This frightened Mary, who also wavered under the censorious gaze of the Boston matriarchs. ("What might one expect of a young woman who cut her hair in a sensational Castle bob, wore monkey fur, and fishnet stockings—and worse!—painted her fingernails pink!") It was more than a year before she sued Dick Peabody for divorce; by that time, the Crosbys had shipped Harry off to France.

Harry, at 19, had seen his best friend, "Spud" Spaulding, ripped open by artillery fire at Verdun. In his diary, he commemorated that fateful day—November 22, 1917—when he "metamorphose from boy into man" and won the Croix de Guerre. Carrying buckets of amputated limbs from a makeshift operating table, he vowed that if he survived in one piece, he would LIVE the rest of his life—on his own terms. "Most people die of a sort of creeping common sense," he wrote, "and discover when it's too late that the only things one never regrets are one's mistakes."

—BUNNY CAN'T STAND ANOTHER DAY WITHOUT YOU STOP SAILING AQUITANIA STEERAGE STOP ENGAGED BRIDAL SUITE RETURN TRIP STOP SAY YES YOUR HARRY STOP—

Once determined on a course, he would not give up the chase. He bet his Paris flat-mate, Lou Norrie—booked for a September 1 sailing home—$100 that he could beat Norrie to Manhattan and at last persuade "Polly" Peabody to marry. The odds were even. Lou arrived in New York, and Harry, who had bribed his way aboard the *Aquitania*, was on the dock to meet him—with Mary. Before she changed her mind, Harry rushed them both to the Municipal Building just before closing on September 9, 1922, where Leonard Jacob, Mary's younger brother, was waiting to give the bride away. (Norrie stood by with the $100, as promised, for the honeymoon.) There was time for a whirlwind round-trip train ride to Washington, D.C., for a strained audience with the grande dame, Henrietta Crosby (staying with Harry's married sister, Kitsa), after which Mary reported that she was made to feel like a two-year-old who had gotten into a forbidden jam jar.

Back in New York, Grandmother Jacob waited at the Belmont with the children's devoted nanny and the little Peabodys, their small Vuitton suitcases packed for the return trip.

"It had to be that way—I wouldn't leave my children behind," Mary insisted.

The passenger manifest for the return trip listed Mr. and Mrs. Henry Grew Crosby, née Mary Phelps Jacob. Passengers noticed the strung-taut young man with intense blue eyes and the attractive woman by his side, obviously on their honeymoon. Theirs was an unusual ménage. An Irish nanny in sensible shoes shared the adjoining stateroom with a towheaded boy just turning six, and Polleen, a girl of almost five. The 24-year-old groom appeared much too young to be their father. Their mother, Billy, had committed the unthinkable treason of divorcing a scion of one of Boston's proudest clans, sailing with her two children and star-crossed lover to the City of Light. "I became a rebel when I married, Harry," she often said.

The Crosbys joined that flock of post-World War I escapists from Puritan backgrounds on Paris' Left Bank. A revolt was growing among young Americans, disillusioned with provincial stuffiness and mores. The expatriates who alighted near the old church of St. Germain des Prés were the vanguard of Gertrude Stein's so-called "Lost Generation." (The difference was that Harry's Uncle Jack (J. Pierpont) Morgan provided a post with the family bank on the Place Vendôme, and his cousin, Walter Berry, intimate friend of Marcel Proust and Edith Wharton, promised letters of introduction to the *gratin, gratin* of the Faubourg St. Germain.)

Fresh off the boat, the young Crosbys took furnished rooms at the Hôtel de l'Université, near the Sorbonne. There were two stuffy cubicles with paper-thin walls—smaller and less glamorous than the boat—and too close together to obliterate the children's noisy laughter during their parents' passionate lovemaking. Harry's first diary entry following the wedding noted a popular French novel of that day, *Les Desenchantées*. In the margin he wrote, in his elliptical scrawl, "Am I?" Harry really wanted an experienced married mistress, not the mother of two. And Mary's loyalty was forever divided between love for her children and infatuation with Harry. Harry usually won out.

At last—with the help of Morgan et Cie.—Mary found more suitable housing for their menage on the bourgeois rue Belles Feuilles, where the children would be out of sight when Harry came home—for breakfast, lunch, and dinner—ready for *amour*. By blocking a door from the front hall to the nursery, Mary solved many problems. But to see the children, she had to go around back through the kitchen, up the back stairs. That routine worked rather well, with one compromise—twice a week, the children were allowed to play jumping games in the sacrosanct boudoir before the *bonne à tout faire* changed the sheets. One Friday, Harry returned early from the bank with college chums and viewed the lively scene.

"My God! What a nursery!" he howled. His face flushed scarlet with anger. He did not return for three days.

Mary, devastated, thought her marriage had ended as spontaneously as it had begun. But to Harry's credit, when he did come back, he was laden with gifts for the children, and a cloth-of-gold Mandarin coat for Mary.

Polleen later recalled her life "blessed and burdened by eccentric, wildly self-indulgent parents." The first time Harry really noticed her:

> I was about six years old at the time, sitting on the steps taking off my shoes, when Harry suddenly appeared.
>
> "Why are you taking off your shoes?" he asked.
>
> "So you can't hear me," I answered, eyes downcast. "I'm not supposed to make noise."
>
> He thought that was hilariously funny. Immediately, he scooped me up and put my shoes on and rushed me off to the Ritz Bar. It amused him that other customers looked on disapprovingly, as I was given glass after glass of champagne until I was giddy. I was taken home absolutely blotto. That was the beginning of our friendship.

Mary was determined to avoid future escapades at the Ritz Bar. She sent Nanny home and hired a French widow, Mme. Doursenaud, as governess. The much-beloved *Petite Mère* was rechristened "Doosenoose" by the children, and for several years, she provided the love and attention their parents never found time for. Polleen and her brother Billy were packed off with Doosenoose to the more wholesome environment of a *pension* near Versailles that summer.

With the children away, the long-delayed, romantic honeymoon began. They moved to a dramatic setting on the Ile St. Louis, the towers of Notre Dame framed between their bedroom windows. Harry's transportation problem was easily solved by tying a red canoe below at the dock on the Quai d'Orleans. At 8:15 each morning, Mary climbed into her bathing costume, and with Harry stashed in the stern, she paddled their "crimson bark" to the Place de la Concorde. Harry stepped off with his briefcase to walk a few blocks to the Banque Morgan. Mary pulled hard against the oars going home upstream: "Good for the breasts," she said, when whistles greeted her from the bridges overhead. While Harry was at the Bank, Mary loved browsing and marketing in the twisty back streets of the Ile. Every night was like room 943 at the Belmont all over again. Harry recorded in his diary: "Pink intimate nightgown. Kissing. Loving. *Over the top with Polly!! Marvelous!*"

A Puritan conscience was inexplicably missing from Mary's passionate nature. Once awakened, she enjoyed a pagan's sensual delight in lovemaking. She was a giver, and she could never give enough to the man she loved—at that moment. "Once one has known rapture, security is not enough," she explained to her critics. The reason she left Boston and Dick Peabody was clearly not because of Dick's drinking problem. It was *"to marry the man I love."* From the first moment to the last—only seven short years—"My love for Harry blinded me like a sunrise. It joined me to him indivisibly, like wind to storm," she recalled 30 years later.

When the leaves began to turn that autumn, and the chestnut vendors set up their stalls on the streets, the Crosbys moved to Pavillon No. 1, rue Boulard, behind the historic Cimetiêre Montparnasse. Mary fantasized about the lovers on the tombs who were joined in eternal repose. The Pavillon was only two rooms deep, but it had a picket fence, a garden gate, a vegetable plot, trees, a sundial, and a flagged terrace to remind them of home.

Harry remained irrevocably opposed to any signs of domesticity. At his suggestion, the outside tool shed was reserved for the nursery. (That Polleen did not catch pneumonia, Mary admitted, was a "tribute to her cheery adaptability.) After the first year, Billy was trundled off to one elite boarding school after another—Le Rosay in Switzerland, later Cheam in Surrey.

Several years of cramped quarters in furnished flats became increasingly difficult, until Mary discovered new lodgings in a more accessible and orderly part of Paris—accessible for Harry and orderly for me," she commented. Thus her New England upbringing triumphed briefly. They settled into an 18th-century hôtel (townhouse/mansion) at 19 rue de Lille, in the aristocratic Faubourg St. Germain *quartier* where the characters in Proust's novels might have lived, loved and entertained. No. 19 has been designated an historic monument with a plaque commemorating *Charles Fioquet, Deputé de Paris, qui est mort dans cette maison 16 janvier 1896*. Christie's, the antique dealer, occupies the ornate building next door. Then as now, hôtels were converted into three-storied apartments, the entrances marked by massive doors between columns topped by large sandstone urns overflowing with chiseled fruit and garlands of flowers. There is a vast porte-cochère with a concierge's lodging on one side of the courtyard paved with cobblestones. In the past, elegant horse-drawn carriages drew up to the marble steps. Through vaulted windows which face on the small, formal garden in the rear, one can still see sculpted woodwork and crystal chandeliers perilously dangling from bas-relief ceilings.

The children, when home, and servants were banished to the *rez-de-chausée* near the entrance. Up the first flight of stairs was a formal drawing room—seldom used—a vast, so-called Sicilian dining room, master bedroom, and bath. The latter was an ornate affair with inlaid wood and a fireplace, the massive, sunken marble tub large enough to accommodate the Crosbys and several guests.

On the third floor, Harry's library ran the length of the wing, with three windows opening onto the balcony overlooking the narrow *rue*, so narrow that the mansard roof of the building opposite almost overlapped. Harry called his library the *tour grise*, not only because of its gray walls, but because of the collected clutter—animal skins, spears, chests, ship models and a skeleton, its St. Jerome's head with hollow ghoul's eyes welcoming trepidatious intruders.

The exchange rate had risen from 5 to 22 francs to the dollar, when Archibald MacLeish, an old friend, visited them. He remembered that the rue de Lille menage was "very comfortable, but not grand or grandiose" for its time and place. The Crosbys had evolved a comfortable "Upstairs, Downstairs" way of life, reminiscent of Beacon Street, adapted to the unconventional milieu in which they now lived.

Their good friend Gerard Lymington (later Earl of Portsmouth) recalled his most vivid memories of the 1920s at 19 rue de Lille, where one might meet André Gide, or Hart Crane, or Goops the Gunman, models from Chanel, bookies or photographers, artists or

Archibald MacLeish; where the party that began on Wednesday persisted throughout the weekend. Guests were "a purée of wit, beauty, and bitchery." (Mary herself was absolutely without malice, her friends agreed, but she was quoted often as saying that "a woman without bitchery is like milk without Vitamin D!")

"*Paris* is a bitch," amended Robert McAlmon, one of their frequent guests, a chronicler of the Paris scene. "One shouldn't become infatuated with bitches . . . particularly when they have wit, imagination, experience, and tradition behind their ruthlessness."

The next year, Harry decided to resign from the Bank to devote his entire efforts to writing poetry. In Mary's view, the life of a poet promised more immediate joy and possible fame than the life of a partner of Morgan et Cie., with "a fat income and a life on the Park Avenues of the world." ("Money weighed very little in the balance of my decisions . . . our inherited incomes of a few thousand dollars were carrying us along very nicely . . . .") Tongue-in-cheek, they wired Harry's father in Boston: "Sell ten thousand in stock. We have decided to live mad and extravagant lives."

In Stephen Crosby's view, his son had committed the second deadly sin of dipping into capital to become a dilettante. His reply: "I assume that the idea of your writing poetry as a life's work is a *joke . . . .*"

Some 3,000 miles away, the young Crosbys were indeed serious about poetry. Inspired by a recent reading of T.S. Eliot's *The Wasteland*, Harry replied to his father:

> . . . Perhaps it is: "we intend to lead mad and extravagant lives" that upset you . . . . There is, I think, a crime in ending life the way so many people do, with a *whimper*. When we think of the comets and meteors and the moon and the stars and planets and the sun all whirling far above us in the great harmony of the spheres, how trivial become dinner parties and auction bridge . . . the investing and selling of stock. For the poet, there is love and there is death . . . and for other things to assume such vital importance is out of the question . . . that is why I refuse to take the question of money seriously.

Harry found his champion and mentor in his cousin, Walter Berry, a distinguished man of letters respected in Parisian social and literary circles. Even Stephen Van Rensselaer Crosby could not look down his aristocratic beak at Walter Van Rensselaer Berry, himself descended from General Stephen Van Rensselaer and the original patroon of New York.

At 76, Berry was the epitome of elegance in an Edwardian morning coat, striped trousers, and highly polished black-button shoes, his small head poised above a high wing-collar like a brilliant bird, given to sudden turnings and bright glances. In an enduring friendship and lifelong correspondence with Marcel Proust, the novelist had written to Berry: "You must choose the art wherein it seems . . . most creditable to have displayed an 'unrivaled ability.' Is it eloquence? Is it style? You have so many intellectual gifts that one is confronted with the difficulty of making a choice."

Berry advised his young cousin to follow his own inclinations: "I'm so glad you chucked the Bank! If this keeps up, you'll have better things in your account that fat $$$'s," Berry wrote. Thus began a surrogate father-and-son relationship that continued until Berry's death four years later, when Harry was designated to take charge of the pomp and circumstance of Berry's funeral cortege and became the legatee of his magnificent library of rare books.

Until Harry discovered Cousin Walter, Uncle Jack Morgan had been the greatest man in America in his nephew's eyes. But despite the Morgan bank loan of two billion dollars to France and the other war-ravaged countries of Europe, Harry now wrote to his mother: "Uncle Jack is as *unstimulating* as Berry is stimulating. Uncle Jack is interesting to talk to, but altogether devoid of the spark which *inspires*."

Berry viewed his cousin as unshaped clay that he took pleasure in molding. In his new role as mentor, he suggested that Harry write a biography of Rimbaud, one of their mutual passions. He advised Harry to "put aside daily hours for work and stick to them regularly," if he wished to become a poet.

A lifelong bachelor, Berry was gallant with women and enjoyed amorous "flirtations" with the young belles of the day. He responded warmly to the admiration of his cousin's vivacious wife, and invited Mary to sit at the head of the table when he entertained at his stately mansion on the rue de Varenne, thus displacing Edith Wharton who, having given up hope of a brilliant marriage to Berry, had settled into the role of official hostess.

"By our background, we were privileged, by our actions we were ostracized: but [for our work], we gradually came to be recognized," Mary wrote. Her creative bent was first manifested in sculpture under the renowned master, Antonine Bourdelle, at the Atelier de la

Grande Chaumière, where she held her own among far more gifted students, Isamu Noguchi and Alberto Giacometti. There, she sculpted the most revealing likeness of Harry extant, a glimpse of the private persona behind the façade, a look that only she could capture: "more expression and mood than man, electric with rebellion." At the atelier she began lifelong friendships with other painters and artists and the master, Fernand Léger, who inspired the renowned coterie.

As a lonely child, she confided her innermost thoughts and feelings to verse, but she never considered these immature outpourings publishable. That summer, in a little whitewashed villa at Etretat ("square, like a cube of Domino sugar") perched among rocky cliffs and dunes with gulls swooping overhead—the view that inspired a generation of Impressionist painters and poets—Mary took up her pen again.

Harry cherished a photograph that dates back to that time, side by side, their hands linked, with Mary in profile smiling adoringly at Harry. He inscribed it prophetically: "You and me at Etretat. It is perfect, and if we ever get to be famous, we should destroy all others in favor of this one." Mary appears strikingly contemporary in a sleeveless plaid cotton sundress with blouson top, skirt falling just below the knee to reveal sun-browned skin; an Oriental-print *para sol* protecting her eyes against the glare of the hot noonday sun. Harry, in a rumpled white double-breasted suit (carelessly cut, falling two inches above his shoe tops), squints nearsightedly into the light. There is no distinguishing characteristic to mark this photo above all others, save as a remembrance of a happy time; they were just embarking on new careers and particularly in tune with each other, in full sun. Estrangement and the variable storms of winter would come later. But the diary entry for that summer interlude recorded: "Mary . . . looking very pretty and younger than ever. Everyone adores her . . . I most of all."

Characteristically, whatever Mary did, Harry was sure to follow. He began to write for the first time in the disciplined sonnet form. Mary recorded: "The next week we spent composing sonnets to each other in traditional iambic pentameter."

Back on the rue de Lille, Harry struck out in new directions for himself. "While I wrote in my own room," Mary remembered, "I could hear his light footsteps passing overhead in the *tour grise* as though he were training for the 'big race.' His steps had a good thoroughbred sound. I was sure he was going to win. My bets were already down."

After several attempts at publication by the "little" magazines and commercial publishing houses, the Crosbys decided that the simplest way to get a poem into a book was to print the book themselves. The Black Sun Press was born, "the foal of necessity out of desire." What began as a simple literary dabbling evolved into a serious commitment to practice and support literature and the arts. If to the proper Bostonians the Crosbys' lifestyle appeared to be selfish and hedonistic, the press they established was to become a serious vehicle for creative literary and artistic expression, in itself a work of art.

"Writing is not a game played
according to rules"

—HARRY

Chapter II

BLACK SUN PRESS

Roger Lescaret, printer of birth announcements and wedding invitations, must have wondered what benevolent fate guided two elegant young Americans to look through his fly-specked window at the shop on the bend of the rue Cardinale, 200 yards from the Deux Magots, the outdoor café-cum-club frequented by Hemingway and other improvident expatriates. The day they arrived on the doorstep simultaneously with Lescaret, he had been delivering printing orders on his bicycle:

> . . . a bird-like little fellow in a black printer's smock came to a very sudden stop . . . a fringe of unruly hair hung over his clouded glasses . . . he seemed quite unaware of the smudges on his face, as he took a huge iron key from the folds of his black alpaca, and opened wide . . . his domain. There was a desk bang up in front of the door and three straight uncompromising chairs . . . already occupied by toppling piles of printed matter . . .

Harry stooped to avoid the beams overhead as he entered.

"You do your own work?" he asked.

"*Oui, monsieur.* All except for the young girl *en haut.*" He pointed to the ladder at his back, leading to a loft which later would become the Crosby editorial office.

"And you print by hand?" Harry continued.

"Entirely," Lescaret answered, pointing to the old-fashioned hand press protected by a large cloth cover. "I cannot afford another."

Harry suggested that their job would be a large one; he soon might be able to afford a new press.

Lescaret protested, "A *whole book* is a lot of work!"

The Crosbys asked him to copy the layout and typography of the handsome deluxe edition from their own library they spread out before him.

Lescaret's confidence returned.

"*Mais oui, mais oui!* But it will be *très cher,* the paper alone; and *astrée italic,* we must buy special type."

Harry assured Lescaret that the cost was no object, the quality of workmanship was more important.

Roger Lescaret was a man with the skills of a master printer and deep pride in his craft. Two days later, he responded by producing proofs that exceeded all expectations, to the obvious surprise and delight of the Crosbys. Thus began a long-standing and successful literary collaboration that was to continue for more than 20 years.

To begin, Mary toyed with designs for the colophon of her first slim volume of lyrics, to be called "Crosses of Gold." One of her first considerations was the name to imprint on the title page. The nickname "Polly" she considered unpoetic, too reminiscent of Boston and the Peabodys. The bluestocking Mary Peabody nobody used but the bank. Harry always referred to Mary as "Bunny" or "The Cramoisy Queen" in his diary. He suggested a new pen name to go with her artistic persona. They consulted the dictionary for names beginning with the alliterative "C" to go with Crosby and "to form a cross with mine," Harry added. "Cara" was close, but they dismissed it as sounding too harsh. "Caresse" with a final "e" to conform to French usage was Harry's final creation; it sounded right. Thus, at 32, Mary Peabody was born again as Caresse Crosby.

The change was registered at the *mairie,* and announcements were dispatched to the family in Massachusetts. Outraged comments arrived by return mail from the Boston matriarchs: "It's like undressing in public," one cousin replied. Undaunted, Caresse linked her new name with Harry's in a golden cross for the colophon.

Of the evocative poems from the collection of Caresse Crosby's early verse, "One Way Like the Path of a Star" emerged as an interesting example. Eulogizing the great lovers of the past—Tristan and Iseult, Thisbe and Pyramus—she draws the comparison with Harry and Caresse, contemporary lovers, who "choose the immortal path of love's bright star," going "hand in hand against the unknown . . . Forever to be, Harry and Caresse."

The critics were kind. *Poetry* of London caught Caresse's irresistible *joie de vivre:*

> . . . a book that shows none of the pretentious gravity of the minor poet. Rather, it is a devout and joyous wantonness. It shows that there is one, at least, upon whom the shadow of our smoke-palled civilization has not fallen . . . if we do well to sorrow for those who weep, we must do well to rejoice that there are others whose laughter is naked and unashamed . . . . We may thank God for a poet who is intoxicated by the beauty of the world around her, wherever she may be.

Cousin Walter encouraged Caresse to submit her work to a commercial publisher. "I shouldn't change a word, but if I were you, I'd send it off, exactly as it is, to Houghton-Mifflin in Boston. . . . They have just lost Amy Lowell," he suggested.

"But I'm not in *her* class," Caresse protested.

"You're a lady poet from Boston . . . that's a beginning," Berry replied.

Such acclaim was heady wine for the young poet. She began to plan the next publication, Harry's "Sonnets for Caresse." Caresse, the designer, chose the paper, the typeface, the layout of the second handsomely-bound volume of *Editions Narcisse.* With a typical blend of serious intent and fey whimsical humor, they named their first imprint after the black whippet, Narcisse Noir. Caresse designed a pool-gazing Narcissus for the title page.

For the young publishers, dropping into Lescaret's small shop to see the pages emerge from the hand-worked press became an irresistible new diversion. The next two volumes of poetry, *Painted Shores* by Caresse and *Red Skeletons* by Harry, were more professional than the first private love messages and illustrated with attractive designs. In *Painted Shores,* Caresse's verse is still personal and provocative:

> All of the day's delight
> And half of the moon's mad rise
> I fling at the feet of "I saw you once
> With deception in your eyes."

This title poem was inspired by Harry's current liaison—only one of many through their chaotic years together—this time, with Polia Chentoff, the Polish artist, who had just completed portraits of both Crosbys. Polia's portrait of Harry, Caresse thought "strange and portentous." Later, when the poet St. John Perse saw Caresse's portrait by Chentoff, he remarked, "I've never seen the distaste of one woman for another so skillfully and subtly portrayed."

Another poem revealed a disquieting personal life, an outwardly giddy façade superimposed on a suffering psyche:

> For you remember that the voyage was made
> To be a holiday of flight and thought
> Since we have loved and learnt, and wept and played,
> Have we not realized everything we sought?
>
> Though you and I, my heart, are sealed with pain,
> Would we not turn and seek it all again?

Caresse also dedicated a poem to her maestro, Antonine Bourdelle, who responded with this tribute: "I am very touched by your kind thought . . . . Your poetry is very beautiful and emanates from your luminous and spiritual personality . . . . The artist and the poet, the two are one . . . ."

The frontispiece portrait by Manolo Ortíz showed the author reclining on a divan in a toga-like gown. Her friend Kay Boyle captured and interpreted Caresse's persona:

> Everything you write has that almost distressingly feminine and alluring *you*. Your letters are like bits of powder puff and a lovely smell—that graciousness of offering one's young, strong lovely arm to help old gentlemen crossing streets—and you, like a very arrogant little figurehead carved in wood on the prow of a ship, going straight through the waves, because you are at the head of an adventure. Well, the poems have all of this, all of that enchantment in life.

The Crosbys first met Boyle through the Jolases' circle of writers. (In time, Harry was listed on the masthead of *transition*, the avant-garde magazine the Jolases published.) Boyle was then living in the artists' colony in Neuilly founded by eccentric, toga-wearing Raymond Duncan. According to Caresse, Kay was "built like a blade," her black hair "arranged with panache to one side, her silver-green eyes the color of moss accented an oval face with high cheekbones like a Seminole maiden."

Eugene Jolas had described the Crosbys to Kay as "madder than hatters and freer than the wind." Boyle provided this vignette of her first meeting with her future publishers and lifelong friends:

> That very early morning (two or three o'clock, it must have been) Eugene Jolas took me to the Bal Nêgre to meet Caresse and Harry Crosby . . . we eventually found them on the perilously high and crowded balcony of the night-club that had become the current rage (it being the thing to have two or three negro friends, provided they were in the jazz scene) . . . Caresse and Harry were drinking champagne, talking, laughing . . . looking down on the chaos of the dance arena below . . . . The Bal Nêgre, near dawn, the wildly stepping dancers with no more than an inch between the coupled men and women . . . are as vividly alive to me today as a Lautrec canvas; the saxophone wails louder and louder, the beat of the drums is almost deafening. In the white blaze of the lights . . . I see the features of Caresse's face, her bronze hair cut in a bang across her forehead, and Harry's face, already then committed to the look of the skull he paid daily and nightly homage to in the rue de Lille . . . .

Harry's poetry, in time, was more significant, more *driven*. *Red Skeletons* was inspired by his reading of Poe, Mallarmé, and his idol, Rimbaud. One sonnet was dedicated to Baudelaire: "Within my soul, you've set your blackest flag." Bearing such titles as "Necrophile," "Lit de Mort," and "Uncoffined," with grotesque illustrations created by the Hungarian artist Alastair, his verse was far more than an exercise in the macabre. Rather, Harry wanted to exorcise the war experience. One critic perceptively commented, "It was a litmus paper of his life, past and present."

Edgar Allen Poe's *Fall of the House of Usher* (also illustrated by Alastair) was next, the production by which the Crosbys' press broke into the English and American markets. For the first time, the credit page read *Maître Imprimeur Lescaret*. In limited edition, Poe's *oeuvre* was an artistic success. In recognition of their determination to expand the publishing venture, the Crosbys changed the name of *Editions Narcisse* to the Black Sun Press. The new name was indebted to Harry's favorite color, black, and his idolatrous worship of the Sun God, Ra. At this time also Harry began to adopt the eccentric habits that followed throughout his brief life—black suits, a black cloth flower in his buttonhole, wire-thin black whippets and black racehorses.

Kay Boyle recognized that Harry was one of the early social dissidents. His black was

> . . . more of a means of blacking out obstacles, imposing the black of oblivion on conventional standards . . . so that he might be free to function unencumbered in his almost frenzied response to other writers, other poets, and to their work. Yet he believed that the black of this undeviatingly practiced sacrament did not for a moment signify the absence of *light*.

According to Harry, "Writing is not a game played according to the rules. Writing is a compulsive and delectable thing . . . writing is its own reward."

Caresse was the driving force behind the Press, with an uncanny knack of picking winners among the vast smorgasbord of unknown writers in Paris. She had a rare gift for nurturing the poets, painters, and novelists who came, seeking recognition, tea, and sympathy. To those who drank from her cup, Caresse was the Life Force. Kay Boyle gratefully dedicated two of her books to "that small woman with the fierce courage of a hummingbird, whose belief and fervor never failed . . . ."

During this era, the Crosbys subscribed to Shakespeare & Company, which in the 1920s functioned as informal club and mailing address for the American literary circle in Paris. Sylvia Beach, the legendary proprietress, was supportive of their efforts. She wrote that "Harry used to dart in and out of my bookshop, dive into the bookshelves like a hummingbird extracting honey from a blossom. The Crosbys were connoisseurs of fine books, but better still, of fine writing."

On Beach's recommendation, they first encountered James Joyce, whose *Ulysses* was brought out by Shakespeare & Company after

U.S. publishers unanimously rejected it as pornography. The Joyces lived near the Boulevard des Invalides, back of the Gare Montparnasse, in a "tidy but unimaginative" apartment, Caresse noted after their first visit, "its only ornaments, an upright piano and a goldfish bowl." Joyce was uncommunicative, "and seemed bored with us . . . retreating behind those thick, mysterious eyeglasses" (possibly because of the pain caused by glaucoma attacks, and the remedy, usually a large dose of Irish whiskey). Nora Joyce was heard to comment in an acrid Irish brogue: "You're dumb as an oyster, now, so God help me, Jim. What is it ye all find to jabber about the nights you're brought home drunk for me to look after?" Then something was said about Sullivan, the great Irish tenor, and Joyce suddenly came to life "and asked if we'd like to join them after the concert next week."

At the post-concert party, "there was much song and ribaldry—I think we drank *beer!*—and Nora had cooked a special Dublin dish. Archie and Ada MacLeish were there, and Maria and Eugene Jolas. Maria took turns with Stuart Gilbert at the piano."

Several weeks later, Caresse plucked up her courage to return and ask if the Black Sun Press might publish a section of Joyce's *Work in Progress*.

"How many pages would you be wanting?" Joyce asked.

"It's the meat not the water that makes the broth," Caresse answered, which seemed to please him. She left with his promise to deliver a manuscript for a single limited edition, paid in advance.

The manuscript of two colorful Irish tales, "The Mookse and the Gripes" and "The Ont and the Graicehopper" soon was delivered by Joyce's emissary, Stuart Gilbert. It was Black Sun's most important acquisition to date, and Caresse determined to enhance it with an important illustration. She thought of her friend from the Grand Chaumière, Constantin Brancusi.

Brancusi loved Americans, and as one critic observed, "pranced about as the spirit of the jazz age, although at times wearing wooden sabots." He was a great bear of a man, who seemed like a peasant saint to Caresse. She went to his whitewashed atelier on the rue Vaugirard, where he lived alone with his white spitz dog, Polaris. A plump pullet and potatoes were roasting on red-hot coals on the hearth, and he invited Caresse to join him for lunch à deux. He set the work-table with crisp white sheets of drawing paper as placemats and carved the pullet with a sculpting knife.

Brancusi responded favorably to Caresse's request. Of the two sketches of Joyce he submitted to the Press, the Crosbys selected an abstraction to illustrate the new title, *Tales Told of Shem and Shaun*. The realistic line drawing is also a classic of its kind, but the two perpendicular lines and the spiral curve represented Joyce's inward-winding thought, they believed. As always, the Crosbys' vision of contemporary art was well ahead of their time.

"The Black Sun Press writers and artists on the Paris scene in the 1920s were workers *first* and party-goers *second*," Caresse later wrote. "Unlike the popular image, we were *not* forever drinking at the Dôme or getting into scrapes in Montmartre. Most of the BSP writers guarded their desks like fortresses, and only relaxed in the evenings when the one electric light bulb or gas jet in the studio up six flights cast a very meager light, then they gathered at their favorite eating places." From the time he left the Morgan Bank until he died, Harry brought out 15 volumes of poetry and his diaries, *Shadows of the Sun*—a considerable output for any dedicated young poet. "Harry Crosby and I rigidly divided the work day in the rue de Lille: 9 to 12, closed in the library; 12 to 2, lunch (Harry went out *alone*, unless we had friends to luncheon); 2 to 5, more *work*."

When the Crosbys entertained in the Sicilian dining room, it was a baroque affair at midday, with the black whippet Narcisse Noir seated next to Harry at the head of the baronial table. On his crimson cushion, Narcisse looked "like a Delta dog on a royal sarcophagus . . . very effective, black against red," Harry wrote Henrietta Crosby. At first, Parisian guests were delighted at the novelty of dining with the trend-setting Crosbys on American cuisine spiced with a soupçon of French imagination: clam consommé with whipped cream, *canard à l'orange*, mashed sweet potatoes, tomato-cheese salad, and marshmallows with hot chocolate sauce. On one occasion, the madcap Douglas Burdens, just back from Africa, brought an uninvited guest—a honey bear!—to lunch. Led in on a leash, the lumbering brown beast was cuddled by the women, ignored by the men, and engaged in pitched battle by Narcisse Noir before they were pulled apart. "Worst of all, the dessert was gone before we others had a chance," Caresse complained.

Nights *en famille* were rare. On such occasions, the Crosbys retired early to the ornate four-poster. (It was a practical necessity in winter, when Paris apartment furnaces seldom functioned until mid-November, thereafter at a meager 60 degrees.)

"Harry loved bed. He loved to write in bed, to eat in bed, to entertain in bed," Caresse noted, with a hint at double entendre. Caresse rarely complained when Harry read in bed until one o'clock.

"Our bedroom light was very bright, but I learned to sleep in spite of it," she recalled years later, with a sense of déjà vu. "Sometimes Harry would get up and dress and go out mysteriously, alone. I was never invited. But he was always there when I awoke in the morning."

The nightly ritual was a game they played, in which Caresse conspired. Caresse and Harry always had enthused about the same people. It was Caresse who discovered the beautiful Bostonian, Constance Crowninshield Coolidge Atherton (more recently, Comtesse de Jumilhac), at a ladies' luncheon, an event Caresse was loathe to attend. "From the moment she hurried in late, all sparkle and flutter, I was captivated. All through the Paris years, she was my most formidable antagonist, but I could not help immensely admiring her." She had lived in a temple, raised Mongolian ponies, and defied convention as the wife of an American ambassador to Peking.

On the surface, at least, the glamorous "Lady of the Golden Horse" did not penetrate Caresse's armor. "One marries a man because one likes him as he is, not as he will be whipped into some other shape," was Caresse's philosophy. "Harry made me believe that my children balanced our account . . . I had to play both the lead and the sustaining role in our drama, very exacting and dissimilar parts—a saint and sinner combination."

Harry's frequent, transitory flirtations, in addition to permanent *belles amies*, were assigned code names in the diary: "The Sorceress," "Nubile," and later, "The Fire Princess." "All were substantial props to the poet's dream . . . I was jealous of only one rival, the imaginary 'Jacqueline'." (Harry had become enamored with a Zorn etching—a shepherdess, "Val Kulla"—whose coincidental likeness was most extraordinary.) "Jacqueline" was Harry's *ideal* Princess, the only one he could *never* touch, save in his dreams. Caresse knew very well that she was the Favorite: Among many Princesses, there was only one "Cramoisy Queen." On his 30th birthday, Harry had written, "Our *One*-ness is the color of a glass of red wine."

"Harry and I were free to do as we wished—alone, if not together, but *alone* was never really as good as *together*," Caresse wrote. She had a healthy appetite for men, and early on, determined that what was sauce for the gander was sauce for the goose, particularly in the moveable feast of France. That summer, restless under the strains of Harry's search for clandestine fires, Caresse went off to Cannes with Manolo Ortíz, the painter described by Polleen as "Mama's Gypsy Lover." In the diary, Harry jotted: "Caresse believes that woman is the equal of man; I, that woman is dependent and the slave of man."

Kay Boyle described Caresse's sexual promiscuity as "not anything she herself wanted or enjoyed. It was one of the demands Harry
made upon her. She talked to me, almost in guilt, about these things,
trying to make them funny . . . gallantry and humor were part of her
courage."

Harry was always ready to seduce her back home. Few wives have
received a letter of equal intensity on their seventh anniversary as this
one from Harry:

> I have been feeling very physical. I hope you feel the
> same way. We don't make love often enough. I wish we
> were making love together . . . . I think we are absolutely
> and entirely made for each other. I know it . . . . I wish my
> head right now between your legs. I love kissing you more
> than anything in the world. I am all strong and excited
> thinking about it . . . . I kiss you and kiss you.

Nights when they entertained at home were "a merry round of
madness," Caresse wrote. When it was time to change from daytime
gear to dishabille, Harry wore his regal Magyar robe, embroidered
with red and gold to match Caresse's dressing gown. Both wore gold
bracelets and gold necklaces they had purchased in a bazaar in
Cairo—from King Tutankhamen's tomb, they claimed. Half-moon
tables were set up around the bed, on the bear- and zebra-skin scatter
rugs. When astonished dinner guests arrived at eight—if novices, in
formal evening dress—they were ushered into the bedroom by the
parlor maid, in full uniform with fluted cap and apron.

First caviar and champagne were served, followed by a simple
American dish—perhaps chowder and corn pone. Guests were
invited to bathe after dinner in the Pompeian tub. This divertisse-
ment was welcomed by even inhibited newcomers from the Latin
Quarter, when bathtubs were more often down the hall or didn't
exist.

"We liked to experiment with bath oils and bath salts, rose and
geranium," Caresse wrote. A Boston friend was shocked to be
invited by Harry to watch—through a concealed peephole—Caresse
sponging off in the bubbly tub!

Not everyone was intrigued by these nocturnal fêtes. Some never
came back. Harry described the dissenters as bourgeois bores, and
thereafter, expendable.

But for mischief and spectacular hijinks, drunkenness and fornica-
tion, no private party could equal the Quatre Arts Ball, marking the
end of the academic year at the Ecole des Beaux Arts. When spring

came around, the Crosbys and others began preparations for the orgy. Held in the huge halls at Luna Park or the Porte d'Auteuil, as many as 3,000 artists and models and ladies of the evening (if French) or well-connected ladies slumming (if American or British), joined the students in the confetti and confusion.

The motif in 1924 was Incan, a memorable first to be followed by many others. Costumes consisted of not much more than body paint and loin cloth, with an elaborate headdress. Harry, always macabre, rubbed down with red ochre paint and around his neck, festooned a necklace of dead pigeons. He was carrying a bag of live snakes. Caresse, as mascot of the atelier, recalled that she "was hoisted into our paper dragon's jaws, my long blue wig flowing over painted shoulders, proudly displaying my *nichons*, as on the prow of a New England whaling ship . . . we marched undraped and wholly uninhibited up the Champs Elysées."

While back at the hall, all hell broke loose, if one can believe Harry's diary: "At one o'clock, it was WILD . . . men and women stark naked dancing . . . from our *loge*, I opened the sack, and down dropped ten serpents . . . Later in the evening, I sat next to a plump girl who was suckling one of them!" Lord Lymington, lance in hand, was dancing savagely with Caresse, when "one brave knelt in my path, embraced my painted knees, and covered them with kisses. I felt deliciously pagan! Stepping over entwined bodies, returning ardently the kisses of passers-by, I reached home before Harry, and found him with three pretty girls soaking in pink bubbly soapsuds together, scrubbing off paint. That crazy night, our bed slept seven, not counting Narcisse. We never knew who the seventh was. He wandered in, in a loincloth, and pushed us over. He left early the next morning, pinning a note to the pillow, 'Had to get to the Department by nine.' What Department? We never saw him again. I wonder if he arrived at his desk in the loincloth?"

During this era on the rue de Lille, Polleen came to know the servants well and depended on them for survival, "like a passenger depends on a lifeboat in a sinking ship." Downstairs, on the other side of the green baize door, there was a bell system: one ring for the personal maid, two rings for the parlor maid, three rings for the chauffeur, and four for the children. "Four rings were seldom heard," she recalled wistfully, "but I never stopped listening for the extra buzz."

Louise, the cook, with the figure of a stevedore and a splendid moustache, shared a room off the kitchen with Henriette, the parlor maid, who giggled when Louise pinched her bottom. (*Les Chansons des Bilitis*, required on Harry's reading list, enlightened Polleen about their lesbian relationship.) The lady's maid (who answered the No. 1 bell) was the Downstairs stool pigeon. "I hated her! I used to call her '*La Reine*' because she gave herself superior airs when Mama visited friends or relatives, clutching the keys to the suitcases, carrying the expensive boxes and parcels that accompanied them. But it was rumored in the attic quarters where the footmen were lodged that she was not so dignified."

Caresse's secretary was a pathetic woman who came in by the day, her limp hair framing a pale face that registered her many disappointments in life. "She had dreamed of being a ballet dancer on the Opera House stage, instead of spending her days banging the typewriter and walking the dogs . . . ."

The daily *bonne à tout faire*, Hélène, was a pretty girl with bright eyes and a tantalizing derrière—Polleen's favorite, and Harry's, too. He dallied with Hélène while her husband worked the night shift at the Champs Elysées restaurant, and Caresse soon dismissed her.

Turnover was also great among chauffeurs, assigned a daily list of expendable chores on a few francs, and fated to long waits. Victor, the most memorable, was the shortest in stature and longest on patience. He could barely be seen over the steering wheel of the "green dragon," a magnificent 1920 Coupe-de-Ville Voisin, with spare tires encased on the running board, an open box in the forefront for two footmen. The two black whippets, in Hermès-designed coats and gold collars, sat inside with the passengers as befitted their rank. (Narcisse had acquired a mate, which Harry christened "Clitoris," telling Polleen the bitch was named after a Greek goddess. It was several years before his stepdaughter caught on to the origin of the name.)

After Mme. Doursenaud, governesses came and went, not because of Polleen's behavior, but because the pay was stingy, the atmosphere so Bohemian "they were consistently shocked by my parents' lifestyle, from which they half-heartedly attempted to protect me."

Polleen caviled that on the rare occasions *she* was invited Upstairs, it was likely for a dinner of corned-beef hash—or coconut cake with homemade ice-cream, churned in a wooden bucket immersed in crushed ice and sea salt. Downstairs—whether to suit the servants' tastes or the meager kitchen allowance—meals were more imaginative. Caresse took pride in "making the coppers glow," her euphemism for pinching pennies on household expenses. "I never balanced a budget in my life, unless I added the necessary heading of Experience or Fun," she boasted.

Polleen learned to savor the servants' gourmet fare: pigeons stuffed with olives and bread, fish flavored with herb-spiced sauces, pigs' "trotters" and—to her horror—pigs' ears, flattened with a hammer and cooked in bread crumbs.

But all was not fun and games in the nursery. Once, when Polleen became very ill, the resident doctor called on his little Choulette. When he left, he kissed her tenderly on the forehead, and was very grave.

Some time later, Harry appeared, squeezing along a narrow passage used to stack the musty tomes he inherited from Cousin Walter's library to the child's tiny cubicle. He entered brandishing a glass of champagne. "Here," he said, "drink this, my Wretched Rat. The doctor said you might die, but this *might* help you!" He disappeared as miraculously as he had come, not lingering to explain.

From that time, Polleen adopted the "Wretched Rat" as a term of endearment. In her eyes, Harry could do no wrong. (Polleen had very exceptional eyes, and learned at an early age to use them.) "Even when I was very young, I understood that my stepfather's flirtations with me were very different from the normal love of father for daughter. I was passionately in love with Harry. He alone was allowed to kiss me on the mouth, which he did frequently, hiding under the rug at the back of our Voisin so the chauffeur could not see, or sometimes in the nursery when no one was about. It was a deep secret between us, and remained so until he died."

Harry had an incredible talent for make-believe, and could talk anyone into indulging his wildest fantasies. Total strangers fell under his spell. Polleen recalled that he read Hans Christian Andersen and *Grimm's Fairy Tales*, and told stories of his own creation, in which he played his part with utter conviction.

> One evening, I was dressed for bed, in my pajamas and robe, when he spontaneously decided to pretend he was the Prince and I was the Princess. Grabbing a bag of pennies he brought home from the Bank, he took me by the hand and rushed into the street, hailing one of those old fashioned taxis with a rolled-down top. He told the driver to take us to Le Marais. In those days (before the Centre Pompidou of course), Le Marais was a very poor *quartier* of Paris. There we were, sitting on the folded roof of the taxi, throwing coins to our startled "subjects"!

"Harry was mad, no doubt about it . . . in a sort of extravagant, glorious way. He had a child's mind. I could understand his sort of madness."

* * *

When Harry entertained Polleen's brother Billy on infrequent school vacations, the two of them dropped beer-filled balloons from the balcony onto the heads of passers-by on the rue de Lille, to the delight of Billy's school chums.

Billy was always on a more formal footing with his mother. Perhaps, because during his first Easter vacation, he climbed into her bed and "fell asleep on my pillow, almost before his head touched it. While I was still drowsing in the morning," Caresse wrote, "I felt his fingers combing my hair at the nape of my neck, as he cuddled close."

"I love you," Billy whispered.

"I love you, too," Caresse answered. Frightened of—or unwilling to acknowledge—the latent sexual attraction a mother has for her young son, she jumped up and fled into the bathroom.

"Time to get up, Billy," she called over her shoulder, slamming the door shut behind her.

"I never dared unfathom half my love," she said. But through the years, they were good friends and conspirators.

Polleen, like Billy, spent much time away—at Chalet Marie Jose, a *hôme d'enfants*, or other boarding schools—"23 between the ages of 5 and 15" (if her diary is reliable)—perhaps because of Caresse's jealous fears about Harry's clandestine liaisons with his stepdaughter. Harry had forwarded to her schools precocious reading material: James Joyce's *Ulysses*, Oscar Wilde's *Salomé*, the poets Rimbaud and Baudelaire. "He wrote the most beautiful love letters, which I read, hidden away in the gymnasium, also learning vicariously about sex, love and romance from books hidden in plain brown wrappers. It was frustrating to be so young, to be stuck away in school, unable to enjoy such diversions," she wrote.

But despite such unconventional upbringing Polleen was not a withdrawn, wistful child. To the contrary, the headmistress reported that she was: "*plus emancipée, plus independente . . .* lovable *et* loved . . ." more than the other girls in her class. She had a lovely face and carried herself well, like her mother. All of the children wanted to dance with Polleen, to sit with Polleen; Polleen had the rare ability to count each one special.

On May 20, 1927, the historic date when Lindbergh arrived in Paris, Harry, Caresse and Stephen Crosby (who was visiting at the time) were among the thousands converging upon the Route de Flandres, the highway over which Marshal Joffre had led his taxicab army to stop the Germans at the Marne in 1914. Their friend, Major "Pete" Powel, a World War I ace, had gotten passes through the police cordon onto Le Bourget field.

A $25,000 prize was offered for the first transatlantic flight, but four American and two French pilots had already lost their lives in pursuit of it. Charles Lindbergh, a 25-year-old mail pilot, was making the latest attempt to fly 3,000 miles over treacherous seas in a Ryan monoplane with wooden wings. There was no radio communication to guide him, no backup team of mission control. He took with him a bedraggled kitten for company, a thermos of coffee to keep awake, and a half-dozen ham sandwiches: "If I get to Paris, I won't need any more, and if I don't get to Paris, I won't need any more either."

At the military field where the Crosbys waited, the afternoon crowd of 45,000 had swelled to 150,000 by nightfall, when the kleig lights were trained on the runways; police and airport personnel were erecting barriers to keep the growing crowd at bay. Anxious and confusing reports came through—the lone airman had gotten off course, was forced down in Ireland. Then someone who *knew* announced that Lindbergh had been sighted over the Eiffel Tower and could not seem to locate Le Bourget. Caresse reported:

> My ears, which are unusually keen, of a sudden picked out a delicate hum of lightest calibre away up in the clouds, which were now scudding across a misted moon . . . a small clear burring as of a toy, and then it was lost. . . . Suddenly, there was a silver flicker like the fin of a darting minnow out of one cloud into another.
>
> "He's circling the field. *C'est lui!*"
>
> "*C'est* Lindbergh!" the cries grew.
>
> Suddenly, from the nearest cloud the bright wings flashed and veered downward, straight and sure to the waiting lane of flare-lit faces. He hit the runway precise and clean.

When Lindbergh climbed down from the cockpit to be hoisted onto the shoulders of the waiting crowd, Caresse reported that he looked boyish and tousled and *very much like Harry*. "I heard a Frenchman say, '*C'est n'est pas un homme, c'est un oiseau.*'" For his part, Harry would have given his life to change places with the Lone Eagle for that brief moment of triumph.

"What thunder and fire for breakfast."

—HARRY

Chapter III

MOULIN DU SOLEIL

In the early spring, Caresse was growing restless for the smell of country air, real countryside where one could bask in the sun and evoke the muse. It was in this frame of mind that the Crosbys discovered the Moulin du Soleil, a dilapidated mill on the property of the Chateau at Ermenonville, which Armand de la Rochefoucauld had inherited on his twenty-first birthday. Armand, whose mother was a Radziwill, was the most sought-after young man about Paris in the late 1920s; his scrapes and peccadillos were legendary among the *beau monde*.

The Crosbys attended Armand's housewarming, and Caresse immediately fell under the Mill's spell. Jean Jacques Rousseau had lived there when he was enamored of the Duchess of Montmorency. It was rumored that Cagliostro, in retreat at the nearby abbey, devised his magic formulae beside the mill stream. Varda, the mystery-loving Greek painter in the Crosby entourage, offered the theory that if one establishes one's dwelling on ground beneath which water flows, one will have a touchstone with magic. Indeed, from the "enchanted" mill stream, Caresse observed that little fish

26

leapt mysteriously several feet in the air and landed safely in the pool above. Some 500 years before, sand had filled the hollows in the surrounding forest of Senlis, creating a *mer de sable*, a phenomenon that still exists. (Atlantis receding beneath the waves was Caresse's explanation.)

Harry, who as usual had no idea how many francs were in the Morgan Bank account, promised to draw a check for the total balance if Armand would sell the Mill to them on the spot.

"Right now?" Armand asked, incredulously.

"Yes!" replied the impulsive Harry. Since he never carried a checkbook, he wrote an IOU on the nearest blank object at hand—a white cuff ripped from Caresse's shirtwaist. (He once used a plate for the same purpose at Zelli's, one of their favorite bars. The bemused waiter took it, without comment, to be cashed at the Place Vendôme the next morning.)

Henceforth the "Moulin du Soleil" became the Crosbys' country retreat. To Caresse, the three buildings built around a courtyard were reminiscent of the Adirondack camps she had loved as a child, save for the 19th-century stagecoach, with *Gare du Nord* painted on its side in large red letters, in the courtyard. A white palisade fence ran along the front of the quadrangle, where five donkeys cropped the grass and sunflowers stood guard. At the front gate, signposts like the spokes of a wheel pointed to the different paths through the forest. The locals claim that the forest of Senlis is so vast that a man can ride through it to Germany without ever leaving its shade. The most often-used path led to the old well, the Poteau du Perth, to which Harry ritualistically walked the half-mile, every morning and night. In spring, the sweet scent of lily-of-the-valley was almost overpowering.

To the left of the main building, the old mill survives today, though the great water wheel has rotted away. Even in the 1920s, the stream that once activated the mill wheel was overgrown and silted up, but the water still flowed in a pleasant trickle. Polleen recalls that "our swimming pool was no larger than two postage stamps, and most unappetizing to swim in, because all sorts of marine life and slimy bugs infested the brown, murky water."

The millstones, like mantic rings, rested on the granary floor. The old wash room and cellars were turned into a vast kitchen, adjoining which was the bedroom of the local gravedigger and his wife, Monsieur and Madame Henri, whom Harry, with his lugubrious wit, hired as loyal retainers. The Henris' duties were endless: to look after a dozen disintegrating rooms, a garden, five donkeys, two dogs, a parrot, a cheetah, 15 pigeons—and the usual weekend complement of ten or more guests. No wonder that M. Henri walked three miles to the village every day for his measure of cognac.

The center building—the former stable—became the dining room. Its rafters, manger, and hay boxes were left intact under a Roman villa-type roof. The trestle-table rested on uneven cobblestones, and Polleen remembers forever shoving pieces of crusty French bread under its legs to keep the table from wobbling. Inside the entrance, under the staircase, visitors were asked to sign their names with colored paints on the whitewashed wall, which served as an impromptu guest book. (D.H. Lawrence scribbled a Phoenix next to Salvador Dali's interlocked "I"s.)

On the first floor were the master bedroom, a guest room, and the only bathroom, installed by the Crosbys; such amenities were unknown at that time in rural France. Under the arched roof of the attic was another small room where the bats made their home, "hanging upside-down over whoever slept there. On crowded weekends, that was usually me," Polleen recalled. "I had to leave the window open wide at night, otherwise the bats couldn't get back out. They would swirl 'round the room with high-pitched screeches, swooping over my head and banging into the window panes!"

This tiny room opened onto a small terrace where Harry communicated with the Sun God Ra. A slab of dove-grey marble grave marker—inscribed with the Harry/Caresse cross, their dates of birth, and their (projected) date of death—was placed atop the tower where the sun struck first.

Harry had selected the date—October 31, 1942—when the earth would be closest to the sun at the perihelion. By age 44, Harry predicted he would have had enough; he didn't like the idea of lingering on, after the party was over. He was obsessed "to die at the right time," quoting Nietzsche's "Thus Spake Zarathustra."

Le beau monde and les boulevardiers soon discovered the Mill, and poets and artists were invited for longer stays to complete their creative work. At one time, the then-unknown poet Hart Crane was installed in the tower with a bottle of Cutty Sark and a ream of paper, condemned to work on his monumental opus, The Bridge. According to Harry's diary: "Hart Crane here, and much drinking red wine; he reads aloud from Tamberlaine, and is at work on his long poem . . . ." At that time Crane was young and cocky, "stocky and bristly, rather like a young porcupine," Caresse described him. "He had gusto and a Rabelaisian laugh" and was a welcome guest at the weekend parties. He stayed on at the Mill for three weeks, faithfully attended by Monsieur and Madame Henri.

In Polleen's childhood memoirs, she recalls: "M. Henri liked to eat snails, collected in profusion from the garden plot . . . . One evening, when the escargots were being prepared for dinner, M. Henri bellowed from the floor below, '*Mais il est fou . . . il est fou!!*' [He is crazy!] Crane had invaded the kitchen and stamped out the snails, presuming they were the larvae of butterflies!"

Hart was inspired by the "solitude of the place," and for the first time in many months, worked consistently until he delivered a draft of the "Hatteras" section to the Black Sun Press. Harry prophetically predicted its success:

> Hart, what thunder and fire for breakfast! By Christ, when you read something like that, all the dust and artificiality and bric-à-brac are swept magnificently aside . . . . Someday, when we are all dead, they will be screaming and cutting each other's throats for the privilege of having it . . . . I am no critic, but I know gold when I see it!

Later, in the season of daffodils, Frieda and D.H. Lawrence were guests. The previous winter, on the Crosby's trip to Egypt with Harry's mother, Harry had discovered a first edition of *The Plumed Serpent* in a Cairo bookstore. He avidly read it, sitting cross-legged on the deck, as the boat plied slowly up the Nile. He proclaimed it the most inspiring novel since e.e. cummings' great work about the war, *The Enormous Room*. Quoting: "I without the Sun that is back of the Sun am nothing," he rushed off an enthusiastic letter to Lawrence in care of his London publisher, describing the impact of the strong Egyptian rays on his psyche and proclaiming his faith in the Sun God, Ra. He hoped that Lawrence might have a story on the same theme for a Black Sun Press Limited Edition, and promised in payment $20 gold pieces, "the eagle and the sun." Lawrence and his wife Frieda (daughter of the German flying ace Baron von Richthofen) were invited to bask in the sun at Le Moulin du Soleil.

Also in Cairo that winter—on leap year day, February 29—Caresse discovered the Sun Ring that was to become Harry's wedding band, "the eternal circle, the letter 'O'" to endure forever. (She was told it had been stolen from King Tutankhamen's tomb.)

Soon after the Crosbys arrived back in Paris, they received a large brown envelope postmarked Florence, enclosing a manuscript of the short novel, *Sun*. Lawrence noted in the attached letter that he hoped it would be printed as written, *un*expurgated. Lescaret immediately began setting the type, to be printed on fine Holland van Gelder paper, with the title emblazoned on a cover of "sunburnt red."

The Crosbys were quite accustomed to unannounced guests on their doorstep, so it was no surprise when a curly-haired painter, Bill Sykes—a friend of Ted Weeks, Harry's old comrade from the Ambulance Corps—arrived at the rue de Lille. Sykes limped up the long flight of stairs, and took off his low tan shoes in front of the roaring fire. Out fell the promised "golden eagles," smuggled from the States following Harry's urgent request.

Harry carefully wrapped and placed the coins in an empty Cartier box, as an afterthought adding another treasure from his ample stock. Then he rushed off to the Gare de l'Est to put them aboard the Rome Express. The first "honest man" he saw, leaning from the First Class window, was a starchy, Chesterfield-coated Englishman, who promised to deliver the package to Lawrence. (Harry's instincts were sound. He had unknowingly entrusted his treasure to the Duke of Argyll.)

Lawrence replied warmly:

> My wife went to Florence yesterday and brought back the Queen of Naples' snuff box and the pieces of gold, to my utter amazement. I'm sure you're not Croesus to that extent, and . . . what right have I to receive these things? . . . How beautiful the gold is! Such a pity it ever became currency. One should love it for its yellow life, answering the sun . . . I feel almost wicked with it! For the first time I know what *embarras de richesses* means . . .

Soon thereafter the Lawrences turned up at the Mill. Harry and Lawrence disagreed on almost everything at their first meeting, except their mutual love of the sun. Harry wrote: "He is direct, I am *in*direct; I am a visionary, I like to *soar*; he is all engrossed in the body and the complexities of psychology." For his part, Lawrence perceptively saw in Harry "a glimpse of chaos not reduced to order . . . but chaos *alive*."

Caresse took Lawrence for a turn in a donkey cart, with a shawl tucked over his knees, his collar turned up and soft hat pulled over his ears. He liked to sit for hours on the sun terrace using the gravestone as a backrest, hoping to cure an ominous, hacking cough. He reflected later that "Harry was really so well, *physically* . . . and my nerves are healthy, but my chest lets me down . . . So there we are, Life and Death in all of us . . . ."

Caresse described Frieda as "upholstered, petulant, and full of pride." She played the gramophone all evening, which put Lawrence's nerves on edge until—in a fit of exasperation—he smashed record after record over her head. (Some years after D.H. and Harry both were gone, Frieda wrote to Caresse: "It's all so vivid to me, that weekend. They were both such vivid creatures, Lorenzo and Harry. I see you in the sailor suit and the [sun] bracelet Harry gave you.")

Almost every weekend at the Mill was festive, "an unreal atmosphere," as Polleen described it. "We had no electricity and no telephone, so attempts were made to communicate with Paris by carrier pigeon." Soon, the news flew around when there was to be a party at the Moulin du Soleil. Harry recorded a typical weekend—and what Hart Crane called "the new atrocities"—in his diary:

> Mobs for luncheon—poets and painters and pederasts and lesbians and divorcées and Christ knows who and there was a great signing of names on the wall at the foot of the stairs and a firing off of the cannon and bottle after bottle of red wine and Kay Boyle made fun of Hart Crane and he was angry and flung *The American Caravan* into the fire because it contained a story of Kay Boyle's (he forgot it had a poem of his in it) and there was a tempest of drinking and polo *harra burra* on the donkeys, and an uproar and confusion so that it was difficult to do my work. . . .

A small cannon, mounted near the front gate, was fired in lieu of a starter gun, as a party of very reluctant guests were forced to mount the frisky beasts and race down the homemade track.

Champagne flowed more abundantly than water at the Mill, and the weekend nights usually ended in orgies (perhaps not *enchantée* in the eyes of young Polleen):

> The top floor of the Mill was one large room (once the hayloft) with a huge fireplace at the far end, and two sofa beds on either side; zebra and bear skins covered the floor. There were candelabra and oil lamps, but the wood fire gave out most of the light. When night fell, the guests would retire to this hayloft, and out came the roulette wheel, the horse-racing games. The dice rattled, the wheel

spun, and great bottles of champagne were uncorked. Couples intertwined on sofas beside the fire-place . . . helped along by opium, a large jar of which was kept in my toy box. This brown sticky stuff with a funny smell, I was told on no account to touch!

Of the rich tradition of drug lore in literature, Harry had sampled a large portion, from De Quincey's *Confessions* to Cocteau and Rimbaud. Opium was his drug of choice, a quick trip to Nirvana, and smoking it in his pipe became "almost a religious act, almost a prayer." Caresse tells us that only once did she accompany Harry in the ritual of the pipe, which they observed "in a most sybaritic manner."

Stories circulated among the bourgeois neighbors about the scandalous orgies at the Mill, "but I presumed it to be a fairly 'normal' way of life, if one belonged to the artistic and smart sets of those times," Polleen observed. Salvador Dali, also a frequent visitor, described the Mill's allure: "A mixture of Surrealists and society people came there, because they sensed that in the Moulin, *things were happening*"—that's where the action was. Caresse collected titles, and even royalty appeared on the cobblestoned doorstep. GEORGE (of England) added his name to the whitewashed entrance wall; the Prince joined a stagecoach race from Mill to Chateau (not without crashing into a tree), accompanied by a great ringing of bells and firing of cannon. America's royalty, Mary Pickford and Douglas Fairbanks, entertained the houseguests on a glorious October afternoon: Mary read palms and told fortunes, while Fairbanks, in full costume (with white spats), swung on a rope from hayloft to courtyard.

Somewhere, sometime, the music had to stop. The Golden Years, the *passionate* years, ended in '29. For many, they ended with the Great Depression. For the Crosbys (as Harry predicted), they ended with a .25 caliber, pearl-handled Belgian revolver.

"To die at the right time."

—HARRY

Chapter IV

LIT DE MORT

On September 9, 1929, Harry's diary noted: ". . . married seven years, and various rites performed: a firing off of the cannon and prayers into the sun from the top of the tower. In the afternoon, I flew—Aviator, Poet, Lover—all for the Cramoisy Queen." Harry's latest passion was learning to fly. Each day, he went out to the field at Villacoublay, and by September, he was flying twice a day with his instructor, the French ace Detré.

When D.H. Lawrence heard the news about Harry's new hobby, he wrote to Caresse: "An *aeroplane?* Is Harry *really* tired of life?" The daily commentary in Harry's diary noted: "The most simple Sun-death is from an aeroplane over a forest . . . down, down, BANG! The body is dead—up, up BANG!!" (In the margin, he repeated the date [31-10-42] on the Moulin tombstone.) In Harry's view, the accelerated intensity of aerial acrobatics was a beautiful poem.

In the fall of 1929, the world economy was obviously sluggish. A consortium of bankers led by Uncle Jack Morgan steadied the

Market temporarily, then discreetly retired from the field when the Market hit bottom on November 13.

In Paris, large crowds gathered outside the Bourse. The *Paris Herald* switchboard was swamped with calls from Americans in Paris trying to keep informed; at Morgan et Cie., businessmen gathered for reassurance, but when word filtered through, it was far worse than expected. Many of the prosperous expatriates queued up at the Embassy for emergency funds to return home. The cafés of Montparnasse emptied, and letters addressed to the patrons' mail rack at the Dôme piled up, uncollected.

Caresse and Harry heard immediately from Stephen Crosby, but the news failed to inhibit their pursuit of pleasure. They were booked to sail on the *Mauretania* November 16—not to attend to family business reverses, but to see the annual Harvard-Yale football game. Harry never cared much about football, and Caresse recognized better than anyone that her husband would never rush home to "Drearytown" only to attend the game. One of the "special girls," the Comtesse de Jumilhac (née Constance Crowninshield), was sailing with them on the *Mauretania*, and while Harry was exulting in the menage-à-trois on the boat, another Princess cabled "Impatient!"

En route, Harry was also engrossed in making a holograph copy of his latest volume of poetry, *Sleeping Together*, dedicated to Caresse. The ship rolled unmercifully, but Harry accomplished the task without a blot and presented it to her before they left the ship. Her favorite poem was "In Search of the Young Wizard":

> I have invited our little seamstress to take her thread and needle and sew our two mouths together. I have asked the village blacksmith to forge golden chains to tie our ankles together. I have gathered all the gay ribbons in the world to wind around and around our two waists . . . . I have persuaded (not without bribery) the world's most famous Eskimo sealing wax maker to perform the delicate operation of sealing us together so that I am warm in your depths, but though we hunt for him all night and though we hear various reports of his existence we can never find the young wizard who is able to graft the soul of a girl to the soul of her lover so that not even the sharp scissors of the Fates can sever them apart.

Prophetically, the Fates were waiting in the wings to do their dirty business within the fortnight.

The final day in Boston, there was a sortie to the game with Harry's mother and father. It was bitterly cold, and Harry had a flask in his pocket that his friends in the Ambulance Corps," The Hounds," had given him. He and Steve Crosby passed it back and forth. Caresse ominously noted that there was "one small white face in the crowd, turned towards us, far off like an impervious ticking clock."

After the game, Caresse rushed back to New York alone and checked into Room 2707 at the Savoy-Plaza. "You will adore this room," she wrote to Harry in Boston. "Lying in bed, I can watch the tugs nosing up the East River and the most amazing phallic skyscraper [the Fuller Tower], very straight and proud. I adore you, my darling, darling! I sleep with 'Sleeping Together,' but I want quickly to sleep together with you." She was playing according to the rules of their game, but she instinctively knew that Harry was sleeping together— with someone else.

On December 9, Harry finally turned up in Room 2707, and Henrietta Crosby checked in across the hall. The next morning he made a cryptic entry in his diary: "One is not in love unless one desires to die with one's beloved . . . there is only one happiness; It is to love and be loved."

Harry's appetite was never satiated. After a feast of lovemaking with Caresse, the early sun dazzled the windows of their room, and Harry, the sun worshipper, whispered:

"Give me your hand, Caresse. Our window is open wide. Let's meet the Sun-Death together!"

"But why, Harry? We have so much to live for."

"That is why, Caresse. There is too much. I cannot endure it all."

"We mustn't!" Caresse answered. "No. But we must leave here, very soon."

A premonition cast a brief shadow over the morning sun. But Harry always mixed talk of death and love. After the War, he wrote: "I ponder death more frequently than I do any other subject, even in the most joyous and flourishing moments of my life." His letters to Caresse were full of that fixation: "I promise with the absolute Faith that we shall be One in Heaven . . . someday Darling," was a typical closing. "I pray that we shall die together. I can think of nothing more sacred or beautiful."

Caresse remembered—to the last day of her own life—that she had turned down Harry's proffered invitation to die. But that day, she had a full schedule of living ahead. She first went to the travel bureau to book their return passage to France on December 13. Then, she rushed off to meet Harry at the gallery on 57th Street where their friend Kay Lane's sculpture of *Narcisse Noir* was attracting the attention of critics.

Harry had reached there first.

"Kiss me, Caresse, before I go," he said. With his left hand, he took off the big horn-rimmed glasses he always wore, and in a characteristic gesture, leaned across Narcisse's bronze flank to kiss her. He nodded goodbye, and swift as an eagle was gone.

At five o'clock, Caresse met Henrietta at the Savoy to go to Uncle Jack's for tea, an appointment made by Harry several weeks before. Harry had chosen as a Christmas remembrance a volume that must have caused his uncle amusement—if not further disenchantment. It was a presentation copy of the Black Sun limited edition of *Sleeping Together*. In spite of the financial holocaust and the incongruous gift, Morgan received the two women warmly. But at 6:15, when Harry hadn't appeared, they politely took their leave and went back to the hotel.

It was unlike Harry. "We were restless out of one another's sight," Caresse admitted. "Harry was forever telephoning to tell me where he was, and neither of us came late to a rendezvous with each other." Caresse and Henrietta were due to meet Hart Crane at the Caviar Restaurant at 7:30 that evening. On December 7, Hart had given the farewell party for the Crosbys at his Brooklyn Heights apartment, in direct view of the bridge. Some of their old friends were included, but it was planned to introduce the Crosbys as publishers of *The Bridge* to some of the literary lights on the New York scene—e.e. cummings, William Carlos Williams, the Malcolm Cowleys, and Walker Evans, the photographer who recorded the event. When the party wound down, one of the guests, quite drunk, asked Harry to pick a card from the deck. There was a silent moment before Harry spoke—"Ace of Hearts"—and picked. The Ace of Hearts.

On December 8, Josephine Rotch Bigelow hand-carried an envelope to the Savoy Plaza. The "impatient" Fire Princess was known locally as a "strange wild girl who delighted in saying things to shock people." Yet only the summer before, at 18, she had married Albert Bigelow, a graduate student of architecture at Harvard and scion of a conservative Boston family, in an impressive society wedding. Bigelow remained stolidly unaware of his bride's liaison with Harry while traveling in Venice the year before. Harry had introduced her to the opium pipe; she had an ugly temper and mad fits of jealousy. When they made love, Harry confided to his diary, "It was madness, like cats in the night that howl, no longer knowing whether they are in hell or Paradise." He told Hart Crane that he was already growing tired of her.

The crumpled contents of a yellowed envelope are among Caresse's carefully preserved papers. A juvenile 36-line poem, "Two Fires that Make One Fire"—an inventory of the enthusiasms Harry shared with the Fire Princess, ends on an ominous chord: "Death is our marriage." The note attached encapsulated its clear message, "Harry, do you know I love you terribly?" (Caresse noted in faltering hand: "This is the letter Josephine brought Harry the night *before* . . . she had not left town as she promised.")

When Caresse and Henrietta Crosby arrived at the Caviar to meet Crane, Harry was not there and had left no message. They exchanged pleasantries during the first course; then Caresse excused herself to call Stanley Mortimer, the painter, an old friend of Harry's. A telephone call was decidedly against the rules of the game, but she was worried and suspected Harry had gone to Stanley's studio, his usual site for a rendezvous. Only the devil—or death—could prevent Harry from keeping a firm date with Caresse and his mother.

They discovered Harry and Josephine lying together in the upstairs bedroom off Mortimer's studio, fully and fashionably dressed, except for their bare feet. The police report noted Harry's soles, tattooed on the voyage to Egypt with a Christian cross on the left, a pagan sun symbol on the right. Both had beautiful skin like parchment, and eyes sunk beneath strong brows, sensuous mouths with full lips, her dark still-damp curls contrasting with Harry's ripe-wheat shock. Harry's free arm was wrapped around Josephine's neck, their left hands clasped, like a tableau of a fairy tale Prince and Princess. The Jazz Age Romeo and Juliet appeared to have supped from the same fatal love potion to lie for eternity on Harry's *Lit de Mort*:

> I shall die within my Lady's arms
> and from her mouth, drink down the purple wine.

In reality, an almost imperceptible bullet hole had pierced his right temple, her left. The Hounds' flask, half empty, lay by Harry's side, next to his small pearl-handled revolver. The gold Sun Ring, Caresse's wedding gift to Harry, was discovered later on the bedroom floor, stomped flat. Josephine had gone first—the coroner reported— Harry followed several hours later. One can only surmise what took place during the several hours when Harry lay alone beside the beautiful, inert girl, trying to find a clue in her silent body to the *Summum Amor* that awaited him.

e.e. cummings wrote an appropriate epitaph:

> 2 Boston
> Dolls; found
> with
> Holes in each other
> 's lullaby . . .

The yellowed clippings in newspaper morgues are as obscure today as the event they headlined:

SUICIDE PACT EVIDENT: CROSBY POEMS CLEW

A week later, the story was dropped, save for a discreet notice about Josephine's interment in Boston.

Fifty years later, Polleen insisted that "in spite of Harry's crazy ways—crazed by opium and intoxicated with champagne—I am certain that *murder* was not in his making. More likely, the unstable Bigelow woman called Harry's bluff, then killed herself. Since there was no other way out of this grim situation, Harry took his own life."

"All the dancing figures of a world in rainbow colors froze." Caresse passed through all of the classic symptoms of bereavement: disbelief, denial, grief, and, finally, acceptance. Harry had gone— without leaving a clue, an explanation.

"My puzzle was to know what Harry expected of me? Should I follow him?" (Caresse would not read the police report; she never believed the destruction of the Sun Ring.) According to Kay Boyle, " . . . she was too uncertain of herself, too lost to be able to sort it all out. She existed—with her wonderfully human responses and inexhaustible energy, in the nightmare Harry had lived in, this terrible, terrible hell of his making."

Caresse finally rationalized that *no* word at all from Harry was the only way to assure her that they were still and forever, Harry and Caresse. "To explain would have been to destroy. Only his supreme faith in me could have made this departure without words justified. With that as my life raft, I pulled myself back out of the depths into the light again."

As the shadows lifted, she could see again into places that once had been so dazzlingly bright: 'One Way Like the Path of a Star'. "Harry's life, for me, burnt far too quickly, but one cannot say that it burnt in vain or that its *Summum* is unrelated to the law of cosmic progression. It had truth, it had beauty, and for me, it pointed a way that I now believe is the path of every life on earth."

Archibald MacLeish—who sat the death watch with Harry, at Caresse's request—wrote to Henrietta Crosby: "Those of us who knew Harry, knew that he was always . . . on the side of the angels and against the authority and numbness and complacency of life . . . . Recklessness and freedom of soul are sometimes dangerous . . . but without those fires lighted . . . the world would be a dark and hopeless place."

Some 20 years later, Caresse sent an unusual essay to Charles Olson, the poet: "In Defense of Suicide, or Planned Death." In it, she reconciled "the many years I was unable to reexamine my faith in voluntary death."

> Harry Crosby willed himself to die, and I, who was his wife . . . watching this will of his develop into consummation, have come to accept, in the years between, the value of the rightness of his act. During the seven years of an unbelievably perfect marriage [sic], both consciously and subconsciously, I accepted suicide as the *Summum Amor* to which I was ardently dedicated, and for which I promised I was waiting, *though never fully convinced and never quite ready.* [emphasis added]. It was to be the almost too beautiful rebellion . . . the answer of sex to spirit and spirit to the unknown—the full transition into love eternal . . . I was momentarily robbed. . . . But I know now that every man has the right to take his own life; "to die at the right time."

> Let each of us be given 70 years at birth—7, as a magical number, and 0, the full circle, as absolute. These years are given to us to mold, to strengthen, to beautify . . . to live each day as though it were our last . . . every hour of life, whether in study, work or rest will be significant . . . the final, or 70th anniversary of our birth will be a great day of rejoicing. . . .

*"For me, events of last year or
yesterday have lost their content. . .
only persons are memorable."*

—CARESSE

Chapter V

BORN TO MYSELF

At first light on April 20, 1892, Mary Phelps Jacob of New York was born. An Aries baby, she puckered up her crimson face and commanded attention, even while her proud father was still passing out cigars.

The name Jacob is derived from the Jacobeans, who—after the War of Roses—settled into Chale Abbey on the Isle of Wight. Like his father before him, William Jacob was a quiet man, who inherited an islander's love of silence. Unfortunately, he did not fall heir to his father's business acumen. Mary's Grandfather Jacob had arrived in America with no fortune but the good sense to marry an American heiress, Emma Lawrence. The then-popular brougham was the specialty of Riker Lawrence, manufacturer of gentlemen's carriages. Riker also had the vision to acquire large tracts of Manhattan real estate. But his carefully acquired reserves dwindled away with the advent of the horseless carriage, and his shortsighted sons considered the midtown property worthless, and disposed of it as soon as they inherited it.

"Poor father never liked being a businessman," his daughter Mary commented many years later. "He was an idealist who wrapped himself in a mantle of silence because the real world never lived up to his expectations." Most of the projects William Jacob believed in were dismissed by his stern, New England-born wife, Mary Phelps, as "Will's crazy ideas."

Named after her mother, young Mary numbered among her distinguished ancestors the first Governor of Massachusetts Bay Colony, William Bradford, and Robert Fulton, inventor of the steamboat. Four generations later, her Grandfather Phelps inherited a coal and iron business in Irontown, Connecticut, and firmly established, consolidated his position by marrying Eliza Schenk of Philadelphia, a daughter of the first U.S. Ambassador to the Court of St. James. As a youth, Phelps had led the Irontown Brigade at the Battle of Antietam; his dress sword hung in the Jacob living room under a handsome, tinted daguerrotype in full regimentals. Mary later observed: "This may account for [mother's] belligerent and caustic spirit. She was difficult to persuade and impossible to fool—she never avoided an issue." "Stupid" was the word that Mary Jacob used most often. It stung her children to the marrow, and to Mary, she added, "You're just like your father," as reproof. But the oval face—a cameo framed in a delicate widow's peak of dark hair, beautiful by candlelight—belied the inner strength of an unbending woman. Walter Jacob was her victim from the day they met at a midwinter skating party; he was in love with her until the day he died.

Hard and practical, yet an idealistic dreamer, was the child born of this union. At the time of Mary's birth, the Jacobs lived on the corner of 59th Street and Fifth Avenue, in a comfortable family brownstone on an expensive plot of land now occupied by the Plaza Hotel.

"I was the first child, I should have hated not to be," Mary noted. "I'll never forget the day I was born—born to myself, that is." She remembered the feel of soft snowflakes melting on her cheeks as, tucked inside a fur lap-robe, she was pushed by her devoted nanny around the edges of the duck pond in Central Park in an elegant Brewster baby sleigh of white enamel. Other early memories mingle with the faint aroma of baking pistachio cake, the scent of her grandfather's Andalusian sherry, of silver polish and Mark Cross saddle soap; "a world where only *good* smells exist."

Nicknamed "Polly" by her grandparents, she walked earlier and talked earlier than most babies, and at five, she was already lording it over Leonard (Len), only three, when the baby Walter (Buddy) was born. In the earliest photo of the three siblings, dressed in white,

Mary shows the responsible look of an older sister who encouraged her younger brothers in fresh Christopher Robin haircuts to hold still and face the camera.

"As a child, I lived almost completely in a world of make-believe," she remembered. Summers were spent at East Island "in a cottage built entirely of pink and saffron-colored seashells; the encrusted white plaster appeared as a fine mosaic, glowing red when the sunset struck across Long Island Sound." One mystical experience marred the idyll of endless summer days. Mary was lying flat on her stomach, fishing for minnows on the wharf, holding tight to the handle of a cumbersome bait hook, when she was dragged deep into the stream. Len, who was fishing nearby, also on his stomach, spotted his sister going under and braced himself to grab an ankle. Mary's head was being sucked under when her gentle Papa heard Len's shout and rushed to the other end of the pier. He hauled Mary out by both feet, while the heroic Len ran up the hill to tell Mama to call the Fire Department Rescue Squad. As Mary later described the experience:

> Into my ears the waters poured strange sea lullabies—not only did I see and hear harmony, but I *understood* everything . . . and I watched my father at work on his boat, my brother, deathly frightened, hanging onto my spindly heels, and I, my hair like seaweed, pulled flat against the submerged bottom of the float. Thus, while I drowned, I saw my father turn and act . . . I saw the efforts to bring me back to life, and I tried not to come back.
>
> There was no sadness or sickness from which I wished to escape. I was only seven, and a carefree child, yet that moment in all my life has never been equalled for pure happiness. Could I have glimpsed, while drowned (for *I was drowned!*) the freedom of eternal life? One thing I know, that Nirvana does exist between here and the hereafter—for I have been there.

For the most part, her early life was that of a typical upper-middle-class family at the turn of the century. The female children lived in a sheltered world of nannies and governesses. Mary was no exception. In the winter, little girls were fitted and fussed over by family seamstresses. "We were always *completely clothed,* even on beaches," she remembered. "To wear a sunsuit next to one's skin or to drive or ride without a coat and hat and gloves was unheard of." The Gibson Girl was the prototype of Mary's mother and aunts, who wore their hair piled high in pompadours, with sailor hats skewered on with devilish hatpins. Starched collars with bow ties fastened their finely pleated shirtwaists. In a Charles Dana Gibson photograph of 1904, Mary appears in a well-cut tan velveteen coat trimmed with a large Irish lace collar; a floppy hat with layer upon layer of accordion-pleated black chiffon was held firmly under the chin by an elastic band. She was also the subject of a Dana sketch, as a member of The Younger Generation, being pulled along Fifth Avenue by an enormous St. Bernard dog with a governess at her heels.

In fall 1900, Mary's Aunt Annie and Uncle Will Barnum decided that Ben, their delicate and sensitive only child, was to be educated at home by Miss Kimber, a young English governess of good family who came to New York to seek her fortune. Mary was invited to "Windward," the Barnum manor house, to be Ben's companion and weekday boarder.

"I could not have been at Windward long when the most exciting event of my life took place. I learned to *read*." She carried a book everywhere, and rushed through meals to get back to it. She awoke early to read before breakfast. When headaches became a problem, she was forbidden to read more than one hour a day, after supper. (Headstrong Mary smuggled books into the bathroom and stayed there for long intervals.) Thus began her lifelong addiction to books, as a childhood escape from a restrictive environment. "My own world was snug around me like a chrysalis, but the vista before me had no bounds or limits," Mary wrote.

Miss Kimber subscribed to *St. Nicholas* magazine, then edited by Mary Mapes Dodge, author of *Hans Brinker and the Silver Skates*. This broadened their horizons with short story and poetry contests. It also inspired Mary and her cousin Ben to publish their first literary venture, "The Madison Avenue Gazette," on gelatin board with runny, purple ink. Mary wrote the lead editorial on the joys of skating.

The Burton Holmes lectures at Carnegie Hall were also looked forward to with great anticipation. They transported Mary to exotic, distant lands—Paris, Peking, Tibet, and Troy—all of which she vowed she would one day visit. "Seated in a dangling basket, we were pulled by Holmes' seductive voice up the purple crags to fabulous heights of a Tibetan monastery. He would leave us dangling there, while my heart beat like a drum. What if the rope should break?"

After Mary's fourteenth birthday, Mrs. Jacob decided that it was time to select a boarding school, and without any discussion, Mary was sent off to Rosemary Hall in Connecticut. "I was neither happy nor unhappy those years at boarding school. Unintuitive teachers and unimaginative scholars irked me. My life was mostly dreams, and adults were the pale untouchables. It never occurred to me, those years, that I might change the course of my life." Admittedly, she was "as shy as a periwinkle withdrawing into its shell."

In Mary's second year at Rosemary Hall, an invitation to her first Yale prom was arranged by cousin Ben Barnum. Aunt Annie and Miss Flynn the seamstress designed a demure white eyelet dress with a voluminous, ruffled petticoat, high-boned guimpe of Valencia lace, and skirt that fell just above the ankles. With sun-burnished hair hanging long down her back and tied tight with a huge, black taffeta ribbon, Mary was miserable, completely overlooked by the sophisticated college girls in silk ball gowns, with curls piled fashionably high on their foreheads. She led the Grand March with Buster Barnum, but she wished she had stayed at home.

Mary had just accepted in her mind that she was a wallflower when a miracle occurred. Cole Porter of Whiffenpoof fame invited her to dance. Cole was a freckle-faced, equally shy Midwesterner who tripped over her feet, but, with his newly-acquired status as the composer of "In an Old-fashioned Garden," he could be forgiven. While they were dancing, he whispered a coveted invitation to rendezvous in New York the following Saturday, adding, "*Don't* bring a chaperone!" When Mary slipped away in borrowed finery to meet Cole at the Belmont Hotel, the long-anticipated date became a comedy of errors. For even though they laughed amicably about it in later years, she could never quite forgive Cole, an "older man," who called her a "funny kid" and offered what he presumed to be appropriate entertainment—tickets to the Barnum and Bailey Circus!

The next summer, the Barnums rented a camp on the Upper St. Regis in the Adirondack Mountains and invited their favorite niece to join them. While there, Mary met Richard Peabody, who was to play an important role in her life. She noted in her diary that he looked shy and that one of his front teeth was chipped at an angle. But she was smitten with the pint-sized skipper in white duck pants who sprinted ahead of the pack to win the Idem Class with his 22-foot boat, built for speed and endurance.

Several weeks later, Dick Peabody asked Mary to the Saturday night dance at Paul Smith's Hotel on the lake. He was just her age, a sophomore at the Groton Academy. But before the evening was over, he impetuously asked if she would marry him when he graduated from Harvard. Even at that early age, Mary loved to say "Yes." She promised to wait seven years, though Dick was too shy to kiss her goodnight. The next morning, she recalled, they met and sat together in church, "feeling solemn, scared, and very old." Both families, when informed of the engagement, made it known that they were much too young to consider "keeping company." But if they still felt the same way, they would give more thought to the proposal after Dick graduated from Harvard.

That winter, Mary learned the joys of sleigh rides under fur lap robes, of beaux taking the *long* way to Fraunces' Tavern, of cotillion flowers pressed between the pages of Elizabeth Barrett Browning's poems, of a cherished lace handkerchief "accidentally" left in a pocket, of ardent messages written on prom cards.

"Flirtation is the minuet of love," Mary later wrote of that lost art. "It takes grace and precision—a time of ease—to flirt. To flirt is not to court, to 'go with,' or to chase; 'going with' narrows the field and excludes one from fun and frivolous delights."

During the 1908 Christmas season, Mary's gentle, beloved father died. It was one of the great losses of her life, and she cried inconsolably for the quiet man who left her, "before I really knew him." Until she was eight, he had been her "whole world." In recent years, he had lived in the only place where his asthma was bearable, a Utopian community on the Brazos River in Texas. In those early days before the field of psychiatry developed, doctors failed to deduce that his physical symptoms worsened when he came East to face the harangues of his petulant wife. "Idealists are all crackpots until they become heroes or saints," Mary wrote in later life. In her view, Will Jacob was a saint, although her mother never learned to see him as such.

Early that fall, her father had come home from San Antonio for his annual visit. He arrived unexpectedly at Rosemary Hall on a bright Sunday afternoon in October to say goodbye. Mary sensed it might be the last time. "I catapulted into his arms. I saw at once that he was very ill, and I wanted to comfort him." A great surge of maternal love washed over her when she noticed that her father was carrying a white wicker basket of grapes, "like a votive offering."

Another of her father's idealistic experiments was the Home Club on East 45th Street, where the Jacobs stayed in town every winter. Uncle Will and several of his Wall Street partners backed two brownstone fronts with a communal dining hall designed to cut heating bills and other expenses by half. It was there that Mary made her debut in 1910. Forever the nonconformist like her father, she rebelled against the boxlike armor of whalebone and pink cordage locked in place by a "corset cover" of muslin or silk that encased every debutante of that era. It was the cause of great embarrassment, peeping out from the neckline of a low-cut ball gown, forever being pushed back out of sight.

"I'm not going to wear that thing tonight," she stubbornly told Marie, her ever-present lady's maid cum chaperone.

"But you can't go out without a *soutien-gorge*," Marie insisted.

"You'll see. Bring me two handkerchiefs and a needle and some thread," Mary ordered. She pinned the handkerchiefs together, on the bias, and stitched the pink ribbons to the two points below the breast bone. Then she instructed Marie to tie the ribbons tight around her waist.

In the dressing room during the dance, her companions flocked around to peak at her new invention. She promised to have Marie make copies for her friends, if they'd supply the handkerchiefs. Mary called the device a "backless brassière," referring to the fact that it slipped over the arms in front, leaving the back bare.

Several years later she hired a young Harvard Law clerk with the firm of Mitchell Chadwick & Kent to draw up an application for "The Brassière, Invented by M.P. Jacob," registered on February 12, 1914 at the U.S. Patent Office. After her marriage, Mary Jacob Peabody sold copyright #1,115,674 to Warner & Company for $1,500, which appeared to be a large sum at the time. "I can't say the brassiere will ever take as great a place in history as the steamboat, but I did invent it," she was reported to have said.

Through the years, Mary's friendship with Dick Peabody ripened, and although they quarreled often, they always reconciled with chaste kisses. As Dick's graduation from Harvard approached, the families decided on a final test of their young love and sent Mary to London for the social season in 1913. She was presented at the King's Garden Party, and an English spring, crowded with new experiences and admirers, helped her to forget the Harvard boys. But by August, 1914 Mary was back in Boston again, engaged to marry Dick Peabody.

Before she left London, she had written Dick to let him know she was coming home, fearing that by now he might have found someone else. But consistent to the Peabody character, Dick was waiting on the dock when she landed and rushed her off to a glorified summer palace on the North Shore where the family and servants adjourned from Beacon Street and Commonwealth Avenue during the warm months.

The engagement was announced formally at the dinner party of a family friend, Bayard Warren. Across the candle-lit table, in the murmur of polite conversation, she heard the news that England was going to France's aid and had just declared war on Germany.

"It can't last more than a few months," predicted their host.

"I'd like to take a crack at those Huns," Dick added.

"Wonder if we'll get into it?" asked his good friend, Ollie Ames, one of the most envied undergrads in Boston. Ames was seated next to—and falling in love with—a black-haired beauty, Kay Fessenden.

"The British will clean them up in no time. It'll be over by Christmas," Oliver Ames' father predicted.

On that happy night, no one could imagine that Ollie would be among the first casualties of Chateau-Thierry; Kay, the first war widow of their circle. Or that Dick, also at Chateau-Thierry, would return to Mary seriously flawed.

Both families were reluctant to set the wedding date for early January, 1915. "Poor Richard might as well be marrying a Hottentot as Polly Jacob of *New York*," complained one aristocratic Bostonian. Tight-lipped Mary Jacob, the bride's mother, had a premonition that Dick's drinking might become a problem. (At Harvard, alcohol played a dramatic part in academic and social life.) "New York boys are far *better behaved*," she commented wryly.

Despite all the objections, Dick Peabody and Polly Jacob were duly joined in matrimony at the Barnums' Windward estate, with Uncle "Cottie" (the renowned Reverend Endicott Peabody) coming down from Groton to officiate. For the small family wedding, the bride wore a blue dress with the wide sailor collar to please Uncle Will. But for the festive reception afterwards, she changed into white panne velvet and Venetian-point lace. Late that night, after the last guest departed, Mary and Dick walked (ran as soon as they were out of sight) down the hill to the stone cottage on the edge of the property where Mary's mother and father had also been initiated into the rites of conjugal life.

Using the euphemism of the time, Mary had promised to "wait for" Dick. The line was primly drawn at Harvard between "nice" girls, whom undergraduates married, and the "chippies" they consorted with at roadhouses on the Boston turnpike. Exploratory sessions with "Flossie" at Ferncroft had made Dick Peabody an adept, if not ardent lover. That he married a "nice girl" who acted like a "chippie" both frightened and delighted him. If, in retrospect, the "first time" with Dick failed to evoke the most erotic fantasies of Mary's girlhood, she discovered new delights with him. For a brief time, Mary was happy and fulfilled, "busy with my new household toys."

To support his new responsibilities, Dick decided not to return to Harvard in the fall. He took a position in sales at Johns-Manville Company, commuting to New York. When snow covered the ground and made the front steps slippery with ice, the Peabodys moved into Manhattan to be nearer to Dr. Thomas, the gynecologist who delivered all of the "best babies" on Manhattan's East Side. William Jacob Peabody was born on February 4, 1916.

But Dick found it difficult to adjust to married life, impossible to accept his new status as paterfamilias. He himself had been an only child, who was never allowed to play with other children—or even to cry—by his stern New England parents. When he first forbade *his* infant son Billy to do so, inevitably, Billy cried louder than before. Dick fled from the apartment and often took refuge in the corner bar. To his credit, he always returned, but usually long after Mary had gone to sleep.

In April Dick resigned from Johns-Manville as precipitously as he had left Harvard, and the Peabodys moved back to Quaker Ridge. He persuaded a reluctant Mary to invest the small inheritance from her father in a private shipping venture. Some months before declaring bankruptcy, he found an easy out with Groton classmates leaving for the Mexican Border. They persuaded Dick to join Boston's Battery A, the crack militia, and Mary was left behind with an infant son, deposited on his parents' doorstep the day he left. There was no alternative for Mary. Her legacy was gone—and so was Dick.

Bringing up a child in a household governed by her mother-in-law's strict rules must have been penitential for spirited, fun-loving Mary. The house at Danvers, Massachusetts, had been brought over from England, brick by brick, by an ancestral ship owner from Salem, not long after the witchcraft trials. It was too often shuttered to be healthy, quite different from Mary's "enchanted" East Island home. Her mother-in-law, Florence Wheatland, had been a sensational beauty before marrying Colonel Jacob Peabody, a rigid stickler for military polish in manners and minerals. He had ground her down into plainness until she took refuge in illness, both real and imagined. Day and night she wore knitted bed jackets and nun-like dresses in solid grey, brown, or black.

When Mary entered this strange, muted household, marked only by visits from the doctor or grocer, her mother-in-law kept to herself, in the other part of the house, except to mutter complaints about the behavior of a wayward, burdensome daughter-in-law. Mary was sinking deep into depression, with only a six-month-old baby for companionship, when Dick came home briefly, just long enough to sign up for World War I. He was stationed in a Plattsburg, New York training camp, scheduled to sail for France in ten days. The baby conceived in October arrived on an unbearably hot July day. A daughter, she was christened Polleen Wheatland Peabody. Before Dick sailed, they had several nights in New York at the Belmont, which exhausted Mary and alienated Dick. He was ashamed of Mary's conspicuous bulge during pregnancy and couldn't find much to love about a limp, dispirited young mother, carrying a red-faced crybaby.

Again, Dick escaped and Mary was back "in the shadow of disaster," as a young war widow under her father-in-law's roof. "Many of my friends were caught in the same cruel trap," she recalled philosophically, "but I was one of the luckier ones. Dick came back."

Even at this early date, she began to consider the horrors of war, to formulate her future campaign for peace. ("To me, then as always, war was a cruel and brutal form of 'exhibitionism.'")

On the eve of Polleen's first birthday the next July, Dick returned to the States on leave. His orders called for further training in Columbia, South Carolina before shipping out again for France. Mary, who had never been south of Philadelphia, was summoned to join him. She sat up all night on a stifling, wartime train, arriving 18 hours later in a incongruous navy blue taffeta dress. There had been no money or time to replace her winter wardrobe.

Their reunion was brief and ardent. Dick's lanky body looked hardened and handsome in uniform, and he was sporting a new moustache. Mary's desire for him had never been stronger, but there was no room at the Inn, and Dick had to report back to camp by eleven that night.

"I'll go with you," Mary pleaded.

"Wives are not allowed in the BOQ," Dick replied. "But I know a place. My platoon *dug* it this morning. We'll get a blanket."

Dutifully, Mary went along, still wearing the taffeta dress. In her memoirs, she recalled the rude awakening of the Captain and his lady when the caissons came rolling along the path the next morning. She discovered that she had spent an ardent night in a trench.

Resourceful as ever, Mary soon found housing in the war-crowded Southern town, and went North to fetch the children. In the artificial world of belles and courteous gentlemen, of Officer's Club dances and dark-skinned nurses to look after the babies, the Peabodys spent some of the happiest months of their married lives.

Dick was spared by the Armistice from returning to France. By Thanksgiving, they had returned to Back Bay and acquired a Marlborough Street house described as "Boston as baked beans," smelling deliciously of cardamon and spice, brought back by a Yankee trader. "We could have been as happy as we were in South Carolina, but Dick was soon out of uniform, and he had not accepted the reality of our marriage," she wrote later. Jobs were few, Dick was restless and frustrated; whisky was plentiful. "I lived like a nun while he was away, but in France it was hard to live like a monk. Glorious memories of France obscured his vision."

While Dick was at war, Mary had matured in her new role of mother. "Ours was a boy-girl affair," she confided in her memoirs. "I was supposed to remain the perfect playmate." She discovered that it is very difficult to "play" with an irresponsible husband after a full day in the nursery.

After one hopeless, confining winter, Mary had reached a nadir. Dick's health began to suffer, and special nurses were required to watch over him around the clock. Mary's father-in-law was overseas with the Red Cross, her mother-in-law sinking deeper into invalidism. It was too much for Mary to cope with alone. She thought of Uncle Jack. Richard Peabody was his godson and they had always been exceptionally close. He now lived at East Island, which the Morgans bought from her paternal grandfather and rechristened "Matinacock."

Her first visit as a Peabody to her childhood home was a disappointment. Her Grandfather Phelps's house had been swept away "like some cobweb fantasy." The carriage block, the pebbled paths, the spring house, the kitchen garden, and the duck pond were missing. Even "the little wooden pier, the purple mussel shoals, the languorous seaweed, and 'sand-locked diamonds'," Mary remembered were gone. Instead, she found a long, level lawn and a formal, uninviting mansion. But Uncle Jack's welcome was genuine. "He must have known by my voice when I rang up that I needed help—

desperately." The busy financier responded by offering a check and some very sound advice.

"Can you get a friend of Dick's to go with you to my Adirondack camp? And someone to stay with the children?" She assured him that she could. Morgan made two phone calls, putting things in order. His son Junius would see to the railroad tickets. "I'm here whenever you need me," he added, before the phone beckoned again from the Wall Street office.

The dreary winter landscape at the Lake was brightened by good company, an open fire, and a library well stocked with books. Mary hoped that clean air and solitude, without the problems of family and commercial life, would heal Dick's wounded psyche. They took long rides in a fur-piled sleigh and fished through the ice on the lake. But one unfortunate day, a delivery boy smuggled in a bottle of Scotch, and Dick became menacingly difficult again. Mary telephoned Junius. In a last effort to save his life, the Peabody-Morgan alliance rallied to her support and committed Dick to a sanitarium for alcoholics.

"That was the spring I met Harry."

"If two lie together, then they have heat,
but how can one be warm alone?"
—ECCLESIASTES

Chapter VI

LIFE AFTER HARRY

On December 13, 1929—as originally planned—Caresse sailed
for France on the *Mauretania*, accompanied by Henrietta. She
carried the urn holding Harry's ashes, wrapped in his red-and-gold
Magyar robe, when she boarded, along with Harry's holograph copy
of *Sleeping Together*, "dreams for Caresse"—the last poems he wrote.
On the title page, Harry had inscribed prophetically a verse from
Ecclesiastes: "If two lie together, then they have heat, but how can one
be warm alone?"

It was bitterly cold on December 22 when Caresse and her mother-
in-law arrived in Le Havre. They hurried to reach Ermenonville by
Christmas. "There was a fine dry snowfall in the air. The cozy and
twinkling appearance of the Mill filled my heart to bursting as we
approached . . . I was at home," Caresse wrote.

Mrs. Crosby stayed on, and several good friends came as soon as
they heard the news. Gretchen and "Pete" Powel, devoted companions on many Paris escapades, stood by to offer support and
condolences. Gerard Lymington was dispatched to Cheam to break
the tragic news to Billy and to bring him home to the Mill to share his

mother's grief. Bill Sykes, the devoted friend who had smuggled gold pieces in his shoes to pay D.H. Lawrence for the *Sun* manuscript, went to fetch Polleen.

"I was at boarding school when Harry died," Polleen recalled in her memoirs. "I had been awakened before dawn and put on a train from Gstaad, without explanation, on a cold, wet morning. A family friend met me at the station in Montreux and broke the news, not in detail, but in stark reportage, saying that my stepfather had shot himself. I was desolate—not with the feeling of bereavement of a beloved parent, but rather the shattering sorrow of a woman losing an adored lover."

"It was a long journey, and when I arrived late that evening I found my mother in tears. We both cried in each other's arms until I bedded down on the chaise-longue in her room for the night. Just before falling asleep, Mama called to me through the darkness: '. . . anyway, I am glad that he is dead because of you'."

"To this day," Polleen wrote, "I do not know how to interpret her statement."

> I presumed she meant that sooner or later, Harry would have seduced me, too? Or, could it be that she was frantically jealous of the special attention he gave me? His love letters to me—and they were indeed, *love* letters—she later found and destroyed. She was aware that something was going on between us. Her jealousy led her to steal, one by one, all of the little trinkets Harry had given me—a Cartier watch, books and paintings. (I knew she was doing this, but did not dare face her with the facts.)

Rivalry for Harry's affection was so intense between mother and daughter, even before Harry's death, that Polleen's childhood admiration soon turned to cold resentment.

Caresse did not suffer alone in the months that followed. Many devoted friends looked after her.

"The Aviator" (Cord Meier), one of Harry's companions from his flying days at Le Bourget, was among the first to appear. He had a handsome, foxy profile, was rich and worldly, and loved to dance— which Harry never did. "He brought beautiful furs, and he asked me on Christmas Day to marry him quickly so that he could protect me from the cruelty of the world," Caresse recalled. "I'll never marry again," was her answer. "I'm still married to Harry."

Caresse shut herself away in the Mill to capture in verse the essence of her life with Harry. While the snow fell in deep drifts, she gathered her memories around her in front of a bright fire. The poetry flowed, spontaneous and swift, "almost as though some urgent ghost was providing guidance."

When she had finished, Hart Crane critiqued what he considered to be her best work, *Poems for Harry Crosby*. He particularly praised "Invited to Die," in which Caresse described the Crosby's last day together:

> Our eyes were opened to a blaze of Sun,
> Clean sunbuilt dawn the day we owned New York
>   I did not guess
>   I did not guess
> That madder beauty waited, unaware,
> To take your hand upon the evening stair.

The poem, "My Heart," Crane called "another YOU. You are meant to heartbreak people," he added. "Love ways, pain ways, courage ways. I love YOU."

After exorcising the ghosts, Caresse was ready again to say "Yes!" to life. "While I kept the secret place [for Harry] alive and lighted, I trod the hedonistic paths of play and the healing ways of work."

"Mama was not one to be defeated by disaster," Polleen conceded. "A great fighter, she always overcame the many setbacks that came her way."

At 37, Caresse was still a beautiful woman. Life at the rue de Lille resumed its heady pace. Polleen wrote: "Mama draped herself in yards of black crepe, wore sheerest black-silk stockings, and donned a little bell-shaped toque. Clutching a bunch of violets, she set out to reconquer man—that is to say, practically any man in sight! Her favorite black whippet Narcisse Noir, in a Hermès morning coat, accompanied her in the long, green limousine of immense chic, a Voisin Coupe de Ville. She was exciting, wildly pretty, and wore elegant clothes that were delivered in shiny white boxes with labels that read: Paquin, Worth, Chanel, Schiaparelli. Frequently I was dragged along to my mother's fittings—in a blue-serge coat with brass buttons, short pleated skirt, grey socks, and shabby shoes, with long straight bangs I could almost chew! Mama moved fast on those slim, thoroughbred legs, after the first will-o'-the-wisp that caught her fancy, often altering course in mid-flight on some quixotic impulse. Her children were often left stranded in odd places. But I became quite used to this way of life. . . .''

In the spring of 1931, Caresse began the difficult task of editing Harry's collected poems in four volumes. For each volume, she asked ''a distinguished man of letters,'' many of whom were former Black Sun authors, to write an introduction: D.H. Lawrence for *Chariots of the Sun*, T.S. Eliot for *Transit of Venus*, Stuart Gilbert for *Sleeping Together*, and Ezra Pound for *Torchbearers*.

Throughout their long correspondence about the publication of Ezra's *Imaginary Letters*, the Crosbys and Pound had never met. But Caresse liked his introduction best. Ezra wrote that Harry's was ''a death from excess vitality, a vote of confidence in the cosmos.'' As his life was ''almost a religious manifestation,'' so his death was ''a magnificent finale.''

In early spring, ''when we Parisians were rigidly pale with winter,'' Caresse noted, ''Ezra arrived from Rapallo, bronzed and negligé. There was a becoming shabbiness to his beard.'' (Polleen's view of the eccentric poet was quite different. ''In his loud checked trousers, looking a bit crazy with his yellow beard in disarray, smelling of booze, he tried to kiss me on the mouth, on the stairs of our flat. . . . I was outraged for a week, in fact, I avoided him every time he came back.'')

Ezra wanted to savor the flavor of Paris by night. They went to the Boule Blanche, a *boite* where a band from Martinique was beating out hot, tropical merengues at a frenetic pace. Caresse and Ezra had a ringside table, but because of her broken heart, Caresse would not, could not dance. As the music grew in fury, Ezra suddenly leapt to the floor and seized a tiny Martiniquaise vendor of cigarettes in his arms, eyes closed, chin out, as he began a hypnotic ''voodoo prance.'' The music grew hotter, as did Ezra, and one by one the dancers drifted from the floor to form a ring to watch ''that Anglo-savage ecstasy,'' until the music crashed to an end. ''From that time,'' Caresse recalled, ''Ezra and I became the best of friends.''

''After my stepfather's death, the list of Mama's lovers grew longer,'' Polleen observed wryly, ''and was very inconsistent in quality. There was a Tartar prince, who told me the gory tale—and I believed him—that he cut off the ears of his enemies and strung them on his belt. Perhaps that is why he was soon replaced by the gypsy painter, Manolo Ortíz. Ortíz displayed such fearsome jealousy that often I was taken along on outings to his studio to forestall any verbal or physical assault on Mama, who clearly—he declared—'had done him wrong.' With flashing eyes, paint brushes and palette in hand, he stormed around the studio until he ran out of breath."

"Then there was Mother's lover who lived on a barge in the Seine, Franz de Geetere. He was a wild-looking Dutchman, very tall and wiry, with the extraordinarily beautiful hands of a painter—which he was, by profession. (I discovered folio upon folio of erotic drawings in a wooden trunk on the barge!) More interesting to me at that time was the fact that he also made kites, and when the breeze was right, we would fly them from the deck. . . ."

"Mama was always partial to titles, especially the British," Polleen confided. Gerard Lymington (later to become Earl of Portsmouth) she had known from the earliest days, when the Black Sun Press published his poetry, *Spring Song of Iscariot*. Lord Lymington— poet and peer—Harry and Caresse had formed a special trio. Now there were two.

On May 23, Gerard wrote: "Will you be in Paris or at the Moulin if I come over next Thursday? Let me know if you don't want me. Bless you, Caresse. You know so much that lies between these lines, so I won't say [it]." Even after Gerard's presumably happy marriage, Caresse often visited the Lymingtons at Farleigh-Wallop, their country estate near Portsmouth. He never failed to end his letters to Caresse, "With my dearest love and devotion," even through the last year of her life.

"I don't know why he loved my mother so faithfully for so long," Polleen commented, "since he was sorely neglected, and in those early years, often was left alone with me and one of my dreadful governesses. On such evenings, he would put on his pajamas and go out for a walk; perhaps by so doing he felt part of the crazy Bohemian world of the Left Bank. (Meanwhile Mama, in widow's weeds, was dining and dancing with someone else!)"

"It was not until spring that I came alive again," Caresse recalled later, "after I met Jacques Porel, son of the famed French actress, Réjane . . . that is, I remet him for the first time since he separated from his beautiful wife Anne-Marie, and I became I widow." She was calling for her mail in the Morgan Bank in the Place Vendôme, and Jacques was there changing francs. "We met in the revolving doors and revolved together out into the brisk sunshine. So off we went down the rue St. Honoré to Le Cremaillière, the most fashionable small restaurant in Paris, and once inside that revolving door, I realized the die was cast.'' Jacques and Caresse were the hottest gossip item of *le tout Paris*.

There was an amorous evening when they took the Bateau Mouche down the Seine to a riverside cafe beyond Versailles. There was love in the afternoon after a thunderstorm at Melun, with Roquefort and burgundy and a mechanical piano that played *"Et puis ça va,"* over and over again.

That summer, Caresse and Polleen were invited by the Philip Barry's for a holiday on the Côte d'Azur. The Barrys were old friends who had accompanied Caresse on the *Mauretania* to France with Harry's ashes. They had taken a villa in Cannes for the season with the royalties from Barry's *Animal Kingdom*, a resounding hit on Broadway, and offered their quiet retreat with a garden and view of the sea for Caresse's recuperation.

But soon after Caresse arrived, she was besieged with letters from Jacques, writing from the Pavillon Henri IV in St. Germain-en-Laye:

> . . . It's three o'clock . . . my bed is still undone, . . . I feel like having you here in my room . . . if you were here, I should take off your clothes (I have got none) one by one and stand hard against you, kissing your neck, near your hair and your ears . . . and then I would push you smoothly on the bed . . . and come so near you that we would make only one. But I should watch those eyes— when kissing your little mouth—to see in them that grey cloud moving . . . and hear that wonderful and imperfect song you sing . . . . Come back to the Mill and let me have you in my arms again, and kiss you everywhere—and let me remain long in you like I did during those marvelous days in Primavera.

Caresse, who could never be quiet for long, succumbed and invited Jacques to come down. Soon, they shared cold lobster and *vin rosé* on a balcony overlooking an indigo sea, with the shadow of ochre sails dotting the harbor at Marseilles.

In midsummer, Jacques and Caresse motored back to Paris from Cannes, leaving Polleen behind under Ellen Barry's watchful eye. They first visited friends at Biarritz, and while there, impulsively decided to cross the Spanish border into San Sebastian to see the American bullfighter, Sidney Franklin, make his debut. They had heard that Ernest Hemingway planned to be there. He was research-ing a book (later to be titled *Death in the Afternoon*).

For Hemingway, bullfighting was the emotional substitute for war, "the only place where you can see life and death, i.e., violent death, now that the wars were over, and I wanted very much to go to Spain to study it." In his view, the so-called "self-hardening process" was necessary to the experience of a developing writer.

Caresse arranged to meet the Hemingways at a café frequented by the toreadors, on a corner near the bullring.

> Hemingway, Pauline, and his eldest son—a boy of about six—were there already. The child, Bumbi, was being given lessons in the handling of the cape by one of the elderly bullfighters. We found Hemingway straddling a chair in a far corner, the old Spaniard explaining an intricate maneuver. The boy had to repeat it again and again; his father was a difficult taskmaster.

Pauline Pfeiffer, Hemingway's second wife, was seven months pregnant, and they were hurrying back to the States so that the child would be native born and eligible to become President. Ernest was one of the few men who did not succumb to Caresse's charm. From the beginning, the chemistry was not right, and future encounters between the two would be difficult and stormy. Their first meeting was marred by an unfortunate mishap. When they left San Sebastian, Pauline forgot her bag with the passports in the back seat of Caresse's car. The fact that Caresse did not discover the loss until she had crossed the French border started the relationship on an uneasy footing. Caresse attempted to compensate by offering to pay for their return passage to New York in exchange for a manuscript.

But when the promised manuscript arrived at the Black Sun Press, "It looked like a discarded passage from *Farewell to Arms*," Caresse complained. "The whole thing amounted to about 1,000 words—mostly one-word lines of four-letter words—nothing to do with toreadors. I was so indignant and disappointed, I wanted to cry," she later admitted. Instead, she impetuously composed a letter to the author, noting at that price his prose was "mighty precious." In reply, Ernest fired back that no one could call Hemingway "precious" and get away with it!

The Hemingways were back in Paris, stopping at a small Left Bank hotel halfway between the rue Cardinale and the rue de Lille, when Caresse finally located them. She hurried over, manuscript in hand, to demand the return of their advance passage-money in exchange for her "precious" package. Taken by surprise, the Hemingways were still in bed. Ernest muttered something about "that bitch," but on the verge of departure, he was willing to negotiate. With some reluctance, he promised rights to reprint *Torrents of Spring* as the first Crosby Continental Edition.

That autumn—in the library of 19 rue de Lille where the Black Sun Press was conceived in 1927—Caresse and Porel planned to transform the Black Sun from a small press specializing in finely printed limited editions into a commercial firm in direct competition with the prestigious German publisher, Tauchnitz. At that time, it was the only firm on the Continent reprinting English classics. Caresse was optimistic that there was an even larger market for inexpensive editions of the best of the young expatriate American writers and avant-garde European authors.

She wrote to Ezra Pound about her new publishing venture:

> They say they have a big demand for English printed books . . . not to exceed 20 francs each, preferably 15 francs each . . . . [I plan] to do an edition of two books per month to begin with at least 2,000 copies each. The first few books must be good sellers . . . after that, [I have] . . . carte blanche. Hemingway promised me three stories. . . . I've just seen him in Spain. . . . I am going to call it:
>
> The Crosby Library European Editions
> -or-
> The Crosby Continental Library
> Crosby Collection Continental Editions?
>
> I think *Torrents of Spring* the best book to do because, to many people, it will look like something new, as few of Hemingway's admirers have read it, and it has not been reprinted.

Ezra soon replied with wise counsel and encouragement. Thanking him, Caresse wrote: "Your wonderful and enthusiastic letter about bucking Tauchnitz gave me a thrill, for if you really will help, I'm sure we can do wonders." (She appeared to be unaware that *Torrents of Spring* was a satirical, and to many, an unflattering portrait of Sherwood Anderson; she selected it to "get hold of a public.")

Never one to hold a grudge, Caresse mended fences with Hemingway in an Open Letter (which became the Introduction to *Torrents of Spring*, the first Crosby Continental Edition):

Dear Ernest:

. . . Do you remember that torrential day in Spain last August . . . when we all foregathered after the *corrida*, you, your wife, Jacques and I and the boot-black . . . in the little *posada* behind the arena? The place was full of English and Americans; you and Charlie [Chaplin] were the focus of many admiring eyes and I felt very jealous of you. . . . I wanted to do something as you two had done something; I wanted to make something out of all this Anglo-Saxon alertness and zest for discovery of new things in ancient lands.

The barrier that separates us and always will . . . is the difference in language. Local color, bulls and blood are all very well, but one wants to know what the people are saying and thinking . . . that is what I was thinking of, across the din and pageantry of that afternoon—my thoughts were revolving round a new idea, to give all these eager travelers a glimpse into the minds of the people they were visiting; something more than local color, rather the racial consciousness that makes and mixes the color, as the painter mixes the paints of his palette.

I am beginning the collection with an American book, your book, because I admire it and because I know I am not the only one to admire what you write; a few million others do, too. I am going to publish books that I like, that have merit, and that interest me, amuse me personally . . . the colors of the titles should match the countries . . . green for the *Torrents of Spring* in honor of Diana and the woods of Michigan!

I am lucky to begin my collection with a book of yours . . . you and those Miura bulls are, between you, responsible not only for this edition of *Torrents of Spring*, but for many CCE's to come.

Good fishing, and again, many thanks.

The summer romance with Porel intensified in the fall. In October, Jacques wrote to say that his break with Anne-Marie might be a permanent one:

Yes, I was wise in leaving. . . . I have now to decide whether I shall *ever* live again in Laurent Pichat or not. I can't very well be all my life going from place to place, and the exchange of letters between Anne-Marie and myself does not show that things are going to an end of any sort. Anne-Marie seems to think quite natural to go on living in my things, with my child, without taking the slightest care of whatever happens to me. . . .

His ardor for Caresse increased, in spite of this November message: "I received yesterday a cable saying that I was father of a magnificent boy and that he and his mother were as well as could be. I don't know how much he weighs, or how he will be called. . . . Life is strange." Characteristically, he added the only other important news—in his view—of that day: "I lunched yesterday at Dolly Radziwill and played croquet the whole afternoon."

Jacques, who had always been dependent upon his wife or mother for support, added a note in the margin to his new benefactor: "You have been a dear about that *Impremir* . . . . How can I thank you? I shan't thank you, because you are always like that . . . you are *made* like that." Caresse was the quintessential "giver," but the men in her life were more often "takers." They left her emotionally exhausted and financially exploited, and in the end, wrung out like a discarded sponge. Her daughter deplored that in spite of the many acclaimed artists and writers Crosby discovered, "She died without a bob [shilling]."

Later in the fall, Caresse traveled to Berlin to buy inks and fine papers for the press, while Jacques' letters remained constant. He was exceptionally perceptive of her nature:

> Caresse, you don't understand me, and I understand you so well and you are such a dear and I am so fond of you. . . . I like your letters because they're like you, spontaneous and childish. You are more clever than the women I know who are stupid, conventional. . . . I only find beauty in what might happen, in that lyrical and deep interior of a clever mind. You find me dull, funny, incomprehensible, because you are much more "in life" than I am and you want to be happy, as young people want to be sailors or diplomats, and I consider it an accident, not a vocation. . . .
>
> I can see you from this silly little room with a beautiful view, surrounded by dogs, friends, servants and other impedimenta . . . and lots of talk will take place.

*   *   *

Again in January, when Jacques was in the U.S. visiting a married sister while trying to sell Crosby Continental Editions to New York publishers, he wrote from the St. Moritz Hotel:

> Sweet darling,
>   I have already written this morning, but I want again to write tonight. . . . It was wonderful hearing your voice from the middle of the ocean. . . .
>   Darling, you are a wonderful little woman, and I kiss you all over, all around everywhere, and I love you and your little thing of which I am thinking often and often. I am writing from my bed . . . I want to be alone with my little woman against a wall with sun and shade and heat and make love to her with that wet noise that excites me, and for H's sake, no bloody fools, . . . either of the Ritz or Montparnasse!!

After a month's absence, the correspondence from the St. Moritz remained ardent:

> Just one week now and I shall be sailing again towards you. How wonderful it will be to meet again. . . . I will hold your hand, kiss your mouth repeatedly and caress your hair (not forgetting looking into your eyes!) I hope you are well, not too tired, and taking care of yourself. I hope that Polleen business is coming off alright. We spoke of it, Mrs. Stuart and myself, the other evening, and she seems to think also that the child . . . who stayed in the country with her and talked . . . needs a more regular life. Be firm, . . . I am afraid you have to. If not, this is also going to be an awful mess, like the one that was made of *my* stepdaughter.

Polleen, for her part, was not taken in by her mother's elegant Parisian lover. "I believe that Mama was truly in love with Jacques. He was on the scene much longer than most. The servants hated him, because his conduct was truly outrageous. He spent most of his time flirting with anyone in sight, including myself and my classmates when they came home with me. I myself felt that he was *using* my mother and all of her glittering entourage, rather than truly caring for her as he pretended. But he was good looking and clever; he had a sort of seductive charm, even if he was a bit of a *pic-assiette*." [The closest English equivalent for this French idiom is "sponger."] "After one particularly stormy encounter, Mama was ensconced for some time in Lady Carnavon's smart nursing home in London with a heart ailment . . . whether there was any connection between Mama's malaise and Jacques' behavior, I could only guess."

Polleen guessed rightly. Caresse's illness followed a particularly stormy exchange, in which Jacques had written to Caresse "*dans sa langue maternelle*" to better express his true feelings. The line "*Je ne vous ai pas trompée*" [I have never deceived (or cheated on) you] was ill chosen. Caresse returned that page of the letter to Jacques, with the phrase underlined in red pencil. In a marginal note, she added: "*Why?* This is rather beastly and has made me feel physically sick."

A telegram from Jacques followed: "Terribly hurt by your letter."

By the next post, a note without salutation was dispatched to London:

> Caresse:
>
> I have one more word to say. If you are a woman capable of writing what you wrote to me in that short note, because there was one page in one of my letters that did not please you, it means for me to have to regret completely all that happened between us. . . . I am quite unwell here, doped with veronal and tobacco—in an awful state of nerves.
>
> Thank you for this last American punch.
>
> Jacques

Caresse, who had fled to England in an attempt to forget Jacques by enjoying the London season, was stricken with the first of the *crises cardiaques* that plagued her for the rest of her life. She was attending a gala showing of Siegfried Sassoon's collection at Lymington's London townhouse. "As I mounted the great ancestral staircase . . . the stairwell whirled like a spinning top and I quietly wilted down beneath the spangled slippers and heels of polished boots. . . . My heart seemed to suffocate inside the bodice. . . . I tried to pull open the high-boned collar at my throat—and then, all was oblivion . . . . When I came to, a white-capped nurse and other unfamiliar faces hung above me. . . ."

Jacques did not rush to her side.

So your doctor says you have done too much and must not. Well, darling, there is no doubt, you do much too much. You go here and there, and fuss a lot. All that is terribly bad for your heart. It's all very fine to say it is . . . on account of me, but what about the wrong food, the wrong drink, that life of a movie star, and those dresses and fur coats, and [between the lines] . . . *all those attractive boys!*

Caresse recovered sufficiently to return to New York for Christmas, with Jacques following soon after. Spirited and full of charm, he became the most sought-after man about town. "He still possessed a key to the Press, but it no longer fitted my heart," Caresse reported wryly. "When I sailed away, Jacques stayed on as the cavalier of a much-publicized New York matron."

Some six months after its launching, Crosby Continental Editions had taken in profits amounting to only $1,200. The question uppermost in Caresse's mind was whether to continue the series, and if so, for how much longer. She wrote to Kay Boyle, whose opinion she respected, for advice and encouragement.

Kay's response was quick and positive. "Consider how many years it takes to build up most publishing houses, and you have started off with an almost unprecedented publicity bang. . . . I should think you would simply have to give it another year's trial."

In reply, Caresse confessed: "I find it discouraging to have to wait on time. If an idea could not materialize at first trial, I move on to another and another, getting no further in the end. I hate to compromise. I'd almost rather give up."

In one last attempt to sell the idea of paperbacked books—20 years ahead of its time—to American publishers, Caresse returned to New York. Even the editors she knew best (including Dick Simon of Simon and Schuster, with whom she had traveled the *route enchantée* to the Côte d'Azur and shared "adjoining balconies") advised that the American public would never buy paper-covered editions as Europeans did, at any price.

In May 1933, Caresse reluctantly replied to Kay Boyle that the Crosby Continental Editions "had not one cent of working capital" and would not accept any more manuscripts. She explained the reasons for her decision to cease publication in a letter to Ezra Pound:

About CCE . . . I am completely discouraged in that particular form of publishing. I lost lots of money and didn't have any really good fun out of it. I only did one book that hadn't been done before, Bob MacAlmon's (that one you advised), and it was a complete flop. I must sell 3,000 to pay expenses, and I've only sold 800 of Bob's. I've not had one book completely sold out yet!! So I've definitely abandoned the CCE. But I have not given up the Black Sun Press . . . and a wonderful new scheme is in the air. . . .

Between publishing ventures, Caresse concentrated on the Parisian social scene. Her activities were picked up by William Leeds, who reported for the Universal Wire Service:

Caresse Crosby, alone, is carrying on the publishing tradition [of the Black Sun Press] . . . . It is the reality behind her flashing social success of which everyone here talks so much.

It has been said of Mrs. Crosby that she is herself a poem. At any rate, . . . these poems of hers account for her present position, without parallel in the history of society in this capital of art and letters and pleasure. . . . Mrs. Crosby has become one of the great hostesses. . . . Even the French speak of her "salon" with awe. *It has never been done before by any American, or by any foreigner— except the mother of the Empress Eugenie* [emphasis added]—for the French, outwardly hospitable to money- spenders and tourists, close their doors to any stranger seeking to cross the threshold into their inner circle.

There are many explanations . . . the simplest being that she is very pretty and a very charming woman. . . . But fortuitous circumstances also have played a part in the metamorphosis of this society butterfly into a welcomer of the great who come as callers, to create that impressive entity known as a salon.

Even when surrounded by a retinue of admirers, Caresse never ceased her quest for new adventures. Of a typical evening at "Le Jokey" (the famed Jockey Club), Caresse wrote: "We were six . . . all of us old friends, sitting at the best table, receiving the best attention from the lofty proprietor down to the lady of the *lavabos*. We always did receive the best everywhere, and we were the gayest, the most lavish, the most envied in Paris that season. Extravagant in talk and action, I was often the center of an exhilarating group.''

On such a night, she spotted a very young man, tanned a deep brown by the southern sun, whose wide black eyes looked contemptuously in her direction. He drew a pipe from his pocket, lit it, and flung the match beneath her table with an insolent gesture. Leaving the glittery crowd, Caresse excused herself to use ''the telephone.'' She searched for her chauffeur, patiently waiting outside, and ordered: ''Follow that young man, Victor. Offer to give him a lift wherever he is going. I want to find him again . . . tomorrow.'' (Polleen observed that ''Mama's chauffeurs . . . often rebelled at waiting for hours outside the *boites*, not to mention the daily assignations.'')

The next day, Caresse was wearing a blue denim apron-dress with a cartwheel straw hat as she waited at one of the sidewalk tables of La Rotonde. She had packed a picnic basket, with patés and cheese, fruit and a rare bottle of Cointreau. The youth approached, leading a large black-and-white Dalmatian—a perfect excuse for conversation. In the bright light of morning, he looked even better than the night before.

''Wouldn't such a fine dog like a romp in the country this balmy spring day?'' Caresse suggested.

Years later, she reminisced that ''The picnic was a success, *à la limité*. I shall never forget the moist high grasses matted with poppies and cornflowers, nor the drone of the ancient mill wheel. Nor Robert—made of mahogany and the sea—so strong, so gentle.''

That spring season, Surrealist painters and avant-garde writers rubbed shoulders with *le tout Paris* at Le Moulin du Soleil, where Caresse enthusiastically welcomed them. She brought life again to the abandoned Mill. ''I was Queen Mistress of my own small realm.''

Acres of wild strawberries were in full flower in June 1933, when Caresse sent out invitations to one of her fabulous parties. It was to be a ball, in *matelot* and *matelotte* costume. Harry's cousin Nina de Polignac replied that she would transfer the necessary magnums of champagne from the cellars at Rheims to the springhouse at Ermenonville.

''For how many people?'' she queried.

''About a hundred,'' Caresse guessed.

Eighty magnums of Pommery Nature soon arrived as a family contribution from the Polignacs. Max Ernst, the birdlike doyen of the Surrealists and a noted gourmet, agreed to help with the food. He traveled down to Marseilles to buy *lotte*, the necessary prime ingredient of a good bouillabaisse. Armand, now the Count de la Rochefoucauld—"sandy-haired and full of love and the devil"—acted as master of ceremonies. Elsa Schiaparelli produced the prize-winning costume—an above-the-knee skirt over fishnet stockings, with a maribou boa draped rakishly around her shoulders.

"I invited the most amusing Parisians, regardless of society's approval, and a few friends from home—among them Louis Bromfield, the writer, and 'Bunny' Carter (Harry's former chief, president of Morgan et Cie.). Both men arrived without their wives. "I was told later that the ladies were afraid to risk their Boston reputations." With her usual gift for exaggeration, Caresse reported that "We had royalty from England and Spain, princes of India by the score, not to mention Afghanistan. There was only one large bathroom for everyone to share. . . . I caught royalty off guard as I went to brush my teeth."

After all the guests were gone, she sank down on a cushion by the hearth "where I could look up through the chimney into the sky that was filling with stars, just as a theater fills with people—one by one, two by two, until the place is a sea of nodding heads—and now the stars above me were crowding the heavens that way. Are they the audience and we the actors? I wondered. If so, then night is the time to play our part to perfection."

An Eastern religious sect—brothers of the Hare Krishna—has replaced the Crosbys and their glittering entourage at the Chateau at Ermenonville; shaved Yul Brynner-like heads bow in contemplation and leather-thonged sandals flip-flop across the cobblestones. Parisians on motorcyles and tourists in small rented *voitures* come out on holidays and Sundays to picnic. They have pulled up the Lilies of the Valley by their roots, and there are no more carpets of wild flowers in the Forest of Senlis.

"When I stand on solid ground,
I lose my footing."

— CARESSE

Chapter VII
HAMPTON MANOR

Europe was on the brink of another war. With the peripatetic years behind her, Caresse was drawn back to her roots, her homeland. Her son, Billy, enrolled in Williams College in Massachusetts, and daughter Polleen, after a New York debut, determined to follow her mother's aborted career as an actress. Caresse sold the Moulin du Soleil, left Roger Lescaret as caretaker of the Black Sun Press, and headed home—for the duration.

A Greek revival-style manor house that Thomas Jefferson designed for his friend, Colonel de Jarnette, stands today in the heart of Virginia's Historic Homes district. Three dimes, with the date 1937 inscribed beneath FDR's profile, are firmly set in concrete on the third-from-the-top of the stairs, near the arched entrance. To one side of this symbolic talisman, the acrostic M/Y was etched for good luck. Caresse linked her baptismal name of Mary with the surname of Selbert ("Bert") Saffold Young, her third husband. That stormy alliance lasted only three years, but during that time, Caresse was the chatelaine of Hampton Manor, a Virginia planter's wife.

The sound and fury that once accompanied the *persona non grata* "dam' Yankees" long since has died; the de Jarnette post office is boarded up. To the North, the A.P. Hill Military Reservation gobbled up whatever land it could acquire from the impoverished gentry. But Hampton Manor is still firmly anchored to the spot, more or less as Caresse described it. It is not knee-deep in honeysuckle, and the elms that once stood "like glorious sentinels" developed blight and had to be cut down. The pond once "enchanted" by Salvador Dali— overstocked with the poetic *nénuphars* that Caresse loved—was dredged out by descendants of the original de Jarnettes, who reclaimed the property and considered the water lilies a nuisance. The giant oak—Caresse's "Green Hat Tree," so-called after Michel Arlen's fantasy—still marks the fork in the road at Oak Corner. But it no longer boasts the bathtub-white lacquer band with which Caresse circumscribed it to protect from intrepid motorists—and Bert Young, when he speeded home drunk.

"There is something unyielding in earth," Caresse once observed. "When I stand on solid ground, I lose my footing." But Bert loved being Lord of the Manor, and looked the part. He was blond and tall, some nineteen years her junior, and lived up to Caresse's description: "Handsome as Hermes, militant as Mars."

They met in Hollywood when Caresse accompanied Polleen for a screen test with Jerry Rubin at MGM. There was an enchanting night when they watched the moon rise over the Pacific and Bert told her all the crazy, impossible things he hoped to do, places he would go someday. "To me, every word was spellbinding," Caresse admitted. "From that time on, Bert obsessed me."

Bert had no pretentions to acting or literary talent. He never learned to spell her name properly (to Bert, Mary was always "Carress," or "Mimsy"). There were hints, early on, that he would become a mean drunk. But he swore that his one ambition was to have a place of his own, to farm. Hence, Caresse left Polleen behind under the protective wing of Frieda Inescourt, a seasoned trooper, and on September 30, 1936, Mary J. Crosby wrote to the New York Trust Company to forward some 433 shares of common stock (with a total value of $19,976), to buy a dilapidated manor house and 500 acres of farmland surrounding it—a white elephant on the Depression-deflated market. Deed in hand, Caresse assumed a new persona, the proper Virginian, broke but proud. The anachronistic flood-lit pillars came later.

Bert and Caresse first took rooms at an inn in Fredericksburg, with a Ford to drive back and forth. It was 25 miles each way, each day, "with headaches at one end, backaches at the other," Caresse complained. They ordered a registered herd of purebreds from the Hereford Association in Texas. Soon, Bert tired of building cattle slips and drowned his sorrows in Virginia Gentleman. After one particularly embattled exchange, he stormed off to Florida, leaving Caresse the weeds and the mud, the plumbers, the plasterers and electricians to deal with, all by herself.

Alone on a soggy Thanksgiving Day, she wrote,

> Bert dearest:
>
> You went away again. I've spent too many lonely nights lately, baffled and hurt . . . I still believe that if you could go on the wagon—*absolutely*, for six months—we could straighten everything out. I would make any sacrifice possible to help. Will you promise, and do you want to try . . . or stay away?
>
> Your,
> Mimsy

The rains set in. It was a disappointing life, with no companions within shouting distance, save for a few back-country farmhands. "It would have been fun, if I had not been alone," said Caresse—who had always been surrounded by a faithful coterie of sycophants and retainers. She never slept alone, if she could avoid it. "At first, I was too proud to write [Bert]." Finally, one dreary night in February, up to her neck in problems, Mimsy broke down and wired, "Come back—and stay."

When Bert was sober, he was wonderful in the rough and tumble world of contractors and day laborers. He spoke their language. By March 1937, they were ready to move from the inn in Fredericksburg to the new stable—the house would be finished in April. Caresse's need to plunge into an "obliterating" relationship was satisfied.

"We feared and admired each other. We hated and we loved each other. Finally, after months of frustration and hoping, we married each other."

A license had been applied for in September 1936, when they visited Bert's straitlaced Alabama kinfolks, who disapproved, on sight, of the Yankee divorcee who "put on airs" and worse still, was "old enough to be his mother." In Virginia, March 24, 1937—six months later—when the vows were exchanged, Caresse omitted the promise to obey.

Like everything else in her life, the third—and last—wedding was unconventional and done on impulse. The bride wore jodhpurs. "In Virginia, jodhpurs are correct for almost any occasion." The best man was Bob, owner of the Seafood Grill where Bert and Mimsy were eating Chesapeake Bay oysters when they made the decision. A rural clergyman was cajoled into meeting them at the church on half an hour's notice.

"My family was appalled, and so were we—everything about our union was unexpected and unbelievable." Polleen never forgave her mother for this ill-matched alliance. Bert, at 27 only a few years older than Polleen, could be charming when he tried. (He tried very hard on one occasion to seduce her.) In a letter to Caresse, her daughter referred to "a very unpleasant scene in Canada. Surely you haven't forgotten, even though you have forgiven. I told Bert that I didn't want to see him again."

For several months, Caresse waited hopefully for the Lord of the Manor to take hold. While Bert hunted and gallivanted, "it was I who, on frosty nights left a warm conjugal bed to help a princeling Domino into the world—and it was I who drove the harvest truck to market." That was Caresse's version of the stormy days and nights they weathered. Fascination and frustration always played equal parts in their relationship.

Soon, the simple, bucolic life Caresse professed to long for was punctuated by visits from exotic friends. From Park Avenue and Paris, the guests who came for dinner inevitably stayed on—all summer long. In 1940, Anaïs Nin recorded an idyllic interlude in her *Diary*. Caresse was supervising the tying up and loading of the wheat sheaves when Anaïs arrived, and as the bundles were thrown into a truck, "the wheat dust flew around her, lighted by the sun, like a gold Venetian halo. She wore a huge straw hat, and moved in her typical way, with airiness and freedom." Anaïs viewed the manor house—"white, classical and serene"—as "the first place of beauty I have seen in America, the first hearth, the first open house." It was as if Caresse had transposed the Moulin du Soleil to the Virginia countryside, a haven for another generation of practicing and potential artists.

Anaïs's old friend, Henry Miller, also appeared one day without warning, walking insouciantly up to the kitchen door. His plan was to complete his Greek opus, *The Colossus of Maroussi*, under Caresse's patronage. He signed the guest book facetiously: "Henry Miller, originally of Brooklyn, New York, late of Athens, Sparta, Delphi—

with him 'in spirit' come his good friends George Seferiades, George Sarantides, George Theotokas, and Lawrence Durrell, all of Greece."

Caresse wrote of her first encounter with Miller: "Henry came to my Black Sun Press in Paris when he was very hard up—Henry was nearly always hard up in those days. I came down from my little rue Cardinale office—I had to climb backwards, down a ladder—and Henry was sitting there, huddled in the corner with a manuscript on his knees, looking hopeful. At that moment, I forgot something and dashed out into the street, and forgot all about Henry Miller. Afterwards, he came back and finally got the manuscript into my hands. I was horrified! I wouldn't publish it now, either," she said of the classic *Tropic of Cancer*, then barred from entering the U.S. by Federal censorship. (Either Caresse's memory failed her, or this version of their meeting is pure fiction. According to Anaïs—and corroborated by Henry—they met for the first time when he and Anaïs visited Caresse's East 53rd Street *pied à terre* in New York the winter of 1940. Later, when a small back apartment in the same building was vacated, Henry moved in.)

Caresse, the sensual woman, could never understand Henry's enthusiasm for explicit, raw sex. But Henry in the flesh was far different from the violent exaggerations of his writing. Slender and lean, not tall, "he looked for all the world like a rosy-skinned Buddhist monk, with a partly-bald head aureoled by lively silver hair and a full, sensuous mouth. His laughter was contagious, and his voice, caressing and warm, like one of the Negroes," Anaïs observed.

Meanwhile, young John Dudley, suffering from an excruciating writer's block, "penniless and had nowhere to go," had settled in at Hampton Manor with his wife, Flo. Tall, lean and handsome, with curly blonde hair, brilliant blue eyes, a rich voice and sensitive hands, Dudley had a well-earned reputation for captivating women. He spun tall tales of his Scottish ancestors who owned Kenilworth Castle; it was easy to believe that he was a descendant of Queen Elizabeth's favorite, Robert Dudley, the Earl of Leicester. He was creative—in art, writing, and jazz music—but for the moment, his Muses had failed him. (According to Henry, he was "gestating.") When he had nothing else to do, he sharpened all of his pencils, and sometimes went out to raise the hood of his 1926 Ford, to see if any of the vital parts were missing.

In May 1940, Caresse shot off a letter to her old friend Salvador Dali:

I am counting on you and Gala visiting me at my
country place in Bowling Green, Caroline County, Virginia. Your rooms are ready and waiting for you . . . it will
be a tranquil place for you to work. I hear that you now
have enough material together to start the book of
memoirs that I am planning to bring out this fall. It is
absolutely necessary that you be here during the summer
months to work on this with me.

Dali's editor at Dial Press had written to Caresse:

Maybe with your help and persuasion, and with his own
desire to express himself, Dali will be able to learn enough
English to put those finishing touches on the copy.

Theirs was, in truth, a friendship of long standing. "Dali used to
come down to the Mill every Sunday, just after he met his wife. Dali
and Gala were that quiet couple who sat against the wall." (The
legendary Gala—former wife of Paul Eluard and *belle amie* of Max
Ernst—discovered Dali in Cadaques and brought him back to Paris.)
"He was very young and naive, really, and very, very hard up at the
time. Myself and one or two others contributed so much a month
towards an allowance," Caresse recalled. "Julien Levy, just starting a
gallery in New York, came to the Mill to see me. I said, 'Now this is
one man whose work you must look into.' Levy saw the paintings and
was very excited about the new 'Surrealism.' He promised to give
Dali a show. The question was, would Dali go to America? I was going
over, so I said I would take them under my wing." According to
Caresse, Dali was scared to death. He didn't know if he dared to take
his paintings—or himself—across the ocean.

"In those days, there was always great to-do when one arrived at
the Port of New York, and the little tug came along with the press on
board. I happened to be in the news at the time, and the reporters
came up and asked if they could take my picture," Caresse recalled.
"'You're wasting your time,' I said, 'The person you ought to
interview is Salvador Dali.'"

Later that year, at the Coq Rouge restaurant, where the Dalis ate
every day, Caresse concocted a "Dream Ball" to recreate the halcyon
days of the Beaux Arts. She invited two hundred of her most intimate
friends (and their spear carriers) to come dressed as their most
recurrent dream—mantic or Freudian. Gala led the pack. To her face
clung bits of mold and leaves, and around her neck wound a
procession of ants, painted by Dali.

What horrors awaited the guests! A bathtub of smelly fish, tilted at an angle, appeared to be sliding down the stairs. In one corner reclined the carcass of a dead cow, its skull wrapped resplendently in a white wedding veil. In the hollow where its stomach had been was a gramophone grinding out current French love songs. "The effect was disgusting absolutely—but the party was a tremendous success!" Caresse wrote to a friend in Paris. Every newspaper in New York carried the story. "Surrealism" was defined and became a household word overnight—thanks to Caresse.

Now, the notorious Dalis were en route to rural Virginia, and Henry Miller was dispatched to meet them in John Dudley's Tin Lizzie. He brought them back with all their belongings intact, even the bird cage and musical inkwell. From the beginning, Miller referred to the artist, disdainfully, as "that nut Dali." Caresse bedded them down on opposite sides of the Jeffersonian hallway. For Henry, the Dalis supplied the worm in the apple of Arcadia.

Soon, the household was functioning for Dali's well-being. Even Anaïs complained, "We were not allowed to enter the library, because [Dali] was working there." She described Gala as "a little faded," as indeed she might be after such a colorful and eclectic past. Gala never raised her voice—never seduced and charmed. "Quietly, she assumed we were there to serve Dali—the great, indisputable genius."

When the small-boned Dali appeared for breakfast, Anaïs saw him as "drawn with charcoal, like a child's drawing of a Spaniard, any Spaniard—except for the incredible length of his moustache." "I have a bigger one, an artificial one, to wear over it on special occasions," Dali retorted. "The artificial one goes on the real one with artificial glue. You spray it with a little humidity, and it moves. It moves slowly for fifteen minutes. I reserve it for dinner and receptions. I myself move very little. I rarely leave the Costa Brava."

Anaïs liked Dali's strange talk. He lost his shyness when she appeared. "He was so full of inventions and wild fantasies." But John Dudley pondered: "Is Dali truly mad? Or is it a pose? Is he spontaneously eccentric—or calculatingly so?"

Yet, "with all of us sitting around her table, [Caresse] was happy," Anaïs wrote. "Her gift for friendship was the central link. She seemed innocent of all diplomacy or ingenuity, her face burned by the sun, flicking her small pink tongue with epicurean delight, interested in all our projects and activities." Caresse, she observed, resembled very much Max Ernst's surrealist portrait: "an abstraction composed of a curled, frilled flower heart . . . the heart of a sea shell . . . the yielding flower heart which drew everyone around her."

From time to time, Bert Young—the rolling stone—returned to the scene. Forever jealous, he did not approve of Caresse's constant caravanserai of artists. Witnesses to more than one battered-wife sequence observed that the dark smudges below Caresse's grey-blue eyes were not cosmetic interventions. To the Southern neighbors, the Youngs had long been *persona non grata*. There were conjectures about her: Why would a strong, seemingly self-reliant woman put up with the likes of Bert (regardless of his prowess between the sheets)? Looking back, "I must have felt the absolute necessity of assuming responsibility for some baffled soul," Caresse admitted.

One night, Bert arrived quite late—as always without notice— stumbled about, opening all the doors and windows, turning on all the lights. Alas, no orgy in progress. The Dalis were asleep in one room, Flo and John Dudley in another. Henry across the hall, and Caresse in her own bed. Undaunted, Bert shouted drunkenly for everyone to leave. This time, Caresse firmly ordered him off the place. And she meant it.

But that was not the last to be heard from Bert. A brief letter in schoolboy scrawl and Bert's inimitable style arrived at the de Jarnette post office:

> Dear Carress:
> As when all things of import happen to me, I want you to be the first to know. I was sworn in the United States Army today. I have 14 days furlough, then I report to Camp Beauregard then to Officer's Training Camp.
> I would like to spend part of that 14 days with you, if you have and [sic] old bus ticket rush it airmail special and we'll see if we can find a few laughs in what remains of my civilian life.
> Strange, isn't it, that this is what I've been looking for all along.
> Please answer this mail, for as I now have a career, I'm on pins and needles waiting to see you.

This letter evoked the old hypnotic pull on her strong maternal instincts. Caresse liked to say, "Yes!" She made the predictable and spontaneous decision to follow Bert.

One can only imagine what happened during that passionate—and stormy—fortnight in New York. The next correspondence was posted by Caresse from Omaha, aboard the Los Angeles Limited:

> Darling:
>
> I'm on my way without you. I learnt that you'd "pulled a fast one" on me in New York—and I found that after I paid $136 for the week in NYC ($187 overdraft at the bank) and the interest on the note in Bowling Green, I had only about $500 of the $1,000 left to get started on. So I knew the only thing to do was to start at once, the cheapest way—this is it! I'll have to get a less expensive attorney when I'm out here, but everything should go through without a hitch . . . I'll stay at one of the less gaudy ranches and not speak to a soul! I am traveling *alone* except for Salar [the Afghan hound]—He is a great comfort . . . I have a roomette and they allow me to keep him folded up with me!
>
> But now, dearest, what about YOU. I worry and dream and wonder about you. Hoping you are in the right branch of the service, that you are happy in your decision . . . and that you keep out of trouble.
>
> *I'll never love anyone but you*—and my dream is that one day everything will come right again for us—*You can do anything you want to do.* I know it! So the (our) future is in your hands—But I'm tired of subterfuge and false promises—You've forced me to go thus far—but I pray you will find us a way back—
>
> I always miss you in every mile I cover—no fun without you.
>
> Your Mimsy

Legally separated, and filing for divorce, Caresse settled into a *pied à terre* on University Avenue in Reno, and enrolled in a course in Animal Husbandry. Her after-hours conduct was—of necessity—exemplary. For the first time in her life, Caresse was temporarily without friends and without funds. She had never preferred the exclusive company of women and as she looked back, she remembered only the *good* times—with Bert.

Sometime that summer, from an unidentified military base, Bert scribbled a hasty note:

Dear Carress:

You were wrong about my not writting [sic] as you are wrong about the way I feel towards you—*you know that I'm a little odd* [emphasis added]—but you to me are the one thing in this strange life that I belive [sic] in—and always will. You can understand that I'm not overly fond of the way females of the species treat the ones they profess to love.

Hasta la vista, love, Selbert

Meanwhile, back at the Manor near Bowling Green, the summer doldrums were setting in. "When I departed for my eight weeks sojourn in Reno, I already suspected a house divided among my guests," Caresse surmised.

Dali still rose early and painted until the light gave out, whistling and singing while he worked. But the meals were deadlocked by undercurrents of hostility. Henry resorted to his favorite weapons, contrariness and contradiction. Everything Dali said was wrong—even his preference for lamb. Anaïs said of Henry, "He has no need of wine, he is a man whom *life* intoxicates . . . who is floating in self-created euphoria." According to Henry, "When [Dali] finished working, he was *nothing*—not even a dishrag you could squeeze a drop of water from."

In late July, Henry wrote to Reno:

So far everything is fine, birds, trees, animals, swamps and fens and pine forest included. Yes, we are all working, though not full steam, owing to the heat. Dudley is breaking the ice, dictating to Flo, who seems like a wonderful helpmate for him. He's got a great story inside him, if he can deliver it.

I am fascinated by the immobility of the trees in the fierce blaze . . . remind me a little of Gainsborough, no? But back of the landscaping, it's America, all right—that furze, that unshaved countryside, so antipodal to Greece where all was as bald as a knob and tingling and crackling with fragrant electrical herbs.

Last evening, back of the house, where once must have been a beautiful mall, I could see the ancestral swarm doing the pavanne with iron-stringed instruments twanging away like mad crickets. I walk around now and then in the nude, towards the cool of the evening . . . that's a real sensation . . . the air is like a Turkish bath. The young bull stares at me quizzically!

No, Bert hasn't appeared yet. We are on the lookout for him, and not a little perplexed as to what his attitude will be. [Over the phone], he spoke of seeing his place, and we had visions of his coming in the middle of the night with a bunch of Virginia cronies armed with shotguns to sweep us out. He gave the impression of being astounded and injured, and then, bango, he hung up. Will telephone or telegraph if anything unusual occurs.

I expect Anaïs back tomorrow . . . and fierce showers. Perhaps we'll be seeing you towards August? I hope so. You ought to anchor here—it's a shame to leave this place idle.

Calm yourself and come back as soon as possible.

Henry

Anaïs returned and recorded the drive through the soft rolling hills in her *Diary*, ". . . distant roads looked wet—a mirage produced by the relentless sun. The trees [were] heavily draped with moss, a profusion of flowers, ferns, and trailing vines . . . the branches of trees, wrapped in cocoons, spider webs, dried leaves and dried insects." Hers was a romantic European's vision of life in the Deep South.

In the morning, everyone worked. It was the freshest moment of the day. The hypnotic heat would come in the afternoons, when all of us took siestas. In late afternoon, it was wonderful to walk through the fields and woods. Around the big manor house, in the small cabins inhabited by Negro farmers and their families, the children were shy, and hid behind the trees. Now and then, one would come upon them playing naked by the side of the pond. The little girls' hair was braided in "cornrows" tied by bright ribbons. Their eyes were soft, rounded, startled . . . they stared at us and grinned. Night was the best time. I walked in bare feet or sandals, felt the moist grass tickling my feet . . . From a distance, the lighted rooms in the manor house looked like Chirico paintings . . . the ponds, like Max Ernst's scenes of stagnant pools. The nights lie around us like an abyss of unusual warmth, awakening the senses. [It's] almost palpable, the pulse of nature sets our pulse beating. Tropical nights are [like] hammocks for lovers . . .

Henry's version was less romantic.

At noon the next day, it would be 110 degrees in the shade, as usual. We would have to sit in our drawers and drink Coca Colas while Dali worked. We would look at the lawn, the dragon flies, at the big trees, the Negroes working, the flies droning. We had Count Basie for breakfast, lunch and dinner. Toward dusk, we had gin fizzes or a Scotch and soda. More languor and idleness. The universe again. We took it apart, like a Swiss watch.

The nights we had nothing to do except take a stroll to the end of the road and back. I talked it all over with Dudley. I mean, about the universe and how the cogs mesh . . . Sometimes, in order not to let stagnation soak in too deeply, we went over to Fredericksburg and ate an Italian meal. Nothing ever happened. We just ate and talked.

Dudley had broken his writer's block. "[He] was an artist to the fingertips . . . everything filled him with wonder and curiosity," Henry observed. Little by little, he put it all down. "Dear Lafayette, . . ." he began. "I know that will be the best letter one man ever wrote to another, even better than Nijinsky's letter to Diaghilev." It became "A Letter to Lafayette," later included in *The Air-conditioned Nightmare*. Caresse once again had become the muse of genius.

For his part, Dali complained bitterly about Virginia insect life. "I'm still tremendously afraid of grasshoppers. The grasshopper is the *only* animal I'm afraid of," he told a reporter, with a shrug of his Catalan shoulders. "I suppose it's a sexual complex."

With a few early-dawn breezes, offering relief, the long hot summer came to an end. September arrived and with it the long-predicted storm. Henry wrote to Caresse:

Bert arrived in the middle of the night. We have all decided to leave. The Dalis also. They are off to Washington.

*   *   *

This time, Bert had done the unthinkable. He had threatened to destroy all of Dali's paintings, the entire summer's work. Alarmed, the Dalis dressed hurriedly, packing their belongings and paintings, and left.

The *Young v. Young* divorce was granted on grounds of "incompatibility." The time had come for Caresse to pack up the pieces of her life in Reno and head East again.

Once back in Hampton Manor, fall and winter raced by. The Dalis were persuaded to return, and when *Life* heard the news, they dispatched photographers for what might be called a "photo opportunity." They got more than they bargained for. The handsome double parlor was no longer a traditional setting for family portraits, antimacassars, and aspidistra plants. Caresse posed in front of the elegant 18th-century fireplace, dressed to kill, with "Hampton's Pride," a prize Hereford, by her side. (The Pride of the herd had been pulled and tugged, in a sitting position, up the front steps.) Dali had created a surrealist fantasy with the "coffin box" square grand piano from the parlor, hauled by steel cables to the branches of a majestic magnolia. Below, a gossamer-clad effigy, a ghostly crew of one, stroked a scull in the lily pond.

"This gracious and venerable estate is currently undergoing a sea change at the hands of Salvador Dali," *Life* reported. Dali was photographed in the de Jarnette general store, on a marketing expedition with Caresse, drinking cokes, talking with the bewildered and fascinated citizens of this small, drab backwater town, populated mostly by blacks who had never been outside Caroline county. The photographers poked and probed and followed Dali about. "He arises at 7:30, puts on dark trousers, a black velvet jacket and a red vest," *Life* informed its readers. "During the day, he is busy painting and 'enchanting' the garden with floating pianos, multicolored rabbits, and spiders with the faces of girls . . . a bare-breasted window-dresser's manikin is 'Sleeping Beauty,' waist deep in the frog pond."

While the *Life* team photographed, Dali worked on a black-and-white composition in the snow: *"Effet de sept negres, un piano noir, et deux cochons noir,"* he called it. "In the evening, he settles down for a cup of coffee and a game of chess with his wife." ("Three sugars; Gala always wins.") Unaccustomedly in the background, "Mrs. Crosby was editing and typing his autobiography, *The Secret Life* . . . ."

"Personally, I think [Dali is] the most stimulating, vital and charming and friendly man. He's all things nice," said Caresse, the Muse, who never said anything unkind about anybody. "I think he did his best work before coming to America . . . but he has endless possibilities," she added.

The *Life* crew departed, and in that spring of 1941, Dali's enchanted garden became one of the special features of the Richmond Garden Club tour. Gala and Dali left for the West Coast to entrust *The Secret Life* to the hands of a translator, and Caresse noted: "Mother came down from New York, and I was able to enjoy her visit this time without Bert's disruptive presence. I was writing again, and planning my new life—I had no regrets, either about marriage or a future without marriage. There was still so much to see, to learn, to tackle."

As the nation girded for another war, the tranquil little village of Bowling Green, with its one cinema and one café, was becoming a mecca for noisy army trainees. "When the farmhands began to appear in uniform, I knew it was time to leave. I was a lady alone . . ."

"Actually, I sold out with hardly a qualm. I put Hampton Manor on the market, and trucked the costly Herefords over the mountain to Staunton for a much-advertised (but wholly unrewarding) sale. I spread my surplus property out on the lawn for a country auctioneer. Piling all that was left into two monstrous moving vans, I realized then how fully another chapter of my life was ended. Although I was moving on, I felt I was not losing, but gaining a lap on life. At the wheel of the leftover Ford, with Salar at my side, I headed out on Route 2 for points North."

"A painting is not an object to frame and hang upon the wall; it is rather a weapon with which to fight the enemy."

—PICASSO

Chapter VIII

WARTIME WASHINGTON

On a bright, Indian summer afternoon—October 1941—Caresse arrived in the nation's capital. Astute observers agreed that it would be only a matter of months before the U.S. would be drawn into the war. The British were making a last-ditch stand, holding off Hitler's armies invading Eastern Europe, while the U.S. offered lend-lease materials, bases, arms, and moral support. "War as a means of deciding differences between civilized people is as barbaric as throwing Christians to the lions," said Caresse, the outspoken pacifist. But she always wanted to be "where the action is," and at that time, Washington was the capital of the free world. She took up residence at 1533 33rd Street in a temporary rental belonging to General and Mrs. Spaatz, recently removed to Virginia to be near the Pentagon.

"Never have regrets" Caresse often said, but it was hard to apply when comparing the narrow, red-brick row house with the gracious neoclassic manor she left behind in Virginia. There was a small front parlor, a back parlor, and a narrow stairway to a lower level where a closet-sized kitchen and narrow dining room faced a flagstone patio.

82

Only a spot of grass with a row of flowers and a picket fence were in back, and one small plane tree for shelter from the hot, humid summers. Nonetheless, a Georgetown *pied-à-terre*—then as now—was Washington's most coveted and overpriced real estate.

When the van arrived, Caresse began to fit each piece of furniture into new quarters like a jigsaw puzzle: books and bibelots and her Aunt Kate's Sheraton desk and Victorian credenza all fitted snugly between the high, leaded windows. Her seven portraits—several by now-famous artists—stared down from the bare walls like the seven faces of Eve. In this setting, she was determined to create another exciting persona.

It was not long before friends from her other lives caught up with her. Trains ran every hour on the Eastern seaboard, and hotel rooms in Washington were scarce. The Georgetown guest room was seldom empty. It became a temporary bivouac for friends—and friends of friends—who migrated South to aid the war effort, some in high offices.

Her first guest was Major Howard "Pete" Powel, in town from Boston wearing his new officer's uniform. In Black Sun Press days in Paris, Pete and his wife, Gretchen, were the Crosby's most valued companions among the expatriate group. Caresse met Gretchen, a hazel-eyed blonde from Texas, at the atelier of her master, Antonine Bourdelle. Pete, a free spirit from a solid family of Rhode Island Powels, remained on in Paris after World War I as a freelance photographer. Harry nicknamed the Powels "The Crouchers," because of the way Pete bent down to line up his subjects, with Gretchen inevitably crouched down beside him. That night in Georgetown, Caresse and Pete had many memories to share. But like everyone else in the city on the brink of war, Powel was up and out by eight o'clock the next morning.

Archibald MacLeish came next. The young poet who once sat the death watch with Harry had become Undersecretary of State. He took a place directly across the street from Caresse, but after a 12-hour day at the State Department, seldom had time to visit.

Caresse was determined to do her bit to help the national defense. She first thought of the Women's Officer Corps. Her application forms listed as references important friends: Averill Harriman, Secretary of State, and James Forrestal, Secretary of Defense. But the graying matron in uniform behind the desk was not impressed. She viewed Caresse as "*pas assez serieuse* for the deadly business of conducting war," Caresse admitted. For all practical purposes, four years at Rosemary Hall—then regarded as a finishing school for the privileged daughters of the rich—did not prepare graduates with useful skills such as typing. "You'll also have to have a physical check-up to see if you're fit," the matron told her. The indignity of a complete physical, of being poked and probed, was humiliating enough. And after, she was told that she failed to qualify on a technicality—she did not have four-fifths of her original teeth!

Driving home in defeat from the Red Cross's austere headquarters on 17th Street, Caresse's morale reached a low point. She decided to try other branches of national defense, where she wouldn't need 25 teeth. She called upon another old friend, David Bruce, then head of the psychological warfare division of the Navy. Bruce was charming over the telephone when he said, "Of course, my dear Caresse, I'd like very much to see you." But Caresse noted later that she was treated like a possible enemy alien by the guard at his office building, and once inside, intimidated by forbidding stares from behind cluttered desks.

> When I asked David if he had a job for me, he said, "What can you do? Can you type?"
> "As well as you can," I retorted.
> "What do you *really* think you can do?" he countered.
> "Plan strategy," I truthfully replied. "I've been doing that all my life!"

Bruce, a veteran of the old school of diplomacy, deftly turned the conversation to shared memories of Paris and ushered her out with a gallant bow. There was a vague promise to call, but he never did.

Despite such disappointments, there were many diversions in the Capital. Word soon spread that Caresse Crosby was in town, and the usual retinue of admirers found their way to 33rd Street. Juan Cardenas, the Spanish Ambassador, whom Caresse had known in Madrid, deposited a hamper of rare vintages on her doorstep and invited her to dine at one of Washington's most distinguished tables. (Cardenas was *persona non grata* on the diplomatic circuit because of his country's then-Fascist government; but one's political persuasion was not considered important among Caresse's circle of friends.)

Caresse also reported on a lunchtime rendezvous at the Mayflower Hotel with a grande dame of old Washington society. The Mayflower's stately lobby swarmed with a caravanserai of crew-cut young officer-candidates waiting out their commissions, along with munitions manufacturers, lobbyists, opportunists, hangers-on, and the well-coifed wives of generals, admirals, and senators. A long queue always formed at the entrance to the dining room, and tables were pushed together to accommodate the carpetbaggers who swarmed into the once-sleepy Southern city. Perfume and smoke mingled with the starchy smell of newly-pressed khaki. The Mayflower was becoming a nerve center of intrigue, hope, and heartbreak.

After lunch, when Caresse walked home to Georgetown from Connecticut Avenue, she noticed a paint-splashed canvas in a picture window. "Walk In," a sign in the window beckoned. She entered the small corner room of a real estate office where a young man was hanging his paintings. It was a fortuitous meeting. David Porter, she could tell by his flat accent, recently had come from the Midwest; he was to take on a temporary assignment with the War Production Board. Porter and other moonlighting artists of the Chicago School rented space in the real estate office to display their work. Noting Caresse's chic Parisian suit worn with her usual panache, Porter asked her to buy one of his canvases on the spot. "Not today," Caresse said, remembering the paintings still stored in a warehouse by the Potomac. But she thought about the encounter on the way home, and an idea began to take shape.

On December 7—a cheerless, frosty Sunday afternoon—Caresse was at Griffith Stadium watching the Redskins lose another game when suddenly the loudspeaker blurted out the incredible news: "The Japanese have attacked Pearl Harbor!" Men in uniform disappeared instantly from the boxes to report for active duty. Within hours, the supercharged, impromptu air of pre-war Washington turned to a mood of grim determination. The nation geared up to carry out President Franklin D. Roosevelt's promise to obtain only unconditional surrender.

Caresse knew that she would never "fit" into uniform, but she was determined to perform some useful function for the war effort. She thought of her friends in Europe, the artists already beginning to escape the threat of Nazi concentration camps. She would prepare a "home" for them, a place to display their work in the nation's capital.

Before the war, Washington was an inhospitable place for artists and art lovers. The city had no neighborhood or street life pulling artists and their patrons to cafés or coffee houses. The bookstore owned by James Whyte just north of Dupont Circle was the one modest venue for local artists to display their works.

Marc Moyens, an exiled compatriot of the wartime underground and friend of Parisian artists—later a prominent D.C. art dealer—said at the time that "Washington was a village. Cows were grazing on

Georgia Avenue." With few exceptions, the art pioneers were like Caresse, enlightened outsiders; they came to the capital for a variety of reasons—the war effort, a spouse's job, or escape from the Axis powers.

Caresse joined the weary group of apartment hunters lounging on chairs or leaning against the walls in the outer office of Hagner and Company, Real Estate. Many of the applicants appeared to have come directly from Union Station with their wives and families. A receptionist was trying to field requests for nonexistent apartment and house rentals. When Caresse confessed that she was looking for space for an art gallery, the receptionist announced, "There are *no* houses, *no* apartments, *no* rooms to rent. And certainly *not* an art gallery!"

Caresse repeated her request to Mr. Hagner—a friend of a friend in the Virginia hunt country—but his answer was, "Don't you know there's a war on, young lady?"

"That is just *why*," she explained. "Refugee artists from Europe, without a country, need a place to show their work. Can't you find something for me?"

Hagner flipped through his file and jotted down three addresses. "Go to it, young lady!"

The first address called for a trek to a loft in the Maryland suburb of Silver Spring. Caresse checked that one off her list. The second— No. 916 G Place, in the heart of the city—was made to order, an antebellum gingerbread house in a quiet cul-de-sac. There was an iron hitching post near the front steps and a bow window, and the door was open. Caresse made up her mind, the moment she stepped inside, to take it. She could imagine de Chiricos over the fireplace, a Max Ernst on either side. Then she heard footsteps. Hagner had given the address to another client!

To Caresse's surprise, two male voices could be heard from the stairwell.

"You can't afford it, David," said a firm, cultivated voice Caresse didn't recognize.

"But, Dan," a familar Midwestern accent replied, "I can live here and rent out the rest. It's exactly right. I've got to take a chance."

"With no furniture? You're mad!"

Caresse heard footsteps on the stair. David Porter, the young Chicago artist, stepped into the room.

"What are you doing here, Mrs. Crosby?" Porter asked. "What a surprise!"

"I've come from Mr. Hagner's real estate agency." Caresse stood her ground firmly in the center of the long front room. "I'm going to rent this place for an art gallery," she said. "You gave me the idea. Did Mr. Hagner send you, too?"

Porter replied truthfully, "We just happened to see the sign in the window, and the door was wide open. But I was inside *first.*"

"With four stories and two of them magnificent exhibition rooms, why not divide the house?" the curator suggested.

Why not? Caresse thought. I have the furniture, and Porter has the strength to move it. She loved to say "Yes!" and she said "Yes!" on the spot. She and Porter pledged their partnership with a handshake. Later, she signed the lease and agreed to pay half the rent—in 1941, only $55 per month—for so much space. Porter brought his sleeping bag and moved in immediately. Caresse soon moved over from Georgetown and removed the beds, bureaus, mirrors, and rugs of Hampton Manor from the musty storage warehouse.

She researched the history of G Place, a restricted area chained off for privacy—an anachronism in the heart of the city. General and Mrs. Grant had lived across the street in the 1860s, and the General's horse had once been hitched to the posts outside. In the 1970s, the building fell victim to a wrecker's ball, but during World War II, the so-called "cave dwellers"—native Washingtonians of Southern descent—still lived there and came out of their adjoining houses to inspect the new Yankee neighbors. It was too soon to pass judgment, but "good mornings" were exchanged.

Caresse's nesting instinct created a home wherever she chose to light, and Porter rushed back from the War Production Board each evening to transform the walls with paint. A GI carpenter was hired to moonlight, putting up shelves and racks, and a crew of two—a house painter and a floor sander—helped on odd nights and weekends. All winter, she and Porter worked to transform the deteriorating old house into working gallery space. All the while their relationship warmed into more than a business partnership. Evenings after their labors, they fell into Caresse's four-poster bed in an exhausted heap.

In her 40s, she was still an indefatigable lover, a caring woman, always with more than enough love to share. Long after their liaison ended, Porter remembered her as the most seductive—if indeed the most volatile—woman in his life. His creative powers reached a peak with her.

The winter chill soon passed, and spring turned into summer— not the best time for a gallery to open in the nation's capital. Before

World War II and widespread air-conditioning, heat and humidity in Washington—like India—warranted "hardship post" pay for the British foreign service. It was the custom for women and children to flee the city, leaving behind the summer bachelors. In June, Caresse departed for Long Island to become the very elegant resident manager of the Old Post House, born again as the Southampton Inn. Porter was left behind to mind the shop, but not without diversions. He wrote to her:

> Dear Baby:
>
> I wish you had been here last night. The old G Place was a good place to be. Inez Stark Boulton came to dinner, looking very beautiful in a grey turban with four bunches of violets attached. Gretchen [Powel], like everybody, is quite fascinated with her, and it appears we are going to a garden dinner tonight . . . Inez is going to be very helpful to us, also Pietro Lazzari and his wife . . . . Inez used one of her lipsticks to tone one of our new pictures and we had a swell talk—all about Margaret Fuller and K. Mansfield. Pietro's wife is going to type letters for us, and I ordered stationery. We are going to try to get some murals for Pietro to do, to pay for his forthcoming "keed." He is very apt at doing silver point portraits . . . a fine creative person.
>
> Do you still love me? Say yes. 'Cause we will have a cozy winter and 'cause the fireplace doesn't work I shall have to keep you—and keep you warm. How is Matta?
>
> Love, David

Matta Echaurren, the Basque painter first discovered in Paris by Caresse, fled from France to take up residence at the Inn that summer. She planned to show his work at the G Place Gallery. Pietro Lazzari, an Italian Futurist painter, and his American wife, Evelyn, also would become frequent visitors to G Place. Lazzari delighted in telling people that he went to school on the streets of Rome, that he swam under the bridges of the Tiber to study the statues from below. He lived for some years in New York before coming to Washington, like so many others, to take a war-related job in government. At the Gallery, he gained a wide reputation for his paintings and the bronze sculptures he called "polychrome concrete."

When Caresse returned from Southampton, she began to plan with Porter the opening exhibition for late fall. A November 7 press release announced "the first modern art gallery in this city" to Washingtonians. On one floor, Porter would display the work of prominent American artists in "Home Sweet Home, USA." On another floor, Caresse would show the "Summer Work" of leading Surrealist painters—Matta, Ernst, Tanguy, and Lam. Max Ernst and his wife, Dorothea Tanning (an artist of first rank in her own right), had just arrived from Arizona, and Tanguy's latest canvases were shipped down from his Connecticut farmhouse. At a time when Surrealist art was little known and unappreciated, she continued her crusade to bring it to the attention of a wider audience.

Invitations went out to Cabinet members, members of Congress, and cultural attachés at the embassies, and, as a long shot, to Eleanor Roosevelt at the White House. Although the First Lady was unable to attend, she sent Caresse an encouraging response. The first *vernissage* was a resounding success. Pete and Gretchen Powel came, and among other old friends, Selden Rodman, a poet and writer in town on a "classified" mission. Architect Eero Saarinen and his wife, Lily, also a painter, were there to partake of the rare feast Caresse provided along with Raul Cardenas's wine, despite wartime shortages.

After the opening, the G Place Gallery kept the hours of two until eight o'clock daily, including Sunday, so that Washingtonians engaged in the grim business of war could enjoy, after hours, fine contemporary art. "The exhibitions we mustered, the openings we staged, the artists we launched, were proof of our audacity and energy—we had no funds at all," Caresse later recalled. Porter contributed his slim salary of $75 per week. Her income from investments never averaged more than $500 per quarter. Despite such meager resources, they continued to provide gourmet dishes— one guest remembered squid, washed down with cheap white wine but deliciously prepared—that divided miraculously like the loaves and the fishes for the many who came to look. Few stayed to buy.

To those who attended the openings, Caresse followed up by mail with plans for the new gallery and a plea for their help:

> We want to bring the Museum of Modern Art's new Romantic Painting in America to Washington, but this also is beyond our means; so we hope you will take part in our future by contributing ten dollars or more and become one of the Members of the G Place Gallery which should—with your help—offer Washingtonians a so-called Museum of Modern Art comparable to such enterprises in other cities. Lectures by visiting artists, special

movies once a month, and limited editions of prints will be arranged gratis for our Members.

Although many of the plans never materialized, Caresse continued to stage openings at two-week intervals. The second, an early de Chirico show, was part of the "Art of This Century" shipment that friend Peggy Guggenheim sent from New York. Giorgio de Chirico, founder of the *scuola metaf$isica*, later joined the Dadaist movement, but his early works were closer to 19th-century romantic fantasy. No lesser a critic than Guillaume Apollinaire described "De Chirico's work as immortal . . . [he is] the most astonishing painter of his generation." It was a well-publicized and very popular opening, Porter reported to Caresse "the morning after" the preview which she was too ill to attend:

> Yesterday was a social and artistic triumph, with guests like Alla Kent in superb triumphant form, and your North Pole Explorer boy friend in complete touch with the surreal world of Chirico!!! Laughlin with a cold and pining for Siren Kent, appeared. I wanted to tell everybody you had gone off (on the strength of a rumor) to bring Giorgio back in time for the varnish, but Gretchen thought it would be so much more glamorous to be just a little bit ill with fever just over par.
>
> The photographs by Powel run all the way up to the second floor landing. I thought it might be cute to have them go around the bathroom walls—but at the last minute—at one minute to four—we re-routed them down again, so when you come in your eye travels like a dizzy Chirico railroad track up and down and around and around. The biographical material got here just in time. Even Gretchen appeared satisfied with what I wrote. She wore a long black dress and stayed in the kitchen much of the time until darkness set in to form a proper background for her costume. Then with Grace Neas [one of the Home Sweet Home artists] who was made up by a make-up gal, the two of them kind of filled in for you.
>
> I've been sleeping alone and getting up early. I miss all your hairpins and binders and stockings in my bed.

The next show was "Portraits by Buffie Johnson." The Washington *Times-Herald* reported, "In private life, Mrs. John Latham,

A.U.S., a bewitching young person whose portraits have been acclaimed by art connoisseurs and directors of national galleries. Her exhibition . . . has attracted art lovers from all walks of life." Johnson was photographed in the Gallery before a 17th-century toile tapestry, sketching a provocative likeness of Caresse languishing under a phosphorescent sea with seaweed draped around her shoulders and seahorses and cockleshells floating about. In the lower right corner, Johnson had scrawled a line from T.S. Eliot: "Till human voices wake us and we drown." Caresse admitted that it was uncanny how close Johnson had come to portraying her psyche. The years had not erased the memory of the near-drowning accident of her East Island childhood.

In May, the Gallery featured Surrealists again, focusing on a theme of André Breton, "A Day in Spring." Women were invited to wear their brightest, most extravagant Easter hats, for which the Gallery gained much-needed notice in the Society sections of local newspapers. Better still, the Gallery was beginning to gain national recognition in publications such as *Art Digest*: "Washington is in for some vivid presentations. Little doubt such a gallery will be welcome in the Capital City, which has been inexplainably barren in centers of modern art." Henry Miller's vivid watercolors—the result of the long, hot summer at Hampton Manor— closed the first season, after which escaped to the Southampton Inn again.

Porter kept in touch after a business trip to New York:

> Dear Baby:
>
> New York dealers were very hospitable and even the Museum of Modern Art had already heard we had moved into G Place. I can't imagine who told them . . . they couldn't give me any money 'cause their purchase fund was exhausted. . . . The Romantic Painting show is going to encompass the whole country. . . .
>
> Now, pardner Baby. The Nierndorf Gallery is sending about ten paintings for our G Place Gallery branch in Southampton. Five of them are small colored block prints by Kandinsky. One is a beautiful Paul Klee, . . . and one by Mr. Chieu, who is a brother of Madam Chang Kai Check (sp.) [*sic*]. Julien [Levy] was in the country. Alfred Steiglitz was more wonderful. I have a new photograph of him—and am going to write an article about him.

Now for you and for me and the night mist. I feel like writing you a poem and if I find the quiet I shall . . . .

In late fall, Porter wrote of the increased media attention the G Place Gallery was receiving:

Dear Snooks:

Life wants photos. . . . They said they probably will send their own people down to do the exhibition in color. Miss Varga saw your glamourous photo in *Vogue,* so I think that's what did it. Our show is beautiful. I got an inspiration for a new title: "New Names in American Art." Wonderful?

Such a sweet and darling love letter. I am feeling happy all over in the thought of it. I was good in New York and good here, so far at least. . . .

Loads of love from a cold bedroom.

In February, Selden Rodman noted in his diary, "Canada Lee came down from New York last weekend." Porter and Caresse were presenting Lee in a reading from Rodman's *The Revolutionists,* a three-act play about Toussaint L'Ouverture, the black emperor of Haiti at the time of the French Revolution. Rodman noted that some fifty people came to the G Place Gallery, and the evening was a great success. "I read some of it with him [Lee] and between us, we covered the whole action. Whether the secondary purpose—to raise some money for a New York production—was achieved is hard to say. The Haitian Ambassador and his wife, M. and Mme. Liautaud, came, and several other Negroes. For Jim Crow Washington, this was something new. The great problem was to entertain Canada three meals a day for three days without making him over-conscious that we were avoiding restaurants."

It was Caresse's custom to go out to eat with her friends after openings to favorite restaurants of the time—the Salle du Bois, the Occidental ("preferred by Presidents"), or to O'Donnells or one of the seafood restaurants on the Potomac. There was also the Trianon on 17th Street, just above Pennsylvania Avenue, an intimate place with red-checked tablecloths and Joseph, the jovial old headwaiter from Luxembourg who always dressed formally in white tie and tailcoat. Henry Miller especially loved the Trianon, though Caresse's guests from the Pentagon considered it too Bohemian for their tastes. Canada Lee, one of the foremost actors in America, could not join

Caresse and her friends at the Trianon or any of the other "white" restaurants. When Canada was with them, they could go only to the Bengazi, an African place.

Determined to break down racial barriers, in June Caresse introduced at the G Place Gallery, "New Names in American Art," painting and sculpture of black servicemen on duty in Washington. Among the exhibitors was a young sergeant, Romare Bearden, born in the rural South and reared on the streets of Harlem, who developed a unique style of photo-montage and paste-up collage. He later displayed gouaches in a show called "The Passion of Christ":

> The motive-force of my paintings [consists of] certain incidents . . . I have read . . . in *Mark* and *Matthew*. In an explosive world . . . what faiths or systems will emerge in the future I cannot guess—I do believe they can be enriched by a consideration of the great ethical and humanitarian contribution of . . . Christ.

Still later, Bearden's work was exhibited in the Manhattan gallery of Samuel Koontz, who also discovered Adolph Gottlieb and Robert Motherwell. Bearden was awarded a Guggenheim Fellowship and became one of the best-known and best-loved of black American artists, due to Caresse's patronage.

Despite the outstanding success of the G Place Gallery, Caresse and Porter dissolved their partnership in fall 1944. The reason remains unrecorded, though one could surmise that Porter succumbed to another "Baby" while Caresse was away. Or perhaps, as Selden Rodman recorded in his diary, they parted because Caresse alleged that Porter defrauded one of the black artists of some $700. On September 14, she spelled out their agreement:

> Dear David:
> This is to confirm our verbal agreement concerning the house at 918 G Place, N.W., on which we hold a joint lease. As you know, I would prefer to take it all over myself, but as you wish to live there and operate a gallery, and as I can operate my gallery uptown, I am willing that you should take over the entire place for one year from this October paying the rent and upkeep and utilities. . . .
> If, however, you are drafted or for any reason do not wish to live there, I am to have the option of taking it all back, making some proper arrangement with you for the

protection of your interests. In no case shall any third party be allowed to take over without my approval and consent. . . . I will vacate the gallery by October 1st and take away my personal belongings by October 5th. It is understood that your gallery will be called the David Porter Gallery as we agreed, and any bills running in the name of the G Place Gallery will be taken care by us jointly before January 1st. The furnishings which we bought jointly will be divided between us.

I think this covers everything. If you have any suggestions to make please let me know, otherwise, if you will sign the enclosed copy of this letter and return it to me, it can serve as agreement.

With best wishes for a great success.

Caresse Crosby

Caresse again resolved "never [to] have regrets." She looked for— and found—a suitable venue near Dupont Circle. The address was 1606 20th Street, a corner building with an English basement large enough for a printing press, a gallery on the second floor with high windows and good light, living quarters above. She settled in to make another Crosby Gallery of Modern Art the intellectual and artistic headquarters of wartime Washington.

Coping on a day-to-day basis became more difficult as the Capital went all out for the war effort. Wherever Caresse went, Salar, the Afghan hound, was her constant companion and a good excuse for a walk. And walking—because of gasoline shortages—was the preferred means of transportation. It was difficult to make one's way along crowded Connecticut Avenue. When Caresse stopped at Larimer's Market, women of all ages, sizes, and colors were drawing numbers from a spindle on the countertop, patiently waiting their turn with the butchers, "like high priests in a pagan ceremony," she said, "dispensing a leg-of-lamb, a pound of hamburger." The military messes took all the choice cuts. At I. Miller's, there was always a long queue for shoes—one pair to every adult customer with a ration coupon.

Caresse's son, Billy, because of his fluency in the language, had been an interpreter for the Free French. Now he was on home leave from the Navy before being shipped out to his next post. He accompanied his mother to many Washington gatherings and was a frequent co-host at the Gallery openings. She continued to launch new discoveries every month, with martinis—donated from the PX by generous friends—very dry. Members of the military, the government, and the diplomatic corps came to the new gallery; indeed everyone who was of any importance in the Capital found his way to 20th Street, even then-Vice President Henry Wallace.

On December 2ọ, ʌfter a quiet Christmas, Caresse presented to the public Samuel Rosenberg, a young Surrealist from Cleveland, then working in Washington as a photographer for the Office of Strategic Services. War brought Rosenberg into an office with Jo Mielziner, the stage designer, and Eero Saarinen, the renowned architect. Both liked his drawings and suggested to Caresse that she might consider his work. His structures and forms had a psychoanalytical bent, taken from his early environment, where he had been intermittently an iceman's helper and a grocery clerk in his mother's store; he was always intrigued by the sadistic paraphernalia in a butcher shop next door. Vice President Wallace returned a few days after seeing Rosenberg's work at the opening, saying, "I was very disturbed by the drawings, and I wanted to look at them again."

Henry Kaiser, owner of the booming shipyards in San Francisco, was in Washington overseeing the war effort. A husky, domineering man, not used to having his authority questioned, Kaiser came into the Gallery and said to the artist, "I don't understand a damned thing about your Surrealist drawings." Rosenberg, pretending to be offended, challenged the industrialist to a mock wrestling match. They grappled each other on the floor for a few minutes, while the other guests looked on with delight. The Crosby Gallery was that kind of place—a place where notables who had never met before became friends; a place where Pietro Lazzari, who enjoyed being outrageous, pulled a wine glass from his pocket to offer "a little vino" to the genteel Duncan Phillips, founder of the more sedate gallery up the street.

Caresse herself liked to be noticed—and remembered. She prepared a stage set worthy of Mielziner. One wall was covered with a textured purple paper, on which she hung copper plates. According to one of her guests, her hair—then tinted a copper color—and a long, flowing copper-colored skirt provided a striking contrast to the purple walls. She hung a large Japanese-style lantern in the window and created an informal ambiance that made everyone feel at ease.

In January 1945, the Gallery previewed the work of Jean Hélion, a French abstractionist and recent escapee from a Nazi internment camp. After the opening, Caresse and Hélion were invited to speak to the students at Howard University, the major institution of its kind for blacks, on "Modern Art in Paris in the 1930s." Caresse said,

"My tongue ran away with me, as it always does," telling tales about her early experiences with Brancusi and Calder and other then-unknown artists. Not long after, she was called upon by the principal of Dunbar, the segregated black high school in Washington, to address the graduating class.

Like Eleanor Roosevelt, she spoke out strongly against inequalities in the segregated South, especially in the capital of a country then fighting to "make the world safe for democracy." She decided to flout local laws and customs by staging *Othello* at the 20th Street Gallery, with Canada Lee in the title role, Harry Moore as the devilish Iago, and herself as a luminous Desdemona. Later, she tried to purchase or rent an abandoned movie house on 9th Street to open a theater for blacks to rival the National—then the only theater in segregated Washington—but was unable to do so. Ironically, her attempt was 30 years ahead of its time. Her long-standing friendship with Canada Lee no doubt inspired her, but her life-long crusade for desegregation was also rooted in Yankee values and fostered by an idealistic father.

In 1932 Caresse lunched uptown with Lee in the first of the "meetings [that] were wondrous secrets, jealously guarded," as she wrote in her memoir. "I felt strange the first time, going by myself to a rendezvous in Harlem with a man I had met but once to a place I'd never heard of—but from the moment that Canada and I talked together at a party in the crazy atmosphere of 'Jimmy's Uptown' I wanted him for a friend." Caresse again said "Yes!" to a long and devoted relationship that ended only with Lee's death in 1952.

Born Lionel Cornelius Canegata in New York City, Lee had a childhood far different from Caresse's "crystal chandelier" background on the Upper East Side. He began his career as a child prodigy violinist at age seven, but ran away from ambitious parents at 14 to become a jockey at Saratoga and Belmont. He soon grew tired of the racetrack life and entered the prize ring, in which he lost the sight of one eye, but won the national lightweight title before giving it up to run away again. He was working on the docks, down on his luck, when he was discovered as a "natural" actor and given the title role in *Stevedore*. Success followed when he was cast as Banquo in the Federal Theater's *Macbeth* with an all-black cast.

In the segregated days when blacks could be arrested if seen in the company of a white woman below 110th Street, Caresse and Lee had to use subterfuge to meet. Those nights in Harlem Caresse remembered as "among the happiest of my life." Often they would meet in an underground jazz den, or backstage in the noisy, overcrowded theaters where Lee was appearing. "Into one's home as guests, blacks were admitted only rarely and apologetically, to hotels, never," Caresse recalled. When Mary Jacob, her mother, a woman of liberal views for her time, invited Lee to tea at her apartment on East 72nd Street, Lee was ordered by a pompous doorman to use the service elevator.

Anaïs Nin recorded in her *Diary* the first visit, with Caresse, to Lee's apartment on the river:

> I first heard his warm voice say, "Come in! Come in! Hang your coat." I seemed to hear for the first time, since I have come from Europe, a warm voice which means what it says wholeheartedly. Canada was a generous, warm-hearted host. He seemed to be whipping up excitement and expansiveness, creating a sumptuous, creamy evening. His warm voice immersed you, his warm hand led you here and there, linking people. The place is crowded. Half-white, half black. People from the theater. Left intellectuals. Artists, doctors, sculptors, architects. Warm, cordial, natural, spontaneous. There is talk, laughter, and a physical tenderness. People embrace, they touch each other. No deadpan faces, no silence, no closed faces . . . there is much laughter, vibrations, flow, humor.

As the friendship progressed, Caresse became Lee's devoted "camp follower" (her own phrase). At the opening of *Stevedore* in Chicago, Caresse stayed at a black hotel near the theater and gave a party there organized by Lee, the star. "We laughed more than I have ever laughed before," Caresse remembered. "I was sad only once on that visit, but that is a story that cannot be put into print for perhaps another hundred years." She had not counted on the social and sexual revolutions of the '60s and '70s that made all things acceptable. When she said good-bye on Monday to return to a Park Avenue apartment, Caresse wrote that she felt like a "pallid flower that had been plucked from a gorgeous garden plot to be transferred to a lonely vase on a varnished stand."

Another incident that stood out in Caresse's memory of her relationship with Lee was a charity ball for the Harlem Children's Hospital. Max Ernst and Dorothea Tanning were there with Caresse in the box of honor, when she observed that all the black guests were in evening dress. Caresse felt that she and her friends were conspicuous in "Monday tweeds, like sparrows in a peacock cage . . . I suffered and was miserable . . . I have never regretted, as so many females have, that I was not born a male—but I have regretted that I was not born a negress," she wrote in envy of her exotic companions.

On March 24, 1941, Orson Welles staged Richard Wright's famed best seller, *Native Son*, which became an instant financial and critical success, the first of that season to win Broadway's top four-star rating. Lee was chosen by Welles over much competition for the role of Bigger Thomas, which has since become metaphor for the alienation, anger, and fear in the urban ghetto. Even the name "Bigger" is a rhyming reminder of the black's hated epithet.

In cultivated, artistic handwriting that belied the memory of stevedoring and prize-fighting, Lee wrote to Caresse:

> Dearest my sweet:
> Everything in the world have [sic] been happening to me. First! *I am "Bigger Thomas"* . . . I've been rehearsing day and night. You should see me this very minute. I'm in bed nude, lying on my side, writing to you, and wanting you so badly. What have you done to me Caresse, my darling. Ever since I first knew you, and that seems all my life, you've been here in my heart, having closed out all the other people I've ever known in my life. It seems I've always loved you. From time immemorial when *I was an Egyptian prince and you were a Saxon slave girl.* [emphasis added]
> Write me soon, and pray God I keep both things, restaurant and play, for I shall die if I lose either.
> Your own,
> CL

The prospect of financial success in *Native Son* enabled Lee to buy a popular Harlem restaurant and nightclub, which he called "The Chicken Coop." Again he wrote to Caresse: "Last week was one of our biggest weeks—Thank God!" After mentioning all the financial difficulties in keeping the restaurant solvent, he added, "The only sunshine and softness in my life is you—and *Native Son*."

In early 1941, before and during the run of the play, Lee found time to write love letters to Caresse:

> Dearest my love—
> I just got your letter . . . Gee! it's wonderful to know that you're mine, all mine. Aren't you dear? The real

opening after several postponements is Monday 24th
. . . After the show everybody is coming to the Coop and
celebrate. I want you among them. You're the most thrill-
ing person in the world. I do love you so much. Do you
think we can find some sort of happiness and content-
ment, somehow, somewhere? This play may mean just
that, my dear. So keep your fingers crossed—mine are.
Ville vous couche avec mois [sic] . . . How's that?
Dearest my baby:
    Every day I say I'm going to write to you and every day I
come home late from rehearsals with just enough energy
to take off my clothes and get into bed . . . I don't mind it
though, honey. I just hope that I can be as successful as I
want to be. It can mean so much to us—you and me. If I'm
successful we won't have to hide so much honey, and we
can get a little of the happiness that I have wanted with you
in this life. Oh, honey, it's too wonderful to be true. I love
you so much Caresse—There are two tickets at the box
office for you. You're my guest, my lover. I wish you were
at my birthday party last Monday. It was wonderful. I
wanted you so much Darling. I'm getting to be an old man.
Isn't it terrible?

(At 34, Lee was 14 years Caresse's junior.)
    One can only speculate whether, by taking a black lover, Caresse
was making a political statement about sexual freedom, or whether it
was Lee's great animal magnetism that drew her to him. He was
undoubtedly one of the most unusual and outstanding men of any
race in his time. Brooks Atkinson, the famed *New York Times* critic,
wrote: "The quality of life Mr. Lee imparts to a scene is overwhelm-
ing—partly physical, partly magnetic."
    Vera Zorina, who acted with Lee in *The Tempest*, wrote in her
autobiography that Lee was "an immensely touching and kind and
gentle man, with a sad, ugly face. As an actor, he gave a raging power,
when he had to, spitting out his venom, but also a very moving
quality."
    Anaïs Nin, who went to the opening of *Native Son* with Caresse
and afterward joined their friends at The Chicken Coop, described
Lee's "warm, orange-toned voice, his one unclouded eye glowing
with tenderness, and joy, his stance loose-limbed, natural; in life,
relaxed, in music and in acting tense, alert, swift, and accurate as a
hunter." In her *Diary*, Nin noted that

Caresse seemed to think that the only authentic life of emotion and warmth seemed to be right there at that moment, with the jazz and soft voices, the constant sense of touch between them. We feel more restrictions, less freedom, less tolerance, less intimacy with other human beings. Except here in Harlem. The place is a cloud of smoke, the faces very near, the hypnosis of jazz all enveloping and even at its most screaming moments, dissolving the heart, throbbing with life."

Caresse's friendship with Lee continued for many years, even after the romance cooled. Later, when it was possible for her to travel to the Continent again, Lee joined Mark Marvin to form a theatrical production company. They were showing a controversial play about segregated housing, On Whitman Avenue, at the Cort Theater, directed by the renowned Margo Jones. In a letter typed on business letterhead, Lee asked Caresse to find a French translation of Othello for him, and added somewhat wistfully, "hope you're really having fun."

Fortunately, I can write that the show has not closed. The wilting summer heat has been rather cruel, but we will do our best to hold it through the summer until Broadway becomes itself again. If we do, and I have every reason to believe we shall, On Whitman Avenue should become the hit of the '47 season. It has what it takes, I have no doubt of that.

As always, he ended his letter with "Love."

In October, the Crosby Gallery of Modern Art was once again involved in controversy. Eleven Surrealist paintings had caused a stir at the Knoedler Galleries on 57th Street in Manhattan after Mayor Curley of Boston called the exhibition an "insult to the Catholic Church" and the Copley Society banned it. The show was the result of a competition to choose a painting for publicity for the highly-touted Loew-Albert Lewin film based on a Guy de Maupassant novel, Bel Ami. The most daring display of nudity, which barely squeezed past the U.S. customs officials, was a painting by Paul Delvaux, a Belgian, featuring three pink ladies not making use of fig leaves or hands to hide their most obvious assets.

There was even some debate about whether the juxtaposition of the early Christian monk and undressed womanhood in itself was appropriate. Some cited as proof the writings of St. Athanasius, troubled by temptations and assailed by the devil, who sent wild beasts, women, and soldiers to torment him. Dorothea Tanning, who expressed "the temptations" more symbolically than Delvaux in her entry, and at 30 was the youngest member of the Surrealist group, insisted that "a man like St. Anthony with his self-inflicted mortification of the flesh would be most crushingly tempted by sexual desires."

Salvador Dali's entry had erotic fountains, obelisks, and a half-nude or two, with St. Anthony thrusting a cross defiantly toward a procession of white horses and elephants with spidery legs. But Max Ernst took the $3,000 prize with a work that showed the Saint writhing in a morass of nightmare creatures, about which the *Washington Post* reviewer quipped: "You haven't seen such creatures since your last warm beer and cottage cheese midnight snack."

The exhibit was widely covered by the national media, and the Crosby Gallery packed in the crowds from one o'clock until six o'clock daily (nine o'clock on Thursdays). Caresse was at her flamboyant best as hostess.

Also adding to Caresse's media coverage in that era was the forthcoming trial of her old friend, Ezra Pound. Pound had been sitting out the war in Italy, where Fascism—in his view—was the second coming of Jeffersonian democracy. He often broadcast this revelation over Italian radio.

In May 1945, when the Americans occupied Rapallo, Pound was taken into custody and charged with treason for the broadcasts. In November of that year, he was returned to Washington and temporarily confined to St. Elizabeth's Hospital, where a series of sympathetic psychiatrists were trying to convince the authorities that Pound was insane, unfit to stand trial.

Dr. "Tiny" Zimmon, assistant to Dr. Overholser, director of St. Elizabeth's, called on Caresse as Pound's former publisher to help assess his condition. She joined the steady stream of visitors to inmate No. 58102 at the red brick hospital across the Anacostia River, among them literary artists, biographers, students—even Alice Roosevelt Longworth. Allen Ginsberg traveled several thousand miles from California to sit at the master's feet. Ginsberg recalled that after he got there, Pound said almost nothing . . . "The silence for a poet like that is a profound apology." But the scene could be bizarre. On a typical day, T.S. Eliot and Pound could be found sitting on a bench talking and lifting up their feet, one by one, as one of Pound's fellow inmates "vacuumed" the floor with an invisible machine!

When Caresse visited, she reported that the stage was set as if for a Kafka play. Two guards who appeared to be actors in *The Trial* stood on either side of Pound when they led him in. His appearance was deplorable, Caresse reported. Pound was unshaven, wearing a ragged shirt and trousers, his feet shod in dilapidated sandals. According to Caresse, she talked with Pound easily, reminiscing about the days of their friendship in Paris, and when she left, Pound kissed her on both cheeks, according to European custom. Caresse thought—but did not report to the doctors—that Pound was as arrogant and as sane as he had been when she last saw him ten years before.

Pound also received weekly visits from the tall young author of the *Maximus Poems*, Charles Olson. To Olson, Pound appeared confused and depressed, exhausted, living in his own past, "his eyes worried and muddy, his flesh puffy and old." But Olson considered that Pound's "jumps in conversation were no more than I or any active mind would make."

Pound went to trial wearing the new blue suit Caresse had bought for him. He sat subdued, nervously clenching and unclenching his hands, with his head and eyes down. Thanks to the lobbying efforts of his friends and the literary community, the case had already been decided. The jury took only five minutes to declare Pound of "unsound mind." His life was saved, but he was doomed to return to confinement in Howard Hall, a "hell-hole" without windows, behind a thick steel door with peepholes.

In the winter of 1945, one of the coldest on record to sweep the Continent, Caresse—who considered France her second country—thought of the heroes of the French underground who led patriots across the nearly impassable Alps during the war. Her printer in Paris, Roger Lescaret, was one of them.

She invited friends and clients to the Gallery to donate one dollar or more as admission to buy warm clothing and chocolates for the school children of Césaret, France. The exhibition notes for "The Private and Public Life of the Animals" were excerpted from the diary of a 12-year-old, Mireille Sidoine, a child of one of the Resistance leaders.

The photomurals were enlarged from the highly original engravings of J.J. Granville by Sam Rosenberg and Charles Gratz, with color effects by Pietro Lazzari. Granville, a contemporary of the 19th-century artist Daumier and precursor of the Surrealist movement, inspired Tenniel's illustrations for *Alice in Wonderland*, and, later, the animated cartoons of Walt Disney.

Caresse—ever the idealist—hoped that the post-war era would provide

> . . . an opening door to a more enlightened, saner world . . . grown full with hope, with the leaven of vision and courage. Let us have more poets and more painters . . . let us erect public buildings of magnitude and beauty worthy of the peace so dearly bought. [Let us] encourage writers to write for posterity and not for profit. . . . [Let us] aid and embellish with our talents the commerce and government of a new and better world. Let us put on "the full armor of light."

Caresse sent out a letter to a number of distinguished leaders in government and the art world, asking for their support in institutionalizing a modern art gallery in the nation's capital.

> I am putting wheels in motion to endeavor to obtain federal financing for a modern art project here in Washington and throughout the United States. This project is to be housed in a key building in the Capital city with experimental art centers on the same lines in each state that warrants a development of this scope and to be constructed with the help of the government. Plans for these buildings are under consideration by a group of prominent architects headed by Edward Durrell Stone (associate designer of the Museum of Modern Art, New York City).

> The Capital of our nation has no Art Center in the sense that I describe. The Crosby Gallery of Modern Art, where for the last year I have presented small exhibitions of modern paintings, engravings and sculpture, has received acclaim as an "oasis in Washington," and just as I see the immediate expansion and importance of our Capital as the center of post-war governmental ideas, I also see it as the matrix of post-war culture.

With her usual verve and enthusiasm, Caresse next turned her sights to a new publishing venture, a literary and artistic endeavor called *Portfolio: An Intercontinental Quarterly.*

(above:) Caresse in the twenties
with her friend and companion,
Narcesse Noir. (below) With Harry
in Lebanon in 1927. (Morris Library)

(left) Hart Crane, lifelong friend of Caresse. His last letter, before he took his life, was written to her.

(right) Salvador Dali at Caresse's Hampton, Virginia estate. (below) Max Ernst, surrealist painter and long-time friend.

Anais Nin was also a frequent guest
at Hampton Manor. *(shown below)*

Scenes at Roccasinibalda in the 1960s. *(above, l. to r.)* Eugene Walker,
Irene Rice Pereira, Caresse, Roloff Bery *(standing)* and Gregory Corso.
(upper right) Caresse in all her radiance. *(below)* Caresse showing a robe
by Irene Pereira. *(photos by Roloff Bery)*

Caresse with Professor Pirionis at Delphi, projected
site of the World Man Center. *(below)* Caresse's
world-citizen card.

IDENTITY

Surname	C R O S B Y
First Names	Caresse
Date of Birth	April 20, 1892
Place of Birth	U.S.A.

ADDRESS

Street	il Castello di Roccasinibalda
Town/ Place	(Province Rieti)
Country	ITALIA

REGISTRE INTERNATIONAL
Centre International
CITOYENS DU MONDE

This card certifies that the holder
is registered as a world-citizen. He will
try to recognise his responsibilities
as a member of the World Community.

Caresse Crosby

Holder's Signature

(left) Caresse with Ezra Pound. *(below)* In the Great Hall at Roccasinibalda. *(Roloff Bery photo)*

*"Those whose deeds have been
recorded by an artist may live till
the world snuffs out."*

—CARESSE

Chapter IX
PORTFOLIO

"Phoenix-like, the world emerges from the ashes." V-E Day—
May 8, 1945—marked the end of the war in Europe, the
beginning of a new era in Caresse Crosby's life. The Black Sun Press
remained silent for six years while Roger Lescaret fought with the
French Resistance. Crosby's daughter (then married to Count
Albert de Mun) and friends (Cartier-Bresson, Hemingway, and many
others) were there to see the Allied troops liberate Paris, while
Caresse herself was "cooped up in America." She was eager to visit
Polleen, now living in London, and to renew old ties in Europe. Yet
only U.S. citizens on official government business were permitted to
travel abroad. Caresse conspired with several imaginative friends to
find a legitimate means of renewing her passport.

Selden Rodman wrote in his diary about the fortuitous meeting at
the Crosby Gallery on the eve of Independence Day, 1945:

> Caresse Crosby called me this morning about an editorial
> board meeting of her new magazine. She said, "Come to
> the gallery early if you can and meet Léger." When I

arrived, she, Harry Moore and a middle-aged balding gentleman with piercing eyes and a sensitive mouth were going over some drawings. She introduced me. "M. Lèger doesn't speak English too well." He and I talked (in French) for half an hour about art and French literature. When Caresse came back, I asked her, "Have we nothing of M. Lèger for the first issue, not even a drawing?" "My God," she said in amused amazement. "You didn't think this was Fernand Lèger, did you Selden? This is Alexis!" I had been talking to St. John Perse, the permanent secretary for the Quai d'Orsay.

Rodman would be listed on the masthead as poetry editor. Crosby asked Lt. Harry Thornton Moore (future D.H. Lawrence scholar and author of *Priest of Love*, then on military duty in Washington) to act as assistant editor. She persuaded Sam Rosenberg to be editorial adviser on photography. Henry Miller, now in Big Sur, California, missed the planning session, but promised to send a contribution:

> It is wonderful to hear you're going to start a quarterly. You ought to make a success of it more than of the gallery, because you won't be limited to that Sargasso Sea of a Washington, D.C. It's really a morgue, Washington! . . . You say send about four or five pages. How many words does that mean? I hardly ever write anything under twelve or fifteen pages . . .

Miller suggested several contributors, such as Lawrence Durrell and Alex Comfort, and added: "The time is ripe. There is scarcely any competition. There are no good literary magazines that I know of. Write me soon about what I can do for you, what ms. to send. Good luck! But why call it 'Generation'? Why don't you call it 'Caresse Crosby's Intercontinental Review'!!!!"

Transition, which ceased publication in 1938, was called "a workshop of the intercontinental spirit." Black Sun published many of the same authors, the symbolic and avant-garde. Caresse hoped to continue the tradition of Eugene and Maria Jolas.

Paper during wartime was difficult to find in bulk, so Caresse bought odd lots of printer's endpapers in any color available. With long-practiced skill, she designed each page with elegant typography and clean reproduction as "a moveable unit to carry away, or to have bound or to frame upon the wall." The oversized 11" by 17" papers were gathered in a posterboard looseleaf binder, a "portfolio" tied with red ribbon. W.P. Tompkins, a specialist in poster reproduction with an office at 931 D Street, printed *Portfolio: An Intercontinental Quarterly* in large red and black script on the cover. Dedicated to world unity through the arts, the first issue of 1,300 copies appeared in fine bookstores on August 6. It sold for $3.00 a single copy ($10.00 a yearly subscription), a bargain considering that each of the original copies is now a collector's item.

Caresse planned a party to celebrate, but when V-J Day broke, there was dancing in the sedate streets of Washington. Moore reported:

> In a wild crowd at the Balalaika I saw an old friend, Thornton Wilder, in the uniform of a lieutenant colonel. I asked him whether I could bring the girl I was with over to meet him, but with his eager politeness, he said he would come over to our table. I took the liberty of inviting him to the *Portfolio* party at Caresse's gallery the next night, where he would for the first time meet David Daiches, who had come to teach at the University of Chicago after Wilder left. Wilder appeared at Caresse's, met David Daiches, and even suggested a book to him—which David then proceeded to write. Such episodes were typical of Caresse's gatherings, at which the air was electric with potential creative activity.

In the introduction to the first issue, Caresse commented on the challenge of the post-war world: "Never before has so much depended on the courageous vision of the artist. In every age, there have been men to lead peoples into treacherous conflict, but human achievement lives on through the medium of the artist, be he historian, poet, or painter."

The list of contributors (who received little or no compensation) was an eclectic group of lively experimentalists, outspoken on social issues. Henry Miller sent "The Staff of Life" (an excerpt from his book *The Air-Conditioned Nightmare*), a biting critique of contemporary American life.

> What do I find wrong with America? Everything. I begin at the beginning with the staff of life, bread. If bread is bad, the whole life is bad. On the whole. Americans eat

without pleasure. They eat because the bell rings three times a day.

Gwendolyn Brooks's "We're the Only Colored People Here" pointed out that all faces are the same shade of gray when the lights go out in a crowded movie theatre. Alex Comfort, an English anarchist, called for civil disobedience to avoid the draft, anticipating the response of the young to the war in Vietnam some 20 years later. David Daiches commented on "The Future of Ignorance," and Kay Boyle contributed a sensitive translation of a chapter from René Crevel's posthumously published novel, *Babylon*. Rodman introduced three war poems, translated from the French, one by the controversial editor of *Ce Soir*, Louis Aragon. "Sleeper in the Valley" by Harry Crosby's youthful idol, Arthur Rimbaud, lamented the death of a young warrier. Harry Moore's review of best-sellers in "a particularly low-grade market place" concluded that there were no rivals for Proust, Mann, Kafka, or even Hemingway, and added the hope that "the publisher's faith in Fitzgerald's work will be justified by sufficient sales to keep it in print . . . Much of his talent was washed down the *Saturday Evening Post's* glittering drain."

Art included Romare Bearden's "Nativity," Pietro Lazzari's "Horses," and contributions by Jean Hélion, Lilian Swann Saarinen, and the British sculptor Henry Moore. Sam Rosenberg's "Practical Joker" was a Rube Goldberg-type contraption designed to confound the sensibilities of the average reader. Loyal to the memory of her dead husband, Caresse included Harry's 1927 photo, "Anatomy of Flight," a surrealistic glimpse of the engine of a World War I fighter plane (which looked for all the world like the innards of a giant land crab). It was a tribute to Crosby's genius as a muse that she recognized and promoted this impressive list of talents, long before their reputations were firmly established. Seventeen-year-old Naomi Lewis admitted that she "had never exhibited except on the bulletin board at school," where her drawing for the first issue of *Portfolio* had recently been thumbtacked.

When Caresse announced alternative issues will be brought out in Paris, she presumed on her long-standing friendship with then-Undersecretary of State MacLeish, counting him as a valuable ally:

> . . . I have talked with Mrs. Shipley in the Passport Division regarding a two-month trip to Europe this summer to gather material for the fall and winter issues of *Portfolio*, my new quarterly review . . . She felt my request "a rea-

sonable one." When I told her that you knew my publishing activities and had been published by the Black Sun Press in Paris days, she said it would be most helpful to me if you would write her a letter to the effect that certain of the younger European authors [should be] included in such a publication. I hope you do feel this to be so, as I am most ardent about creating a following. . . ."

Armed with additional letters from David Finley of the National Gallery of Art and Huntington Cairnes of the Censorship Bureau, Caresse again called upon Shipley, "expressing my belief that ideas could prove of more value than guns, and that peace must be sought through international understanding. Shipley—God bless her!— realized that the plan had value, and the letters I brought with me assured her that I was capable of putting wheels in motion."

As Caresse described the encounter:

Shipley said, "I'll give you the passport, but you have to get yourself over there. You are not attached to the military, you know, nor to any branch of government. I doubt if you can manage transportation."

"I'll try," I said, and the next day, I returned to pick up the precious document, duly signed and sealed.

My first idea was to ask Mr. Foster, travel agent in the Mayflower Hotel. "Absolutely no civilians are allowed on American planes or transports going to England," Mr. Foster said. At the door he stopped me. "There's just a chance that BOAC might take you on. They are hungry for dollars. Their office is up Connecticut Avenue."

When I inquired of the charming lieutenant behind the desk at British Overseas Airways, he said, "If you have a passport and five hundred dollars, I can fix you up. When do you want to go?"

"As soon as possible," I answered.

"Tonight?" he said. "Not tonight, but tomorrow?"

I hesitated.

"Then will you settle for Friday?" the lieutenant asked.

"Of course," I said, "yes!"

Caresse was told that a BOAC limousine would pick her up and drive her to Baltimore, where the nearest flying boat was anchored in the harbor. She was a bit nervous about this odyssey, her first transatlantic flight, and asked her daughter-in-law Josette, who lived around the corner from the Gallery while Billy was on Navy duty, to accompany her to Baltimore.

Caresse was one of the two women en route to London. All other passengers were returning Army personnel in uniform. Wearing her usual travel clothes, she boarded with her Schiaparelli hatbox, her red silk umbrella and zebra jacket which, she recalled, "caused some consternation on that military transport."

The flight was as luxurious as one could expect in the aftermath of war. The old "flying boats" had spacious accommodations for overnight passengers, seats that reclined so completely they could be made up into beds. Each compartment had a washstand, a long mirror, and a curtain that could be drawn for privacy. Despite post-war shortages, the dinner was ample. Caresse joined the gentlemen on the lower level for coffee and cognac in the lounge, but she had to face the troops alone. The other woman, a WAC officer, retreated behind her curtain, and none of the men had much to say to their exotic civilian companion.

The next day, Caresse arrived by taxi at the front door of her daughter and son-in-law's cottage in a mews off Sloane Square. "All were as amazed at my appearance as if I had dropped from another planet, for it was quite unheard of that a civilian not on official business would be allowed on a BOAC flight." The rejoicing carried on into the night. After the reunion with Polleen in London, she crossed the channel to begin the difficult task of starting up the presses again in a city hard hit by war.

The large Schiaparelli hatbox Caresse carried was not a frivolous affectation. In it were the works of two Washington artists for the first post-war *vernissage* at the John Devoluy Gallery. Lorna Lindsley covered the opening in a special to the *Paris Post*, an English-language newspaper:

> Of special interest to Americans is the little show at the Devoluy Gallery in the rue de Furstenberg. The drawings and paintings of two American painters were brought over by Caresse Crosby . . . As she came by plane, she could not bring much, but these are the first American pictures to come here in years. There are line drawings of horses by Pietro Lazzari, an Italian-born American who has worked for the WPA, and a series of watercolors of the Passion of Christ by Romare Bearden, a Negro, which show extraor-dinary feeling and talent. His rather archaic style and

strong coloring suggest the ancient windows of stained glass in the French cathedrals. France needs more art from America. They know little about us over here. Let us hope that Mrs. Crosby, like the first swallows of spring, is a portent of others to come.

"The going is difficult in regard to paper, printing and getting about Paris . . . everything is full of red tape," Caresse wrote to Moore, now stationed in New York with *Air Force Magazine.* In late October, his reply finally caught up with her:

> I wrote you airmail on 4 September. . . . letter was returned yesterday (*retour a l'envoyeur*—I'd so much rather be a *voyeur* than just an *envoyeur!*) . . . it had been addressed to the rue Cardinale. . . .
>
> People are delighted with the magazine [*Portfolio I*]. I don't know how it's selling nationally, but I do know Pietro and Evelyn are selling it to bookstores in Chicago and Los Angeles, etc. And the Gotham's first batch here sold out: Miss Steloff says the re-order shipment is going slower.
>
> I'm so pleased to be in NY, for which I have the true hick's true admiration . . . Our magazine office is down in the Battery region, which has the harbor-smell I knew as a child on the edges of San Francisco bay. I'm in a small hotel, am very broke, but quite happy. I imagine you're having a wonderful time: keep it up! And do let me know plans for the next issue, for I am deeply committed . . .

Caresse dashed off a quick reply:

> Delighted to hear from you after so long . . . From now on, please address Hotel California, 16, rue de Berri . . . This number will stick mostly to the well-known names because the time has been too short to make discoveries and judge the work of newcomers. So in this issue we have ELUARD, CAMUS, SARTRE, PICASSO, CARTIER-BRESSON . . . and a Siamese doctor whose name I cannot spell . . . We have three political articles "Oui-Oui, Oui-non, et Non-non," and a wonderful declaration in prose by Picasso on an artistic-political trend.

No. IV will contain some new names that even the French don't know about and I hope I guess right. We will save the American contributions for the January number, but your review is important because French people are avid for news of American books and tendencies of thought in literature. I am having spiritual indigestion so much is happening!

Moore replied that he hoped [Crosby's] "spiritual indigestion is cured, though I envy the causes of it."

You indicate that a trend-review would be of special interest . . . there isn't too much can be done in that way at the moment. We had no exciting groups over here the way the French have had, with their stimulating café meetings, etc.

How wonderful Paris, even though it is doubtless still a little stunnned from the war, must be! I can just see that magnificent flame-hair of yours against the chestnut trees in the boulevards; do you ride the Bois in a cabriolet, or is it already too cold for open-air travel? The new issue sounds magnificent . . . I have, by the way, secured a promise from Tennessee Williams for an experimental short story; he is *the* boy over here now . . . The possibilities are enormous . . . As I've said, everyone likes the mag . . .

Portfolio II came out in December 1945. Lescaret set the type for a limited edition of 1,000 copies. Published "in the face of material difficulties at a moment when France is with great hardship being restored to its cultural activity," Caresse wrote, ". . . The Editors wish to thank our French friends."

It was a tour de force. Jean-Paul Sartre, leader of the new movement of so-called Existentialists—"the most provocative editorial writer in Paris" (for *Les Temps Modernes*)—commented on the challenge to "young France Today": "This little bomb which can destroy 10,000 men at a time . . . confronts us with terrible responsibilites." Albert Camus, then editor of the Resistance newspaper, *Combat*, appeared for the first time in any English-language publication. Henry Cartier-Bresson captured the "decisive moment" the refugees were freed by the Allied armies, a year before his first exhibition at the Musem of Modern Art in New York.

Henry Moore suggested that the literature emerging from World War II was in the grand tradition of Tolstoy's *War and Peace* and that "Henry James' Americans in Europe in 1875 tell us a great deal about Americans in Europe in 1945."

Pablo Picasso, a frequent guest at Caresse's Mill before the war, sent portraits of Mallarmé and Verlaine and added his personal political statement:

> What do you believe an artist to be? An imbecile who has only eyes if he is a painter, ears if he is a musician, or a lyre on every rung of his heart if he is a poet: or even if he is a boxer, only muscles? He is at the same time a political being . . . No, [a] painting is not made to decorate apartments. It is an instrument of offensive and defensive warfare against the enemy.

In January, Caresse was back in Washington, writing to Henry Miller in California:

> *Portfolio* was received in Paris like rain in drought. I've never realized what aridity for information and ideas and new objects loss of physical contact with the outside world could cause. They hung on to every word, they passed the few copies of *Portfolio I* from hand to hand, group to group; they are as hungry, from lack of contact, mentally as physically. . . . that is why to go there, to eat with them, makes one feel that you are repaying them for the bread and the wine. They long for us to come back . . . the little restaurants—45 francs—taste better than ever before. No-one in Paris looks ragged or starved (although of course "au fond" they must be).
>
> Everyone tells me *Portfolio II* is better than *I*, but I don't think so. I believe that *I* is fresher, more hopeful, and vigorous.

Miller agreed: "I liked *Portfolio I* better too." But he protested he minimal payment to European contributors.

> I understand your difficulties. However, I doubt if our poor European friends will see it that way . . . I would like to say this—a suggestion merely—that you pay such people treble or quintuple the amount, at least, and *not* pay

the American contributors . . . I think most American writers would take it in good part. I just hate to offer, or have you offer, pitiable sums like ten dollars. . . . But try to remember, to see, how they would look at it. *Portfolio looks* like a million dollars. If you can pay the printers and paper mfrs. for such elegance, why not the poor artists who really make the magazine? ENOUGH! . . . This is no reflection on you, please understand. Just a bit of bewilderment. No doubt it will all work out in the last blow of the horn.

Caresse's idealistic view of the world often failed to consider such grim realities as money, but she did follow up Miller's suggestion to seek more funds. She reminded Russell Davenport: "Please don't forget you promised to write me a 'fan' letter for *Portfolio* that I could show to Paul Mellon," but no help came from that source.

Portfolio III was produced on a shoestring in the basement of 1606 20th Street. The masthead listed Rodman, Rosenberg, and Miller as associate editors, along with Moore. Striking yellow posterboard binders lettered with bright orange script held together the kaleidoscope of orange, blue, pink, and cream-colored pages. (To print David Daiches' article about Frank Schoonmaker's selection of wines, Caresse used a *burgundy* ink.) A deluxe edition of 300 copies offered a frameable cover design by Romare Bearden "at a special price." A quotation from Charles Peguy embellished the flyleaf: "He who does not shout the truth when he knows the truth makes himself the accomplice of liars and counterfeiters."

Henry Miller sent Part II of "The Staff of Life," another rebuke to the Philistines, and Kay Boyle contributed a story about a peasant who stubbornly refuses to give up his land in "A Military Zone." Jean-Paul Sartre focused on the dilemma of adolescence, "Boy into Man." The then-unknown Spanish poet Federico Garcia-Lorca contributed "Lament for Ignacio Sánchez-Mejías," a dead bullfighter, handsomely illustrated by Pierre Tal-Coat. Harry Moore praised Anais Nin—whose first commercial fiction, "This Hunger," appeared in *Portfolio*—as "someone to watch." Rodman defied the *New Yorker* review of the highly-touted *Brideshead Revisited* by calling it an example of Evelyn Waugh's "newfound pietism."

Caresse reprinted several significant pages from the 1929 edition of *Shadows of the Sun*. Harry's paraphrase of Walt Whitman provides a revealing glimpse into Harry's own phyche: "it expresses exactly how I feel towards those who love me."

Who is he who would become my follower?
The way is suspicious—the result uncertain,
perhaps destructive.
You would have to give up all else—I alone would
expect to be your Sun-God, sole and exclusively.
Your novitiate would then be long and exhausting.
The whole past theory of your life and all conformity
to the lives of those around you would have to be abandoned.
Therefore release me now—let go your hand from my . . .

(Caresse must have caught the nuances of his message, it so
perfectly mirrored her relationship with Harry.)

She again recognized promise in another erratic young poet,
Kenneth Rexroth, author of an innovative verse play, *Iphigenia at
Aulis.* When she took a change on him, she had no idea she would be
rewarded with this angry outcry from San Francisco. (Rexroth's
letter gives a glimpse of the casual manner in which the "editorial
board" of *Portfolio* functioned.)

Last fall, Seldon Rodman asked me to send him some
things for a magazine he was editing. This turned out to be
Portfolio. . . . He suggested that I "might get fifty dollars"
for them, if I "asked you nicely." I answered that I
considered such a proposition degrading, that it was not
my custom to beg from the rich, and please return the mss.
as I had other places to place them on less insulting terms.
I heard nothing from him, and forgot about the
matter. . . .

Today, in a bookstore, I came upon *Portfolio III*, with my
play. Since I received no final notice of acceptance by you,
no proofs, no author's copies, no pay—I certainly consider this a most extraordinary piece of behavior on your
part. I am not a syncophant—the last thing in the world I
wish is to be beholden to you in anyway—I am well aware
that the literary bon ton is made up of English assistants,
Stalinist gunmen, fairies, professional cunnilinguists [sic]
and other swine, who simply love to be kicked around by
millionairesses. I am emphatically not such a person. I
publish only on invitation, in periodicals, etc. run by my
friends. I loathe and despise the world of cocktail literature and art and want nothing whatever to do with it.

Doubtless you are asked simply everywhere as . . . a fascinating woman, and one of the world's leading art patrons. I hear you have your picture in *Harper's Bazaar*, or is it *view*, as a "Career Woman of the Year." This is at my expense, and others like me who would not possibly afford $3.50 for your simply fascinating magazine.

Of course, I know, when one has so much, one is careless about other people's property, isn't one? Poor dear.

He added a postscript: "I am very poor, and *not* careless about such matters.

Caresse's answer was lost, but she wrote to Moore about the contretemps:

The Rexroth business was the limit. Selden did all the correspondence with him, and he went off to Haiti without leaving me Rexroth's address . . . When I learned that his check had not been sent due to lack of address, I mailed one c/o Selden from Europe. According to J. Laughlin, the $50 I paid Rexroth was more than he received from *New Directions* and when he [Rexroth] wrote me the absurd tantrum letter, *Portfolio* had only been out two weeks, so the delay was not very enormous. I imagine he suffers from a great big inferiority complex. In spite of all this, the *Iphigenia* was one of the very finest things we have ever printed and really worth the row . . .

Caresse was always willing to take another chance on new talent. Virginia Paccassi, a 24-year-old with a distinctive, colorful approach to painting scenes of contemporary life in the streets and docks of the cities, wrote to her benefactor from Bleecker Stret:

. . . Everything seems to have happened today. I got a divorce at noon, lost my train ticket this afternoon, and almost had to walk home from Boston . . . . I found your *Portfolio* at the door when I reached home. I have a three-year-old daughter who Henry Miller was crazy about when he visited us in California two years ago. The painting you reproduced I painted when I was 19, therefore I was a bit in the fog on perspective—still am!

*   *   *

The Rome edition of *Portfolio* was prompted by a call from the cultural attaché of the Italian Embassy in Washington. He noticed *Portfolio II*, edited in Paris, and asked Caresse to make a similar report on the modern renaissance of Italian literature and art. During the Fascist regime, exhibitions were closed the day they opened if paintings did not conform, and liberal books were banned. After 21 years of repression, artists and writers, long underground, "emerged into the light of a modern era." Their interest and curiosity about America were great.

In April 1946, Caresse set sail once again for Europe. It was still difficult for a civilian to enter Italy, so she stopped off in Paris to arrange a flight with the Air Transport Command. "I was not told what day or hour I would depart, only that I should be ready to take off whenever I was notified by telephone," she wrote. She was having dinner with friends and had just started back to her hotel on rue de Bac when "I was met by the little *chasseur* on a bicycle . . . the ATC had telephoned that I was to be at Orly Field in two hours!"

She packed quickly, and as it was almost impossible to find a taxi in those days, the concierge telephoned every place he knew before he finally "ran to earth a *copain* with a car." Even then, the driver arrived only some ten minutes before she was due at the Place Vendôme, the central meeting place for transportation to Orly.

At the airport, she waited another hour for a sudden rain to let up, then piled aboard a converted bomber with bucket seats filled with American G.I.s and officers. "We swooped down to a little shed with 'Roma' on its red rile roof. The day was beginning to dawn and the darkness and desolation . . . were very apparent. I had heard that Rome was not destroyed, but I saw that the edges were badly singed," she wrote.

She was billeted along with military personnel at the Excelsior, once Rome's "swankiest" hotel. Several members of the staff remembered Caresse from former visits, and the concierge welcomed her as a long-lost friend. She had lunch alone in the Officers' Mess, "decidedly PX, but the two martinis at 50 *lire* [then the equivalent of 20 cents] were decidedly pre-war."

Caresse spent the afternoon obtaining "privilege" cards for use in the occupied city and calling at the U.S. Embassy, where Professor Morey, the cultural attaché, won high marks as a man of keen intellect, excellent taste, and good sense. (She discovered belatedly on the day she left that Morey was also a poet.)

"From the moment that I finished my coffee and strawberries next morning in the sunshine on the Via Veneto, I was obsessed by a world of new and exciting work," she wrote. She set about her task of interpreting the Italian scene of arts and letters "for circulation in America." The work of Alberto Moravia ("Malinverno") and Carlo Levi ("Italian Panorama") were published in *Portfolio* well ahead of Levi's best-selling novel, *Christ Stopped at Eboli*. Morandi, an unknown youth—in her view—usurped the high place of Giorgio de Chirico. (De Chirico's "Self-Portrait in 17th Century Dress" was "an abundance of realistic fruit and feathers that seems to spell the word *pompier*.")

Caresse noted other important post-war trends in Italy. New names like Manzu and Savelli added to the rich heritage of sacred art. Architects and sculptors were making impressive strides, and there was a renewal of cultural life in the great castles and estates far from the cities. The great halls of the Castello di Torre Sommi-Peccinardi were converted into a modern theater, where ambitions villagers were offering French and Italian chamber music and attempting a Saroyan play in translation. Before she left for the States, Caresse was photographed by Romolo Marcellini at one of the historic fountains of Rome for the flyleaf of *Portfolio* (a photo later reproduced in a *Madamoiselle* feature, captioning her as editor of one of the "newer avant-garde magazines").

Back in Washington, she announced a special edition of 100 numbered copies with an original lithograph by Roberto Fasola, *L'Autel des Jesuits*. She wrote to Moore, now at Craig Air Force Base, Alabama:

> Back again full of Italian news. *Portfolio IV* is going to be sensational. Half of it is on the way, shipped by the U.S. Embassy. The other half I am getting together now in Washington. Your Lawrence article is to appear in both Italian and English. The translation has already been made. I will send you proofs next week.

Few translators lived up to Caresse's meticulous standards. She wrote to Dr. Felix Giovanelli at New York University:

> I am enclosing my check for $13 to settle the balance of your translating bill. . . . The actual number of your words printed in *Portfolio* were 5,439. I had to discard the Moravia as the translation was not up to standard.

. . . The poems that I used (and you said I could do as I liked about them) were completely revised by me and Corrado Cagli, who . . . said your translation, as it was, could not stand. I am sorry that so much of your work had to be discarded.

Always hard-pressed for funds, Caresse wrote to Bearden:

Dear Romie:

We are sending you a check for $50 for the magnificent contribution you made. I hope that next year, now that circulation is increasing, expenses . . . will be reduced and adequate means available to increase payment for materials used.

. . . In March I plan to go to Greece. The following number I would like to have made up entirely of Negro contributors. . . . I am wondering if you would be willing to act as one of my associate editors, your name to appear on the masthead? There is no salary connected with this, but I am hoping that you may find it of sufficient interest to devote some time to helping me gather an impressive list . . .

Portfolio V was issued in Washington from new editorial offices at 918 F Street. Bearden came aboard as art editor, but Rodman, newly released from the Army, was no longer listed as poetry editor. Belazel Schatz's illustration for Henry Miller's *Black Spring*, a serigraph (silkscreen) of the author's handwriting, was the frontispiece of the deluxe edition of 200 copies. "Handwriting possesses direct contact, carrying a flavor . . . all of its own which is completely lost in type print," the editor commented.

On the flyleaf was Harry Crosby's 1929 photograph of D.H. Lawrence at the Moulin du Soleil, illustrating the feature article by Moore, "Why Not Read Lawrence, Too?" (At the time, *Lady Chatterley's Lover* was banned from publication in the U.S.)

Max Ernst supplied another of his surrealistic paintings from Arizona. Man Ray, whom Caresse discovered in Paris—as yet unrecognized in his own country—contributed one of his photosensitive "rayographs," which he described as "painting with light." René Batigné, director of the French Art collection at the National Gallery of Art, contributed an essay on life and work of Modigliani.

Caresse continued to be a risk-taker in publishing unknown talent, however unlikely the source. Edwin Becker's "Who Cried

Against the Wall"—a short story submitted on Miller's recommendation—was written while the author was serving time in New Jersey State Prison for creatively forging his name to checks. "A young man of sensitive and courageous mind, he has made of his life in prison an opportunity for study and intellectual development," the editor noted. "In one of his letters to me, Henry Miller said, 'Prison is not the worst place in the world in which to write. . . . many eminent men have written great works in prison: Marco Polo, Cervantes, *et al.*, Walls? Bars? Restrictions? . . . against freedom of the mind, NO!'" Becker's byline later appeared in mass circulation magazines, such as *Colliers*, *Esquire*, and *Readers' Digest*.

Of special interest was an excerpt from Tolstoy's last work, "The Law of Love and the Law of Violence," never before published in English. Caresse must have chosen to print it as a personal expression of her philosophy. Protégé Charles Olson sent "Upon a Moebus Strip" from the new experimental school in North Carolina, Black Mountain College, where he was in residence.

Portfolios were getting popular press coverage, not only in Washington and New York, but as far afield as the Toledo *Blade*:

> Remember Caresse? In the post-war heyday of American expatriates in Paris, she sponsored surrealist painters and writers; maintained Le Moulin, popular salon for artists; flashed rhinestone eyebrows at the opening of Gertrude Stein's "Three Saints in Four Acts," wore a white horse costume at the fancy dress ball she gave to introduce Dali to New York.

Now she and her staff are editing "around the world." The next *Portfolio* will be edited in Athens, she says, and will report the artistic and intellectual reaction of the Greeks to their current dilemma.

*"The surreal for me is the
greatest reality of all."*

—CARESSE

Chapter X
SUN AND SHADOW

The Greek edition was the last—and in many ways the most difficult and rewarding—of the *Portfolios.*

> In going to Greece at this time of crisis, I hope to gather into *Portfolio* VI an expression of what new Greece, young Greece is feeling and hoping . . . at a moment when her future is in the balance and the eyes of the world are on her political problems, even her problems of survival, I intend to present every intellectual viewpoint that I find there, whatever its political background, and also to publish an expression of the direction of Greek thought in terms of art, literature, poetry and music.

The *Boston Herald* review of March 28, 1948 was amazed that *Portfolio* VI could come out despite the chaotic political situation under the military government. Caresse's introduction, "Sun and Shadow," described the appalling poverty, the shortages, the gigantic inflation, and wondered "at the beauty of the moon-drenched

127

Parthenon [while] Greeks were fighting in the hills and children were starving just around the corner."

When Caresse first arrived at Hassani Airport in May 1947, "the hills were the color of the sidewalks of New York, stripped bare of all living foliage." During the bleak years of the Nazis, the Greeks survived without gas or electricity, and wood was the only source of fuel for cooking, even to propel the buses that carried the people to work. She noticed that the buses were still "crippled little derelicts with great caverns in their sides . . . they were back on gas now, but each bore a gaping smoke-blackened wound in its side."

Caresse was startled to discover from currency control at the airport that two one-dollar bills brought a huge mound of 10,000 drachmas at the current exchange rate. On the drive into Athens in an ancient taxi, she saw the impoverished Greeks sitting on patched and unpainted chairs at little tables in the cafés that lined the way, nursing a small cup of coffee (Turkish), but more often, only a glass of water. "I learned later," Caresse wrote, "that one ordered water, then scooped a spoonful of a sweet resinous paste, masticha, from a center jar; this is dipped in the water to give it flavor, or licked slowly from the spoon. . . ." (With 5,000 drachmas for the taxi, plus a tip here and there, the two dollars in exchange were quickly spent.)

The venerable Grande-Bretagne Hotel, Caresse's favorite hospice, had no vacancies so she continued on to the other luxury hotel, the Acropole Palace. A threadbare room with an army cot and a dilapidated bath that provided water for only one hour per day was luxury in 1947 Athens (and a bargain at 50,000 drachmas—at the current exchange rate, U.S. $10—per day).

Caresse's first stop was Aetos, the bookshop under the Colonnade that she remembered from her last visit in the '30s. There she met Nicholas Calamaris, a young Greek poet with a rebellious look in his eye, who became her "constant cavalier" and followed her back to Paris. He was a frequent visitor at the Mill, where she introduced him to André Breton and other Surrealists before he acquired an international reputation as Nicholas Calas. (She planned to publish an excerpt from his book, "The Gathering Together of the Waters," in the Greek Portfolio.)

Later that night, she went to dinner with friends. Walking through the narrow streets, skirting the tiny burial ground where Byron lies next to the house where he once lived, they arrived at the little taverna under the Acropolis, deserted then except for three tortoiseshell kittens and a small boy doing his homework. In the back, behind a hanging carpet, a cook labored over the wood-burning stove with glowing brazier and three huge, simmering kettles to prepare the Spartan menu—pigeons wrapped in vine leaves and tiny artichokes the size of walnuts, with special Attica wine and a sweet made of pastry and honey.

Not until the place began to fill up at ten o'clock did Caresse discover that this humble tavern was "the" best place to eat in the post-war city. She noticed that the women of Athens, who had not been able to buy new clothes for many years (or nylon stockings, at a prohibitive $12.00 a pair if one could find them), still managed to dress with flair. The Parthenon shone silver-white under a full moon when she left, and she could hardly believe the poverty-stricken sights of the morning, or that "the starving partisans in the hills were dying in defiance of that corrupt minority of 'quislings' who then held Greece in their grip."

In the face of these difficulties, Caresse set about collecting the finest examples of the work of young Greek artists. Diamantopoulos was working alone in a bare room with only his paints and paper (canvas at the time was too costly, even if he could find it). He fought through bloody campaigns of the war and suffered starvation and imprisonment before devoting his life to creative work with no promise of selling. Krapalos worked in the hill country with home-made tools and clay before returning to Athens with his sculptures packed in straw on an ox cart. A bombed-out building in the outskirts was his temporary workshop. Ghika spent many years of exile in Paris and London before returning to his native island of Hydra to capture the Greek landscape on canvas. The youngest professor at the University of Athens and a leader of the modern Greek School, Ghika was well known in his own country but had no reputation abroad until Caresse published "The Invisible Mirror."

Through Ghika Caresse happened upon the work of Vassilakis Takis—a shy, proud, and hungry young man, "not only belly hungry but spirit hungry"—who was sleeping in his only pair of ragged pants and shirt in Melethon Park "like a fallen Icarus." Hydra was the first of the Greek islands she visited. The daily mail boat from Piraeus deposited her on the pier, where she and her companions ate crayfish, cheese, and bread washed down with *ouzo* at a quayside tavern before a peasant with a donkey led them up the steep cliff to Ghika's summer palace. The huge beds, with freshly washed, heavily embroidered linen piled high with eiderdown, in rooms with casement windows, were a welcome sight. "It was an adventure, as all journeys are, through these island landscapes," she wrote.

The next morning, Rosa, the peasant's daughter, came with fresh eggs, bread, and butter, with lemons for tea. Afterwards, Caresse went down to the sea—skirting ledges and ravines and little gardens—sunbathing "like one of the lazy little lizards that decorate the stones." She could see young men below, bathing "naked as the gods." One of them was Takis. Later, at the Ghikas', Takis showed Caresse his delicate carved medallions and sacred pendants. She took with her an oval with blue and silver mermaids enameled on its surface, a treasured keepsake. Some 15 years later, Takis was artist-in-residence at the Center of Advanced Visual Studies at M.I.T., attempting to achieve "spiritual collaboration" with scientists through the medium of his magnetic sculpture.

Tetsis, also from Hydra, Kanellis, and Moralis produced new and vigorous conceptions of art in fresh forms for *Portfolio*. Caresse soon resurrected the works of Theophilos, a primitive with the naïve richness of a Rousseau, for a retrospective exhibit at the British Institute.

Critics and friends warned Caresse about Engonopoulos, a surrealist painter, poet, and philosopher: "He is difficult. He is shy. He is a little mad." She went to see for herself. "A brigandish chauffeur drove me down long narrow streets and left me in front of a garage," she wrote of the experience.

> I skirted the dark building until at the back I saw a slit of light from a toolshed. I pulled at the door and stepped in. . . . A bare bulb hanging from the rafters lit up thirty or more huge canvases. . . of such vivid unreality that I gasped. . . . At a low table, the artist crouched, pen in hand, with pages strewn about, and from behind the largest, wildest painting issued the voice of Bing Crosby crooning softly, "Goodnight, Sweetheart." I knew then that the surreal for me is the greatest reality of all.

She gathered up the verses scattered about, one of which was printed in *Portfolio*: "The women that we love are like pomegranates. . . ."

Soon after the bizarre experience with Engonopoulos, she was invited to tea in a spacious drawing room overlooking the Royal Gardens by George Theotokas, who was writing a *Portfolio* piece on the intellectual ferment of modern Greece. Five baronial chairs were placed around a center table of highly polished cypress, and in front of each chair was a beautiful string of precious beads—lapis and gold, silver and jade, onyx and crystal. Theotokas brought together

Dimaris, a contemporary critic, Nicolareizis, a poet, and Elytis, a philosopher. "As each young man took his place . . . he lifted the beads pensively in his fingers, and as he talked, he fingered the string as if it were a rosary. I did likewise, and I must say that this elegant and spiritual custom seems to add much to the flow of ideas. The young men were quite as handsome as the beads," she wrote, "and I took away with me a most embellished memory. . . ."

Caresse's reputation was expanding into ever-widening circles. Eleni Vlachos, a reporter for *Kathimerini*, an Athens periodical, described their first meeting:

> I happened a few days ago to meet an American lady at the house of friends of mine, Mrs. Caresse Crosby. She seemed particularly interested in our artistic movement, and to have already become perfectly acquainted with the way it expressed itself. She rolled off titles of Greek books, painters, authors, musicians, she criticized and compared; she had also met actors and discussed recent talent.
>
> "How long has Mrs. Crosby been in Athens?" I inquired.
>
> "One week," was the reply.
>
> "Well, how did she manage to learn all that stuff?" I inquired in amazement.
>
> [She was] possessed by a demon, and by a great talent. What kind of demon, and what kind of talent? The discovery of personalities . . . without artistic experience, she'd spy value in the unknown, in poor and despised painters and authors. She'd fish out talent in the way a cat smells a rat. . . . Nor did she need the support of reviews to understand the value of a work. She started traveling, looking, discovering, supporting, and succeeding. . . .
>
> Now this indefatigable woman is editing an art review, called *Portfolio*, which appears as a large copybook. . . . [She] may well tell us about the present Greek art, and may add a fresh talent to the collection of those already discovered . . . that we in our blindness had not yet detected. [Translated from the Greek.]

Caresse discovered the Arts Theater, founded in 1942 by Charles Koun with the help of Dora Stratos, a dedicated musician who raised funds, borrowed costumes, and roused the public consciousness.

During the German Occupation, the theater was a means of keeping Greeks informed about the Allied world despite strict censorship. The box office "take," divided among the dedicated young troupers, averaged 1,000 *drachmas*—then 20 cents—a day. "With raisins as our principal meal and butts of cigarettes going the rounds, we formed the craziest plans for a theater, hoping to build up a better civilization in a new world," Koun wrote in *Portfolio*.

In the early days, German censors insisted that there should be nothing in a play that could suggest its British or American origin. Koun managed to produce Erskine Caldwell's *Tobacco Road*, wholly unexpurgated, under the title, "For a Piece of Earth." Some of the Anglo-Saxon-sounding names were changed, as subtly as possible, so as not to misinterpret the meaning. "Lines that at other times would have had but a normal effect, under Nazi terrorism touched in each one of us more profoundly our sense of social justice." After a hiatus of several years when conditions were intolerable, the Theater reopened in 1946 to produce Tennessee Williams's *Glass Menagerie*. Mano Hadjidakis, a gifted 19-year-old, composed the score, and Taroukis, who later designed for Maria Callas's appearances in Paris and London, did the sets.

The next-to-last day in Greece Caresse went to visit Angelo Sikelianos in his monastic retreat on the island of Salamis. She joined his wife, Anna, for the long and difficult trip by bus and by boat to the legendary island. Wearing big fisherman's hats and carrying wicker baskets packed with cherries, cakes, and books for the poet, they set out on a sweltering June day through the vendor-crammed streets of Athens to Larissa Square, where a flotilla of rickety buses awaited. Soon,

> . . . we riders-to-the-sea were tearing along the road Ulysses once followed. The signpost at the first corner read: Illis - Thebes - Delphi. . . . All along the roadside roses were bursting into bloom. The way to the sea was fringed with flowering trees, back of them, the olives shimmered silver-green, and the denuded hills rose blue and gray. Then of a sudden round a corner . . . the Aegean, indigo and pearl, lay between us and Salamis like a carpet. I shall never forget the first glimpse of that inland sea or the long, bright day that followed.

*   *   *

At the border of the province, military police stopped them for identity cards, and Caresse discovered she had left hers in Athens. After protesting in fluent "American," she was allowed to pass. Two hours later Caresse and Anna arrived in Eleusina, a remote village of fishing shacks and deserted cottages. At the water's edge, fishermen's nets were hanging out to dry. The two women asked "a barefooted and sun-blackened" oarsman to take them to the opposite shore to the ancient convent of Phaneiomeni, where they found Sikelianos at work in an isolated sky-blue house.

"The blue door opened and I was in a scholar's room, filled with shadows and poetry," Caresse remembered. Her first impression was of a massive form and heroic head, with soft, penetrating eyes. "The poet told me he worked twenty hours a day, breakfasting at five, and that even then, there was not time enough." He signed the flyleaf of his book "To Caresse Crosby, with emotion and friendship." After a picnic lunch and a swim, the women poked about the island and departed at sunset. Sikelianos was standing at the end of the pier, waving his hat slowly back and forth until they could no longer see him.

Back in Washington, Caresse lost no time in writing to members of the Royal Academy in Stockholm, recommending Angelo Sikelianos for the Nobel Award in 1947 for *The Awakener*, "not only by his acknowledged eminence as a literary figure, but by the example he has . . . set forth in his Delphic Idea."

Caresse suffered many headaches in bringing out the Greek *Portfolio*. She wrote to Alexander Xydis in Athens:

Dear Aleko:

After trials and tribulations, *Portfolio* is actually to appear in a few days. The art work that I had printed in Florence has only just reached here due to strikes and customs. They have promised to deliver the shipment Monday morning, . . . I will send twenty in care of USIS Athens so that they may be distributed to contributors and fifty more to Aetos.

The spelling that you drew my attention to has been corrected, but I have been in a quandary as to several other spellings, since the Greek Embassy says one thing, the author himself signs another way and is often spoken of in the reviews written for *Portfolio* by another spelling. All this is most confusing. . . .

The greatest disappointment has been that I have had to postpone the poems of Elytis and Seferis until a future number since I depended on Catsimbalis who did not come through as he promised and Friar's translations are so very inadequate and unpoetic that I feel they would do more harm to both the poetry and to his readers than otherwise. . . . I also had to have the Dimaras article done over and the Hadjimihali, since the first renderings done through the Greek Embassy were likewise a jumble of incomprehensible wording. . . . Your article was the only one that was sent to me in condition to be given to the printer, for which I was most grateful. I miss you all very much as I feel I have been living with the contributors in spirit for these many weeks.

She also thanked the British poet Derek Patmore, whose rendering of "The Woman of Crete" by Andrea Cambas was exceptional:

I am using the Greek translation you gave me and will send off a CARE package the next time I go to New York. *Portfolio* is only just now about to appear because the ship which was bringing the printed matter from Italy was held up for months by dock strikes in Marseilles and has caused the greatest delay and difficulty on this end. However, the material in the Greek *Portfolio* seems to be even more timely than a few months back and as soon as it can be launched, I will send you, say 500, copies to try out in London.

Despite such obstacles, *Portfolio VI* came out almost on schedule in spring 1948. Caresse wrote to Bruce Blevin, editor of the *New Republic:*

Herewith is a copy of *Portfolio VI* . . . in brief, a review of the contemporary art and literature of that country whose problems are now so vividly in the news. I have attempted to gather together under one cover the aesthetic expressions of a people whose ardor for the arts neither war nor famine has quenched. . . . [I]t is a modest attempt at the objectives our Government's cultural program advocates, an exchange between nations of contemporary ideas. . . .

The Greek artists, most of them in dire need, . . . have received the minimum for their work, . . . but I did promise them an audience in this country, and it is in hope that you will help me keep this promise that I am sending you *Portfolio* VI for possible mention in your paper.

From the beginning, *Portfolio* was subsidized heavily from Caresse's personal account. From Greece she wrote to Arthur Wagman, newly hired as business manager and public relations liaison in Washington: "I have great confidence in your ability to create a good market and to manage the business successfully, for," she added realistically "we'll either fold or flourish now."

She explained her dilemma to Miller:

After trials and tribulations *Portfolio VI* is on the way to subscribers and one will reach you before long. I have had to reorganize the selling of *Portfolio*. It got very much out of hand while I was away, and unfortunately Mr. Wagman not only didn't sell, but *unsold*, which was quite disastrous financially. I tried to find assistance from some of my well-heeled friends and from some gilded Greeks in this country, but not a soul has come across and I have had to falter along on my own resources. I hope the result will not be too inferior.

For three years, Caresse had accomplished the impossible with these handsome productions, and as she confessed to Wagman, "Never has so much been done on so little." "Let no one account this a small effort," the critic Carley Dawson wrote.

Whoever has worked with his hands, and has slipped a thin wedge under a weight apparently impossible of moving, will know how effective a slender wedge can be, even when it may be only a small hammer that continues its persistent blows. Caresse Crosby, in her eager, knowledgeable mind, has that wedge. In her dynamic energy, her obstinate faith in and love of people, she has that hammer. Successive numbers of her *Portfolio* should be awaited with respect and interest, not only by intellectuals everywhere, but by all those who sense the world longing for a creative, universal, and lasting peace.

*　　*　　*

After *Portfolio VI*, Caresse was bringing out Charles Olson's long poem *Y & X*, hoping to have it completed before Christmas. In answer to Olson's request for payment, she wrote:

> I'm in a jam myself until December 1st—if that is no good to you I'll try to arrange the accounts so you can have it sooner. I saw Corrado but we are no further on *Y&X* because (1) I have too much at present to get out *Portfolio* (after this week, the checks will be cleared) and (2) I myself have no funds just now to work with. I always pay as I print—I hate bills piling up! So I am solvent but broke. . . .

Y & X finally came out early in the new year, a handsome limited edition in palindrome format, handset in astrée italics, illustrated by the line drawings of Corrado Cagli. It was an appropriate swan song.

Caresse wrote:

> Here are proofs of the text—but all you can check is the text—this actual printing was done on a proof press and I can't get final proofs actually *en page* until the day it goes to press. If you were on hand we could watch the first sheets together and rectify any spacing, etc., but you will just have to trust me—I fuss and fume and work and space for hours, to my heart's content, until I get things right. . . . Well, let's keep our fingers crossed. . . .

Olson replied:

> I return the proofs (which have just come) with the greatest pleasure in the type, congratulations. It seems to me perfect. Preface stands out like some revolutionary broadside, and it couldn't be better. My own wish is that a little more breadth of space be put where I have indicated, even if it means crowding the margin a little in this case. For it is a difficult poem typographically and must be given all its chance, no?

Caresse was going ahead with plans to publish the work of black artists and writers in *Portfolio VII* until late 1948, when she abruptly announced to disappointed subscribers: "I regret to say *Portfolio* has been suspended due to lack of funds. You ask if publication will be resumed. We hope so, but we need financial support. Do you know of anyone who might contribute to this very worthwhile expression of cultural exchange?" When no angel appeared, there were no new issues of *Portfolio*.

Caresse was again a woman ahead of her time, in the vanguard of creative thought, apart from the crowd. In the post-war world of "pop" culture, she spoke out loud and clear against "the Philistines," a voice crying in the wilderness in her time. Without an academic background or special creative talent of her own, she was blessed with an intuitive artistic sense to evaluate the work of others and was utterly fearless in printing anything of real merit, as long as it was sincere. She must have foreseen the importance of her role as muse, of a lifelong commitment to the arts, when she wrote: "The poet or artist is the longest life-giver in the universe. . . . Those whose deeds have been recorded by a poet may live till the world snuffs out."

At the mid-century mark, a mushroom cloud appeared on the horizon that threatened the world "snuffing out." Caresse cast aside creative concerns to take on a new role as political activist.

*"Idealists are all crackpots until they
become heroes or saints."*

—CARESSE

Chapter XI
A CITIZEN OF THE WORLD

As Caresse reached another turning point in her life, she was still her father's daughter, and William Jacob was a man who "dreamed of, believed in, and planned for a better world for rich and poor alike." The cause she was seeking turned up on her doorstep in January 1948. "A young lawyer, Rufus King, and his wife Janice came to my editorial office in Washington, bringing a beautiful idea with them in manuscript," she wrote. "They appealed to me as an independent publisher to print their work. Other publishers had turned it down as, at best, 'ahead of its time,' or at worst, 'crackpot.' These young people aimed to *do* something towards making this earth of ours a better habitat."

> We have just survived a cycle of three decades that carried us from total war to total war. This time, the cycle may be shorter; and this time it promises a holocaust. . . . We are young, with good years ahead of us in this life. . . . We believe that our lives could scarcely mean more to us than yours to you. . . .

138

This document of some hundred pages—*The Manifesto for Individual Secession into a World Community*—was couched in legal terms, but the thrust was obvious: A small number of national leaders had unleashed a weapon of total destruction. Only by pledging allegiance to a higher, international authority could mankind avoid the total disaster of a third World War.

"That night, in reading over their conception of World Citizenship, I realized that I had in my hands the cornerstone of a new World Order," Caresse noted. "Their greatest appeal was to my heart and conscience. I knew it [the *Manifesto*] would have no immediate political or financial success. The best I could promise was to get it into print in Paris in the spring, and to distribute review copies."

She began by placing announcements in Washington newspapers inviting anyone interested in world citizenship to gather at the new editorial office at 2008 Que Street. Some 50 people came, a cross-section: "the religious man, the artist, the soldier, the diplomat, the housewife, the businessman, the student." The movement failed to gain momentum until April, when Caresse flew to Europe with Rufus King, taking the *Manifesto* in his briefcase. At their first stop, Hyde Park Corner in London, the tall, lanky young American impressed passers-by with his well-expressed ideas. In Paris, Roger Lescaret's press put the *Manifesto* into production, with the publication date May 15, 1948.

Also in May, the Black Sun Press produced the first World Passport:

> This passport has little meaning in itself. You will note that you have made no pledge or promise. You are simply identified as one who "will endeavor to recognize" his responsibilities as a member of the single, total World Community. . . . The number on your passport is the number of human beings who have accepted this trust already. Their numbers grow. We welcome you and honor the step you have taken.

A young American in Paris, Garry Davis, was the first to act upon the idea of individual secession. A slight man with sandy hair and a self-effacing smile, Davis was deeply moved by his experiences as a bomber pilot in World War II. "No one really understood except those of us who had been out there with them and heard them laugh the night before it happened, heard them jeer obscenities . . . and then seen them die the next morning." The son of Meyer Davis, a popular society orchestra leader, Garry planned to make a career as an actor before the War. When he returned, he was not the same carefree young man who left for flight training. After he read the *Manifesto*, "The only thing that was clear in my mind was that I, Garry Davis, was in some way responsible for the march of nations toward World War III."

In a dramatic gesture, Davis walked into the Passport Division of the U.S. Embassy in Paris and renounced his American citizenship. To prove his point, he camped on the steps of the Trocadero, at that time the meeting place of the United Nations, designated an international territory. In a filibuster lasting for several days, Davis lectured the passers-by about U.S. history and the Founding Fathers—Madison, Monroe, Jefferson—self-declared "Americans" who relinquished citizenship in their native states to declare allegiance to a higher authority. Citizens of contemporary nation-states—particularly the Big Four—should renounce their own national interests on behalf of world government, according to Davis. (Lescaret, hero of the French Resistance, infiltrated the crowds to take meals to Garry.) The crowds thinned out as soon as the novelty wore off, but one young American stayed on.

"Are you Garry Davis? I'm Rufus King—from Washington."

"I've heard about you, Rufus. Good to know you."

"I thought you could use some professional advice. Say, I'd like to help you to put this thing over. . . . We could draw up a *world* Constitution, a Bill of Rights, a Pledge of Allegiance, etc., for world citizens."

Despite Rufus's offer of legal aid, Davis was a young man without a country, subject to extradition by the French. Caresse knew the day would come when gendarmes would move in to arrest him, and she did what she could to prevent such injustice. Reporting back to Olson in Washington, she wrote:

> I am now official printer to the Citizens of the World! Youth movements, World crusaders, etc., etc., flock around my door. I am printing leaflets for "followers of Garry Davis"—it's growing—60 countries heard from. Youth is against the Atlantic Pact—or any military pact; they're scared, they want to rise up soon and assert their right to live in peace. You'd better come help us—or prepare to help me have a big rally in Washington in September!

The international press at the time discredited and caricatured Davis and the World Citizens movement. As publisher of its "Bible," the *Manifesto*, Caresse Crosby was tarred with the same brush. The Sunday *News* in Washington noted on June 27:

> World Citizen No. 3! Mrs. Caresse Crosby has a world citizenship movement of her own, in which she follows Mr. and Mrs. Rufus King on an informal citizenship roll. . . . Puzzled State Department officials have no answer. Millions outside want "in," desiring the most useful citizenship in the world, and others clamor to renounce the privilege.

Several periodicals returned the published *Manifesto* to Caresse without reviewing it. A few enlightened individuals—such as Norman Cousins, editor of *The Saturday Review* and leader of the United World Federalists—praised the World Citizens movement as an idea whose time had come.

A major breakthrough occurred when Robert Sarrazac, leading French intellectual, risked his reputation by recruiting a distinguished group to meet at the Cité Club, a *Conseil de Solidarité*, with André Breton, the poet, and Albert Camus, the novelist, among them. With such substantial backing, the world press began to swing in Davis's favor. *The New Yorker* acknowledged: "Mr. Davis, whether he acted wisely or foolishly, is in step with the universe. The rest of us march to a broken drum." *Life* noted that Davis had aroused a deep longing for peace. An editorial in *Harper's* magazine stated that "Six months ago, young Davis was a pathetic and somewhat absurd figure, staging a one-man sit-down strike on the doorstep of the U.N. Assembly. Now . . . he is supported by a group of intellectuals which astonishingly includes Albert Einstein, the novelist Richard Wright, and a number of French literary figures such as Albert Camus, Jean-Paul Sartre, and André Gide."

In the busy summer of 1949, Davis took the *Manifesto* to the first World Citizens' rally in Belgium, and Caresse printed an agenda for the Peoples' World Convention to be distributed by the British Parliamentary Committee for World Government. She was also invited to become sub-editor of *Across Frontiers*, a world newspaper edited by Jerry Kraus in London. Never one to play second fiddle, she decided to form her own organization.

A new idea began to take shape, of finding a home for World Citizens in an international territory. Pietro Lazzari, the Italian artist whose works Caresse had shown at the Crosby Gallery, thought of the town where his mother was born in Rieti province. "You must go there and see the ruined castle at Roccasinibalda," Pietro suggested. "It's just the place to start your 'one world' idea. Artists would love to live in that place."

The next summer, Caresse took a lease from the Vatican with the option to buy, a million *lire* as down payment. "My idea was to provide an atmosphere where the poet and the philosopher, the artist, can really create ideas that will lead the world to peace and sanity. It's a very big idea, but this is a very big place to start. . . . In this ancient fortress, with a new idea, with *ideas* for a world where artists are important, I can carry on my own activities and help others. . . . There's a sense of beauty, of eternity. . . ."

Once settled in, she determined to declare her own small fiefdom a *Citta del Mondo*. She invited the women of the village to come up to the castle to sign the petition. At that time, there were three women for every man, so many men had lost their lives during World War II. Their hostess offered *vino* and an attentive, sympathetic hearing of their problems. Before the *signoras* left, they voted to be recognized as citizens of the first World City. They marched back down the cobblestoned path to convince their men and the Mayor of the Commune that their town should be declared an international territory. Caresse wrote to a colleague in Washington:

> During the past two months I have been living here in an ancient castle . . . in a pitifully poor, but humanly beautiful community (500 souls) in the foothills of the Abruzzi. . . . This mondialization has drawn a great deal of public and journalistic attention to Roccasinibalda. But while its women have taken a courageous step forward in time, their present surroundings remain pitifully inadequate. They look to me and to America as their saviour.

To another Washington correspondent, Caresse urged help for "these men and women . . . I have visited the rubbled homes of the poorest citizens and know that with a small contribution of materials and of willing minds and hands we could mend and restore. . . ."

> We will need an engineer for advice, an architect for plans, some handy-men and white-washers for manual work . . . the use of a buzz-saw for cutting planks, the use

of a cement mixer, a sewing machine, and one or two young women to sew curtains, etc.

At the end of another busy summer, the Vatican refused to grant Caresse the option to buy the Castello. Her dream of establishing a World Citizen center at Roccasinibalda would be postponed for another ten years.

*"The story of the phoenix holds good in the
life of ideas more truly than in any other
sphere . . . Whether or not we are successful
in our generation, we shall have lit the lamp
by which future generations will see."*

—CARESSE

Chapter XII

WOMEN AGAINST WAR

The mushroom cloud of the first atomic bomb that ended the
second World War still hovered as a permanent shadow.
Caresse's son survived four perilous years in the Navy and returned
home with a Brazilian bride, Josette. But Caresse considered she had
"lost" two husbands as casualties of war. Both Dick Peabody and
Harry Crosby returned with scarred psyches and died prematurely.

"We who have known war must never forget war," Harry Crosby
wrote. His widow never forgot. She listened intently to the last
speech of the wartime President, Franklin D. Roosevelt, whom she
strongly supported: "The work, my friends, is peace—more than an
end of *this* war—an end to the beginning of *all* wars."

When press reports first hinted that Albert Einstein and Robert
Oppenheimer had discovered the secret of the atom, Caresse sent a
telegram to President and Mrs. Harry Truman, at Blair House while
the White House was undergoing reconstruction:

—WE PRAY THAT THE NEW AND INFINITELY DESTRUCTIVE ATOM BOMB WILL NOT BE MADE—STOP—LET THIS GREAT NEW FORCE BE USED ONLY FOR PEACE AND PROGRESS—STOP— WE TRUST YOU—

Caresse considered that trust broken at Hiroshima. In earlier wars, women waited behind the lines for their men, but in the nuclear age, every man, woman, and child lives in a battle zone. With the threat of nuclear war looming in Korea, she joined the chorus of wives and mothers in protest. "Now it's up to the *women*."

In her view, women *bear* children, and children are the future. Men who control and direct the military and foreign policy hurtled America into two major wars in half a century. It could no longer be left to men to make life-and-death decisions. Women—53 percent of *all* Americans—must bear their share of responsibility too.

"Until I reached fifty, no matter how hard I tried to act independently, I never matured," she admitted. "If ever there was a job which we women ought to tackle, it is this question of war and peace." At a press conference, she made an emotional appeal to women everywhere: "Stop, stop, for God's sake, stop!"

The collision is just around the bend, the train-loads gain momentum. . . . Perhaps the bodies of all the women of the world kneeling on the tracks from East to West could *stop* those trains. It may well be that from the rubble of World War III, here and there, one survivor of the East will at least climb forth to lift up one survivor of the West from the cinders of civilization, and naked together, will start anew. A man, a woman, a world; but before this can happen, all man's power, his wealth, and his hopes may be sown into limbo.

While her plans to save the world were taking shape, Caresse happened upon a line from William Butler Yeats: "In dreams begin responsibility . . . ."

What do they know of love
Who do not know
She builds her nest
Upon a narrow ledge
Above a windy precipice?

Inspired by Yeats's vision, Caresse wrote to Charles Olson that "love is the answer" to the horrors of war:

> . . . I think I have hit upon the philosophy that the world has been waiting for, the philosophy so simple . . . that one wonders why it has never been expounded before. *The philosophy of love.*
>
> Even *philosophy* means *"love theory"*—there is no other doctrine that can compare for universality. . . . Enthusiasm, affection, and desire are all degrees of the same power. . . . The power of love is far greater than the power of hate; love is faith, and "faith will remove mountains."
>
> We are now moving, herded, against our natural desires in a direction that we neither desire nor enjoy, and can we not realize that by turning away from resistance we can flow back into the stream of acceptance and ease and *love?*. . . I must preach love, not [only] the Christ love of "Love thy neighbor as thyself." Love is not to be introverted. It is an expansion, a sunrise. The only way to conquer the mistrust and hatred in the world today is with the forces of trust and love.
>
> *Summum Amor!!* This is no Pollyanna doctrine—it is lusty!

Olson's answer was quick and to the point: "God help us, you're right. Love *is* the law—and precisely as you put it . . . tell 'em, the law breakers . . . it's like a preface to the *Summum Amor.* It *is* lusty. To love or not to love. You are down to primaries . . . very exciting!"

> Love is no commodity, but hedged now
> trafficked with by states, vulgarities,
> unburied dead who hid their hates in wrappers, lies;
> steal impulse at its birth, choke off its breath,
> a usury more fierce than money deals . . .

Not to be numbered among Olson's "unburied dead," Caresse wrote to Lord Boyd-Orr, winner of the Nobel Peace Prize: "I propose to form a World Association of women . . . . The united strength of the women of the world will be so great that no destructive force can deter or stop it." She dedicated her considerable energy and talent to organizing "a universal, trans-political association of women, based on the right to life, liberty and security of person" (a phrase borrowed from the United Nations' Declaration of Human Rights). Boyd-Orr agreed that "Women do not know their own power. If they spoke with one voice, governments would grant their requests."

To make her own voice heard, Caresse addressed the

WOMEN OF AMERICA:

Join me in my endeavor to bring about world accord . . . NOW! American women must take the initiative and have confidence in their own ability to lead world thinking. Only by standing together—by organizing for Civilization and Progress—can we exert our greatest influence. The time is here . . . to take positive action to make sure the basic idea of PEACE is not lost in the maelstrom of girding for war. . . .

(The letterhead on her stationery read: "Caresse Crosby, Director—All Women Against All Wars.")

Using the popular "chain letters" of the era, she urged women of the U.S. to form a "chain reaction of friendship around the world—a Chain of Faith, so to speak. . . . If each woman who forms a link in this chain is considered to have the average arm span of five feet, it will take only some 26 million women to circle the globe—in unity, friendship and faith. Until now, my efforts have been personal, and self-financed, but in order to continue, I must have your help— spiritual, actual and financial," she wrote. "Join this Chain of Faith by sending your contributions, even small ones—dollar bills."

Launching a worldwide campaign, Caresse wrote to Maria Rozhneva, director of the Kupava Woolen Mills in Moscow, suggesting an exchange of letters.

I have chosen your name from those in an article which appeared in one of our newspapers, in the hope that you will care to answer and give me the names of Soviet women like yourself to correspond with . . . .

I am an American woman, poet, and editor of an intercontinental review of art and literature. I am also interested in a movement to join women around the globe in an effort to prevent war and promote international peace by better understanding of each other's problems and aspirations. . . .

An impulsive note to Queen Elizabeth II complimented one of the world's great women on a recent telecast:

Your Majesty:
You rejoiced the hearts and gladdened the eyes of my countrywomen last night, when you appealed so warmly for international friendliness and better understanding, expressing the hope in every woman's heart that there can be cooperation between those who desire peace rather than power, and who want to love rather than hate. May I thank you in the name of millions of women associated with me throughout the world?

As one mother to another, she added, "My son went to Cheam [the exclusive boys' school], too."

Caresse made full use of the new medium of television to denounce warfare as mass murder. She announced Eleven Points for World Peace—among them, the end of nationalism, the education of children as world citizens, and the use of atomic energy for peaceful purposes. The idealistic theme of her program was summed up in Point 9: to admire and support goodness, wherever we find it. "As Jesus Christ said, 'I come to you from all the world.' I don't think the world was ever meant to be divided into warring, greedy nations."

In February 1950, Caresse registered to lobby the U.S. Congress "in the name of *Women Against War*, supporting a Peace Bond Bill. . . to create an account in the Treasury for peaceful uses only." She asked Katharine Price Collier St. George, Representative from her native New York (27th District)—a first cousin of President Franklin D. Roosevelt and descendent from the original settlers at Plymouth Rock—to introduce the bill in Congress.

St. George's straightforward manner appealed to Caresse, and her impressive bearing commanded her colleagues to take notice. An early, outspoken advocate of equal rights for women and the first woman to serve on the powerful House Rules Committee, St. George stated that "Women neither need nor want protective legislation. . . they want to be free to *work* as equals, asking for no special privileges, but insisting on equality of opportunity and pay."

The two women drafted a Peace Bond Bill, providing for an issue of U.S. Government bonds to replace the war bonds issued as a patriotic fund-raising effort during World War II. St. George introduced the Bill—H.R. 7596, 81st Congress, 2nd Session—on the floor of the House on March 7, 1950. It stated, in part, that all proceeds of sales of Peace Bonds would be covered in a special account in the U.S. Treasury "to be used for housing, education, hospitalization, communication," and other much-needed social programs. Specifically, no funds raised in this manner were to be used for payment of war debts or any military activity.

The ranking female member of Congress, the Honorable Frances P. Bolton (R.-Ohio), applauded the Bill: "That's a grand idea . . . a smart move. It should make quite an appeal." Edith Nourse Rogers (R.-Mass.), widely respected and influential among her colleagues, also sponsored the Bill, saying "Anything I can do for Peace, I am *for*. . . ." Caresse used her acknowledged gifts of persuasion in the predominantly male bastions of Congress, but her efforts were the target of sexist jokes.

Her small, self-financed secretarial staff wrote to key women throughout the country to "do something REALISTIC about Peace":

> I appeal to you, Women of America, who now hold more than 75 percent of the wealth of the capitalist system. There is no investment in our Government today of which over 70 percent is not used for purposes of war. . . . We can stop this! Let us ask for Peace Bonds for 1950, which we women can get behind with our earnings, savings, and inherited wealth; support our country so that it will grow greater, knowing that no part of what we invest will swell the atom stockpile or fabricate the tools that kill . . . OUR POWER IS COLOSSAL!!

Despite her tireless efforts, the Peace Bond Bill was defeated in the male-dominated Ways and Means Committee before it went up for vote in the House. St. George agreed to try again at the next Session. But this was—admittedly—a major setback for Women Against War.

Viewing the defeat as a temporary obstacle to be overcome, she wrote:

The story of the Phoenix holds good in the life of ideas, perhaps more truly than in any other sphere. If we fail— and I do not, will not believe we shall—it only means that the women of later generations will take up the sword where we let it fall . . . whether or not we are completely successful in our generation or not, at least we shall have lit the lamp by which future generations will be able to see.

In the spring, Caresse launched the first Women's Party in the District of Columbia, a model for other states. "Woman has acquired the right to vote," she wrote, "and now has a sacred duty. She must not shirk or be afraid of politics, but use her moral weapon for peace and for the defense of freedom through law. Woman has come of age!"

Our representation in *our* government is woefully inadequate:

471 Congressmen (only 21 women)
81 Senators (only 1 woman)
1 Cabinet member

In other countries in which women have the vote, they are far more active on a government level . . . England, France, India (only two years), Italy—those other women wonder why we hold back, and I ask, why do we?

Our children need us, you say—but out of a woman's active life, not more than one-fifth is given over to the bearing and care of children, and during those 1-5 years after marriage (usually between the ages of 25 and 35), she can still participate in government by her vote, study in preparation for a political career if she *plans* her life. Career women can and do accomplish as much as a man, help support the home, better the standards of their calling.

Why not do the same in government? We should have equal representation in Congress, equal positions in the Cabinet, equal rights in the manner in which our lives are governed; at present we accept the status of a minority group, but WHY?

Caresse was again a woman ahead of her time, a voice calling out in the wilderness to a generation still shackled by Friedan's "Feminine Mystique."

Not content to make her views known only in her own country, Caresse flew to Paris to assist in establishing the World Center of Women's Organizations in the 8th *Arrondissement*. A press release announced: "Now we must succeed in broadening the initiative, and in creating a national center in every country . . . an International Committee, with representatives of women's organizations working together with National Executive Committees."

She planned to travel around the world to gather the support of of Mohandas Gandhi and other pacifist leaders, to spread the gospel among women "in every walk of life, in every land. We women need not infiltrate [with our propaganda], for in every land, we are already there!"

> My hope, . . . is to appeal simply as a woman to other women . . . to influence the leaders of East, West, North and South to believe that those they serve are citizens of ONE WORLD, with different problems and different faiths, to be sure, but with one hope, one prayer, for Universal Peace. . . .

Caresse was dressed in the height of '50s fashion when she was spotted by a wire service photographer arriving from Athens at Rome's Ciampino Airport. She was wearing immaculate white gloves and a two-piece suit with large pockets and wide lapels, carrying a *para sol* against the damaging effect of the sun. "Fashion is a world citizen," she noted on a scrap of stationery (preserved in the archives). "My dress, from the U.S., my hat from Italy, my gloves from Germany, my sandals from Spain, my watch from Switzerland, my bracelet from England, my necklace from Egypt (a gift from Harry), my perfume from France, my scarf from Greece, my emblem from the World (*i.e.*, the World Citizen's pin)."

Among the press clippings Caresse collected are photographs of the World Citizen's flag flying above the model city of Faridabad (a refugee community built by displaced persons outside New Delhi), a pass to a debate in the Bombay Legislative Assembly (about the use of English in the school system), and a transcript of the interview with Gandhi.

She described her journey to then-Secretary of State Dean Acheson:

> . . . I have traveled to India and back, and have been able to reach leaders who represent, I believe, over 100 million women . . . . I have talked with Soviet Women in East Berlin, with the League of Anti-fascist Women in Yugoslavia, Socialists and others in India, and all parties in Europe and the Middle East.
>
> I realize now that following the Marshall Plan which was so gratefully received and did so much to alleviate the immediate hardships of Europeans, it is now to the *inner* man, that we must offer a belief, almost a religion, that we can all work for . . . not the dollar economy, but a world ideal that transcends all *-isms*. World Citizenship could be that unifying allegiance we so desperately need.

". . . facing universal disaster,
man turns again to Delphi,
the spiritual capital of the world."

—CARESSE

Chapter XIII
DEDICATION AT DELPHI

"I shall never forget my first sunrise at Delphi," Caresse wrote.

It was January, the harshest month of the year in Boetia, the village chilled to its marrow by the night winds that whirled down the slopes of Mount Parnassus . . . through the sacred olive groves. I pulled my heavy Burberry around me as I sat on the topmost round of that perfect Grecian amphitheater and waited for the first glow of dawn. . . .

Her quest for a permanent home for World Citizens led to this site, overlooking the sacred grove of Apollo. There, the first document of human rights was conceived by the Amphictyonic League, almost five centuries before the birth of Christ. The symbolism was not lost on Caresse.

As she awaited the dawn, cocks crowed, donkeys brayed, church bells began to peal, and the strident horn of the morning bus to Amfissa summoned its passengers. Caresse climbed aboard with the

153

women carrying eggs in gaudy market baskets and bundles of kindling tied with woven bands. Beyond the village, where the road to
Amfissa curved around the plateau, she caught a glimpse of a rocky
promontory—a sheer drop of some 300 feet above the town of
Krissa—"no vegetation there, only the silver and amethyst stones of
the fields shining in the morning sun. I knew then that I had to reach
that spot. Something inside me cried out to it."

Once there, she asked the villagers to locate the man who owned
the property. The Patriarch spent most of his days with his herds on
the mountainside, but two young relatives, Iani and Pericles, were
sent to search for him. They hiked for several hours and finally
returned with the oldest member of the clan, a wrinkled shepherd
who was astounded to see a petite American woman in his humble
cottage. Even more amazing was the fact that she wanted to buy the
small piece of rocky grazing land that the Patriarch's family had
owned since the year 900 A.D.

"No good, that land. Not even for goats!" the Patriarch said in his
native tongue, using his gnarled hands in an attempt to put across his
meaning. The young men interpreted that he would not *sell* the land,
but he would *give* it to anyone foolish enough to buy it. Taken by
surprise, she refused to accept the land without a token payment.
Endless, polite negotiations were accompanied by meaningful ges-
tures. In the end, the old man agreed to sell two acres of land for 250
dollars. But the entire family must be present, he insisted, to sign the
deed to make the act official.

Iani and Pericles were sent to round up the Mayor and some 18
members of the Patriarch's family. When all were assembled by
candlelight, Caresse signed the document making Citizens of the
World owners of that symbolic spot. Ceremonial toasts in *retsina*
sealed the bargain and lasted until another dawn was breaking.

Caresse's dreams were never small ones. She planned to build a
marble Thesaurus, or treasury, for World Citizens on the site. She
had researched the classic meaning of the word "treasury"—a
storage place, not for gold, but a spiritual bank for works of art and
rare documents (in ancient times, the documents were often marble
tablets). A press release announced the World Citizens' plan to erect
a pentagon of white pantellic marble—the marble of the Parthenon—
as a meeting place, library, and school for instruction in world
citizenship. Its five points would symbolize Truth, Beauty, Love,
Justice, and CHOICE (emphasis on the latter). Each nation-state
would be invited to deposit its greatest legacy to the world. (In her
view, the Constitution should be the U.S. contribution.) On the

outer rim of the building, CITIZENS OF THE WORLD would be carved in both English and Greek. Delphi would become the spiritual capital of the world.

In Athens, she discussed her plans with Prime Minister Venizelos, with poets and writers, with religious leaders. She never counted the cost of building materials in contemporary dollars, or the high cost of labor, never measured the impracticability of transporting marble to the site. (Since there was no native marble, the giant building blocks of the original temple at Delphi were carved on the other islands, then shipped in sailing vessels to Itea, where they were pulled up the path on the backs of mules.) Nonetheless, she consulted the prestigious architectural firm of Edward Durrell Stone in New York to confirm that she was serious about the construction and determined to see it through.

To followers of the movement, Caresse announced: "A new dawn is breaking! Today, . . . facing universal disaster, man turns again to Delphi." Telegrams were sent from the Hotel Grande-Bretagne to the Big Four leaders of the Western world: Dwight D. Eisenhower at the White House; Anthony Eden at No. 10 Downing Street; Edgar Fauré at the Quai d'Orsay; and Marshal Bulganin at the Kremlin:

—INVITE YOU TO HOLD PRELIMINARY MEETING WITH OTHER MEMBERS BIG FOUR ON MY PROPERTY IN DELPHI WHERE 2,500 YEARS AGO AMPHICTYONI MET FOR WORLD UNITY AND PEACE—STOP—IN THIS INSPIRING AND SACRED PLACE YOU WILL FIND SOLUTION TO PROBLEMS NOW CONFRONTING HUMANITY—

Back in New York she organized an art sale to provide funds for the building, bringing together more than 100 of the finest contemporary painters, a United Nations of the art world, all of whom she knew well: Joan Miró from Spain, Fernand Lèger from France, Alexander Calder from the U.S., Pietro Lazzari, an Italian-American, Michael Lekakis, a Greek-American, and Romare Bearden, a black-American. In Washington, Lazzari held a benefit showing of his paintings at the Crosby Gallery, half of the proceeds of which were earmarked for the Delphi project.

"I plug away and cry 'shame' whenever the unbelievers cry 'Utopia!'" Caresse wrote to newlyweds Charles and Connie Olson. "I am very busy on various projects—Women Against War, the book [*The*

Passionate Years]—soon to be out, Delphi—not developing very fast, and a real Herculean task just now."

She appealed to Dr. Stringfellow Barr, director of the World Government Foundation, in the hope that he might sponsor the Delphi project:

> I have been working continually, largely through women, for a United Nations Government. In every land our numbers increase daily, so much so that I, and my own financial resources, can no longer take care of these vast projects. . . . In the U.S., even a campaign for funds costs money, and too many people are suspicious of worldwide affiliations to sign up.
>
> In May 1952, we World Citizens will lay the cornerstone of a World Treasury at Delphi. World Citizens from England, headed by Hugh Schonfield—also from France, Italy, Belgium and Germany—will be present. A deputation from India, Mrs. Kamela-Devi and Ray Kamari Amrit Kar, are now with me.
>
> Michael Law, a British film producer, will make a 16 mm. color film of the ceremony. . . . He requires only $2,000 capital, but this I cannot supply myself. The architectural schools are interested in a [design] competition for a World Treasury—this competition will need organization and circulars—another $3,000 at least! Time is precious! *This initiative must not die.* . . .

To Hugh Schonfield of the Commonwealth of World Citizens, she wrote:

> . . . a lack of funds is the thing I find most difficult at this point. All secretarial work and postage come out of my own pocket, as well as other incidental expenses, but in this country people seem to steer clear of investments in *world ideology.* However, I think we will get press and radio coverage from Delphi, and that will be important.

Worldwide press coverage came—much sooner than Caresse dared hope. The invitations went out to World Citizens to attend "The Dedication at Delphi" on May 24.

Caresse Crosby, Citizen of the World, will dedicate the land, and Hugh Schonfield, founder of the Commonwealth, has agreed to give the acceptance address.

Other speakers:

The Greek Minister, P. Sifneos
("for Freedom from Fear")
The Archbishop of Amfissa
("for Freedom of Worship")
The Mayor of Delphi
("for Freedom from Want")

Members of the diplomatic corps and the Greek government headed a distinguished guest list that included Albert Einstein, Lord Boyd-Orr, and other Humanists.

The Greek Ministry of Foreign Affairs graciously granted permission to hold a meeting on the Delphi site and issued the permit for a future Office of Information there. After the invitations went out, the Ministry—in an about-face—decreed that the dedication ceremony could not be held without sponsorship of an international organization. Hugh Schonfield agreed to give the official stamp of the Commonwealth.

Then something unforeseen erupted in the Greek press. The act intended to symbolize a world without boundaries was perceived as a threat to Greek sovereignty, flying an alien British flag over Delphi, the "sacred" territory. Caresse arrived in Delphi two days before the ceremony, to be met by someone from Reuters, the international news agency: "Are you going ahead with it, Mrs. Crosby?"

"Yes!" she answered, in disbelief that her attempt for world peace would be perceived as a political affront. Reuters wired, "We are sending reporters to cover the story."

The next communication came from the Ministry of Defense in Athens: "We are sending the militia if you continue." Caresse's humanistic dream was becoming a nightmare, a diplomatic incident. When she attempted to reach the Minister of Defense to rescue the ceremony, he had conveniently left the country. When most needed, the American Ambassador also made a diplomatic exit. Caresse called upon a higher power, King Constantine, but discovered that he was away on his yacht.

Caresse captured in her memoir the comic-opera overtones of the events that followed. At the beginning of the ceremony, the Home

Guard, wearing the traditional short white skirts of a more peaceful time, came carrying flowers to present at the ceremony. After receiving new orders from headquarters, they dropped the drooping bouquets and picked up guns to "invade" the promontory. They looked embarrassed, puzzled, not knowing what to do. According to Caresse, the Ministry of Defense ordered the local Commandant "to stop, by any means necessary, all artistic and spiritual activities near Delphi!" Soon, the guard began firing across the road.

Caresse stood her ground. A reporter from the *New York Times* arrived on the scene. "*We are Americans* and this is your territory, Mrs. Crosby. We will go up anyway!"

She insisted, "I have a right to read the Dedication!" but her voice was lost in the crowd. The apolitical opening remarks—approved by the Greek authorities—were never delivered:

> We Citizens of the World are both new and ancient peoples. We are spiritual, united from every part of the globe in the conviction that wars do not make peace. The world is facing universal disaster. It is now our duty to come forward as men and women with malice toward none, believing in goodness rather than power. . . .
>
> And so it is we return to ancient Delphi, where Humanism was born, to declare to all the world that we are here for friendship and for universal understanding and justice . . . . We believe in one another and in mankind. We believe in the great past and hoped-for future, and it is in this belief that I now dedicate this promontory of earth to the service of humanity and raise the flag of the Citizens of the World.

On her copy of the dedication speech, Caresse noted: "This is what I intended to say at the ceremony on May 24. I agreed not to raise the flag after the police interfered, but I was stopped from saying anything at all. Can it be that the cradle of democracy is to become the funeral pyre of individual liberty?"

The British cameraman started to record the ceremony, but the authorities confiscated his film. Busloads of World Citizens and VIPs were stopped at Delphi and turned back as an invading army. Caresse was left holding the symbolic green and blue flag ("the colors of earth and sky"), with a child's stick-figure of World Man, its legs and arms extended to embrace the globe. Still protesting, she was taken back to Athens under armed guard and placed under house arrest.

Later, when she stepped out on the terrace, a delicate moon was rising over the silent countryside. She could see the heads of the guards silhouetted below. "I will *not* give in," she vowed, with the stubborn streak that sustained her Puritan ancestors during the Revolution and bleak New England winters.

Friends throughout the world who read press reports responded by letter and cable. The Minister of Defense maintained, in interviews, that it was against national interests for large organizations to set up headquarters in Delphi, a Greek national monument. Caresse held firm: "I have a right to peaceful assembly, to freedom of expression, under the United Nations Bill of Rights."

She appealed to the Minister of Foreign Affairs. At first, the Minister pretended ignorance—had she failed to obtain the necessary permission from the Ministry of the Interior? The Consular Section of the U.S. Embassy replied to her inquiry in typical bureaucratese:

> Dear Mrs. Crosby:
>
> You have requested this office to inform you of any decision reached by the Greek Minister of Foreign Affairs, in re. the status in Greece of "The Commonwealth of World Citizens." The Royal Minister has informed this office that it is impossible to give any further consideration to your request. It was stated that according to the concept of the Greek authorities, districts like Delphi are considered sacred areas, and anything which might disturb the tranquillity of such an archaeological site could easily be interpreted as sacrilege.
>
> In view of this decision by the Greek Ministry of Foreign Affairs, it does not appear that this office can be of further assistance to you in the development of your project . . . .
>
> Very truly yours,
> David C. Berge
> American Consul General

Never one to surrender after the first encounter, Caresse engaged Angelo Prokopiou, a Greek associate of the distinguished law firm of Frere, Cholmley and Nicholson of London. She planned to take her case to the highest authority—the Greek Supreme Court. "I firmly believe that the interference of the Greek Government was a gross injustice," she wrote Prokopiou. "The architectural plans for the building site were submitted to a committee chaired by Professor Piccionis of the Polytechnic Institute of Athens, and never had any of my hopes and plans been made without knowledge of the authorities. My aspirations as a Citizen of the World only add to the glory of Greece."

During the controversy, the World Citizens' headquarters in London raised some 200 pounds in British currency for relief of Greek earthquake victims. "This should prove that in spite of the ungracious reception of the Commonwealth founder, its members bear no ill will towards the Greeks."

After she had not heard from Prokopiou for several weeks, Caresse requested an immediate reply to her queries: Will there be more than one hearing? Has the Declaration of Human Rights been ratified as part of the Greek legal code? Do I enjoy the same rights as any other landowner in Greece? (She attached a photocopy of the deed to the land at Delphi.)

The Crosby case was mentioned in the Athens daily, *Eleptheros Logos*, by G. Vassiliades:

> This organization works for international peace. . . and although it may work for a Utopian dream, it nevertheless aims at no subversive purposes. . . .

> The case before the Supreme Court is of great importance. . . . The actions of the Administration . . . are contrary to the Rome International Agreement of 4 November 1950, "on the Rights and Basic Liberties of the Individual" which has been ratified by Greece. Article 10 of this agreement provides for the freedom of expression of personal, philosophical, artistic and political opinions. Article 11 safeguards the freedom of assembly for peaceful purposes, while Article 13 safeguards the above rights to all persons irrespective of sex, race, nationality, color, religion, and national origin. Mrs. Crosby's attorneys will invoke the above Articles, and if her appeal is rejected, she will make a further one to the European Committee on Human Rights.

> We can only express the hope that this last step will prove unnecessary, so as not to present Greece in an unfavorable light to world public opinion which is carefully observing the case. . . . [Translated from the Greek]

Caresse's case before the Greek Supreme Court was defeated, despite Prokopiou's valiant defense. Characteristically, she held no malice toward Greek friends and few regrets. By that time, she was enthusiastically embarking on another international venture, a World Man Center in Cyprus. She wrote to a Washington correspondent, Mrs. Julius Wadsworth:

> I will not be in Greece this summer. I must work on my projects here for awhile. If and when you do go to Greece, let me hear. I will send you some introductions, and above all, be sure to visit Delphi. Stay at the Castalia Hotel and go out on the balcony overlooking the valley, turn your head to the right, and just beyond the little Greek church that looks like a lump of sugar, you will see the promontory that belongs to me and to the Citizens of the World. If you will walk over and say a prayer there for the future of mankind, I am sure the gods will listen.

"Faith and love and venture are the values I have built my life on. I do not think they are going to fail on Cyprus."

—CARESSE

Chapter XIV

WORLD MAN CENTER, CYPRUS

"The world at this very moment stands on the brink of defeat or success, of Heaven or Hell," Caresse wrote to Archbishop Makarios of Cyprus; "why not be the one country to take the forward step . . . toward One World?"

She was beguiled by the island birthplace of Venus Aphrodite, the goddess of love. Cyprus appealed to her sense of history. It was Mark Anthony's love-gift to Cleopatra, the seaport where Desdemona waited for Othello's return. She discovered that Zenon of Kitium, a follower of Socrates and Plato, first considered Cyprus as a neutral territory dedicated to peace. When she met another Zenon of Kitium—His Excellency Zenon Rossides, a suave international lawyer, then Cypriot Ambassador to the United Nations—from that time forward Cyprus and the Cypriots played an important role in her life.

In recent history, Cypriots were ruled more often by Mars than by Venus. The island was the prey of contending faiths and factions, the

162

British, the Turks and the Greeks. The British established a Crown
Colony in 1878 that endured until after World War II, when the
Greek Cypriots petitioned for *énosis* (union with Greece) and the
Turks for partition. In the compromise government, the Greek
majority won two-thirds representation, but violence and the *énosis*
movement still persist.

Against this historic backdrop, Caresse—at the suggestion of
Rossides—proposed to install her World Citizens' Center, ousted
from Delphi, on Cypriot soil. If Makarios agreed, "the Archbishop
would be known throughout the world as the leader who resisted
greed, militarism, and power politics," she said. She knew that
Makarios was no stranger to American thought and ideals. The 37-
year-old Bishop of Kitium had been studying theology in Boston
when—in October 1950—he was called home to become Archbishop Makarios III. Some ten years later, after a plebescite, the
Cypriots elected him as first President of the Republic. In this man of
impressive physical presence, ready eloquence, and mischievous
sense of humor, the Greek Cypriots found a dynamic leader, and
Caresse a man worthy of her unabashed admiration. She asked if she
might come to the island to talk with His Beatitude and the women of
Cyprus.

She flew to Cyprus with Rossides to seek a site for World Man.
From the air, Nicosia appeared to be an irregular row of white
houses, green-shuttered with red-tiled roofs, against a backdrop of
the majestic Kyrenia mountains. On the ground, it was obvious that
some of the native charm was giving way to so-called "progress." The
old-fashioned coffee shops still lined one side of the square, but a
Ford garage now stood between the ancient Kyrenia Gate and the
Convent of the Dancing Dervishes. A large municipal market had
taken the place of the old trellised bazaars, and a beauty-shop
replaced the spice-sellers' stalls. Outside the walls, where once there
were fields of barley, were now blocks of suburban apartments,
shops and offices, and a movie theater.

Caresse knew that she could not complete her Herculean task on
the first visit, but she began by purchasing eight acres of land (with
$2,000 from her personal account) near the ancient Abbey of Belle
Pais. British writers have compared the site to Wordsworth's Tintern
Abbey, but it was difficult for her to imagine this exotic southern isle
transposed to a northern setting. In the spring of the year, the sea and
sky were an unbelievably clear blue, the olive trees and cypresses a
deep green. Anemones and cyclamen carpeted the ground, gladioli
and wild irises and tulips were just beginning to peek through, and

the red oleanders were already in full bloom. Rosemary and thyme were growing like wildflowers on the hillsides, and the air was fragrant with the scent of orange blossoms and bitter lemon. As Caresse approached the Abbey, she could hear the distant, doleful pan-pipes of a goatherd, as Euripides must have heard them. The sun's reflection tinged the ancient stonework with gold. It was love at first sight. Caresse said "Yes!" to Cyprus.

Back in New York, she began to take practical steps to realize her idealistic dream. Incorporating the World Man Center with offices at 866 United Nations Plaza, she named herself president and called upon Rufus King—whose *Manifesto for Individual Secession into a World Community* Black Sun Press published in 1948, now a respected international lawyer—to act as secretary-treasurer. The Greek artist Michael Lekakis and architect Buckminster Fuller agreed to serve as vice presidents. In addition to Rossides, 15 important names were listed on the letterhead as members of the executive committee: Norman Cousins, John Huston, Philip Ives, Elsa Schiaparelli, Cyril Connolly, Kay Boyle, and Jean Hélion, among others. Her granddaughter, Lorraine de Mun, now living in New York, would provide secretarial backup.

Caresse's long-standing friendship with "Bucky" Fuller dated back to the Depression days of the '30s, when he came with Isamu Noguchi to Romany Marie's restaurant in the Village. By the '60s, Fuller's star was rising. As architect of the U.S. Pavilion at Expo '67, the world's fair in Montreal, Fuller was featured as a cover story in *Time* and the subject of an in-depth article in *The New Yorker*. Bucky's active participation as architect of the World Man Center was regarded as a coup by Caresse. It lent credibility to her idealistic Cyprus project.

Fuller wrote to Caresse on Valentine's Day 1966 from Carbondale, where he was then research professor at Southern Illinois University:

> Very dear Caresse:
> This letter confirms my agreement with you to act as your architect for the Cyprus undertaking. It also confirms my agreement to go with you sometime between June 15 and June 30 from Rome to Cyprus to inaugurate our design task. Now that you have substantial funds pledged to the project and Makarios' assurance of an adequate portion of the whole of the island for a world headquarters, and have substantial friendly support of both Greek and Turkish youth, and probably with United

Nations support from U Thant, I see no reason why you
should hold back any longer on publicity.

With greatest love, faithfully yours,

Bucky

That summer, Fuller wrote to Rossides proposing the construction of a building suitable for World Man's oasis on "space-ship
earth," a large, geodesic dome "to act as a vast umbrella to protect the
activities below it from rains, winds, and too intense sun." He added,
"I foresee that the Cypriots heretofore agitated by external sovereign
nations to fight against one another may wish to cross the line for
sovereign nation control into the World Man area, or may even
request Archbishop Makarios to extend the World Man land to
enclose their own homes on Cyprus. . . . We are trying
to . . . become transcendental to the international concept, wherein
nations become as obsolete as sovereign boroughs, cities, states,
countries. . . ."

Yet political disturbances erupted again on the island. On June 17,
Fuller wrote to Caresse:

> Mr. Lekakis called me today to say that Mr.
> Rossides . . . had become truly disturbed to learn that
> you had written to Makarios regarding talking with Dr.
> Kutchuk about our undertaking. Mr. Rossides feels, as do
> I, that it will be easy to upset this situation due to the
> smoldering conditions of yesterday's fighting. I urge you
> to talk with nobody about the situation until we all meet in
> Cyprus, and some firm arrangements have been made.

She well might heed Fuller's warning to use discretion when
dealing with the political leader of the Turkish Cypriot community,
Dr. Fazil Kutchuk. He was a heavy-set, stubborn man with a gruff
voice who presented a sharp contrast with Makarios, the shrewd
tactician and patient bargainer. Kutchuk's second language was
French, not English; he was inclined to miss the point of much of the
conversation and to assume that the jokes were on him.

While Fuller was dictating a letter to Caresse, a reporter from *The
Washington Post* called to confirm a news item picked up from an
international wire service: "Is it true that you have been retained by
Mrs. Crosby to design an International Peace Center on Cyprus?"
That was the first question. She then startled Fuller by quoting
without a source the beginning of a sentence of his letter to

Ambassador Rossides: "I foresee that the Cypriots, heretofore agitated by external sovereign nations to fight against one another, may wish to cross the line. . . ."

Fuller was alarmed that the reporter quoted the sentence out of context. To the best of his knowledge, he replied, none of the proposed agreements had occurred, and "*if* the proposed center was realized, it would be *super*national. . . . I am not interested in anything *inter*national."

It was a matter of semantics, but Fuller was agitated by the exchange, and warned Caresse:

> It is my experience that nothing will bring about the perishment of a good idea more swiftly than premature publicity. My only hope is that we are dealing with something so evolutionarily solid in respect to emerging World Man that we will be able to weather the complex of misunderstandings and emotional disturbances and geo-politics in general. . . .

He added a native New Englander's word of caution: "When caught in a sudden lethal squall, experience has taught me that swift attention to cleaning up the ship and getting it on an even keel quickly enough sometimes prevents a following knock-down from sinking the ship." He closed with a strong vote of confidence in Caresse:

> The ramifications of your life are great. Nothing I have to say should make you feel that I have anything other than the greatest affection, admiration, and enthusiasm for you. . . . I am confident that if we weather this we may be about to establish the first true freehold of World Man. His numbers will multiply rapidly to hundreds of millions. In 2000 A.D. all humans will have become Universal Citizens. The concept of man as a citizen of a geographically limited ward, county, town, state or nation will seem as strange and foreign to the life and thoughts of 2000 A.D.'s "Universe Citizens" as now seem the lives of slaves in a Roman galley or the cave-dwelling events of Stone Age man.

Caresse was "terribly distressed and frankly astonished and angry about the abusive report" of the *Washington Post* reporter, she wrote

Fuller. George Weller from the *Chicago Daily News* had lent her his house in Kyrenia, and she suspected that that was where the story originated. She had shown the portfolio of documents about World Man and enthused about Fuller's participation in it over cocktails between 8:00 and 9:00 p.m. on June 14. "He must have put the story on the wire that very evening or next morning . . . I was flabbergasted—what can I do to help get the ship on an even keel again? It *does* look as if it were rocking."

Caresse mentioned to Fuller that Rossides was disturbed by the letter she had written to President Makarios, urging him to seek the cooperation of *all* Cypriots, including the Turks, in the World Man project:

> I know that you have many enthusiastic friends among the young people in England, in America, and in Greece, and I hope when I come to Cyprus with Dr. Fuller . . . that I will be able to meet the Vice President of Cyprus and talk with him about the possibility of interesting the artists and the youth of Turkey as well as the Turkish Cypriots in this concerted effort.

"I can't play at secret diplomacy," she admitted. "I believed that Makarios was the President of the Republic of Cyprus . . . *not* just a Greek puppet President. . . . I still have faith in his integrity." She planned to meet Fuller in Nicosia on the Fourth of July, she added, and "I hope you are not too upset, for nothing is stronger than an idea whose time has come. . . . Our ship must not founder once launched."

On July 7, she issued an official statement in the name of Makarios from the Presidential Palace in Nicosia. As the first head of a sovereign nation to cede land to World Man, Makarios offered the 200-acre property in the vicinity of the Abbey of Belle Pais, to be administered for 50 years under a trusteeship "of the highest order of intellectual and scientific capability." (The World Academy of Art and Science, which included in its governing body a number of Nobel Prize winners, was one possibility.) Of the estimated cost of the conference building—about one million dollars—the Archbishop was to contribute $200,000.

Referring to the continuing violence on the island, Fuller used the opportunity of the Palace press conference to point out that armed conflict was always the result of the Malthusian principle that mankind multiplies far faster than the capacity of Earth's physical resources to support human life. If mankind could succeed in increasing the world's resources to support *all* human life, then war—even political systems—would become obsolete.

In August, Caresse met representatives of the WAAS, Dr. Max Habicht and Dr. Boyko, in Rome. She wrote to Fuller:

> You will guess that I am not completely happy at the turn our planning has taken. . . . I am wondering just what influenced you to name the Academy as caretaker at that first press conference in Nicosia? We know so little about their activities and their members. . . . I liked Dr. Boyko and Dr. Habicht very much, but from their point of view, my usefulness would be to raise money to enable them to make a year's study for their report. . . . Their need for delay seems even a bigger hump than the hump the *Washington Post* gave us to hurdle.

Two weeks later, she wrote again: "I have not heard from you since Beirut and my last letter was a cry for 'Help!' I am waiting for your advice about the World Academy, and whether I should go ahead with the art auction . . . ?"

From his summer home on Bear Island, Maine, Fuller replied that Ambassador and Mrs. Rossides had appeared there "in the wilderness," on the same day the "cry for help" letter arrived. Together, they had re-read all the documents, including the letters from Boyko to Makarios, and it was "not as bad news as it at first seemed."

Fuller had written to John McHale, who was in turn making it clear to Boyko, that there were several alternative trustee bodies that would be just as appropriate as the WAAS, but he found the WAAS roster of members impressive. Fuller himself recently had been accepted as a Fellow of the WAAS, along with Dr. Doxiadis, head of the Architectural College of Athens. Doxiadis gave their program his vigorous support, and "since . . . [he] deals with the high powers of Cyprus, this is good news," Fuller reported.

> I am confident that everything is in good shape. . . . I am also confident that Caresse Crosby . . . will be in a leading position of authority in respect to . . . the World Man Center, . . . the unique consequence of her long years of dedicated work. . . . Very dear Caresse, I am sure that in taking the responsibility of being your advisor in your great undertaking that I am not going to let you down.

*   *   *

In October, the World Man Center received one encouraging letter from Philip Isely, Secretary-general of the World Constitutional Convention, with headquarters in Denver, Colorado. Isely asked Caresse to serve on the World Committee of the WCC as a member from Italy, her official residence. She preferred to represent Cyprus—"I actually own some land on Cyprus, aside from the World Man Center"—and would seek the approval of President Makarios on her next visit to the island. The fact that the WCC and other world organizations accepted Caresse into their membership shows that her efforts were highly regarded by those in positions of authority—that her activities were not viewed as the hobbies of a dilettante.

Just after the 1967 New Year, Caresse drew up a Cyprus Plan of Action. She listed the people and organizations to contact for loans and/or advice: the American Ambassador to Cyprus, Toby Belcher; Aristotle Onassis ("who is already interested"); the Hilton hotels and TWA (for an airlift from Nicosia to Kyrenia); Hormousias, editor of *Kathimerini*, the Athens newspaper; the president of the Bank of Greece; and Constantinos Doxiadis.

Her son-in-law, Polleen's then-husband Stephen Drysdale, was among British investors in a Belgian real estate venture on Cyprus, which—Caresse observed—could also be a point in favor of keeping Cyprus peaceful. The Ford Foundation had expressed interest in World Man, but they would have to wait to appeal to other foundations until tax-exempt status was granted.

In addition, she proposed a Cypriot referendum to determine the greatest needs—schools, hospitals, roads? She supported the plan submitted to U Thant by the Parliamentarians for World Government to offer a military unit from Cyprus as part of the U.N. peacekeeping mission, thereby replacing the British troops on the island.

In first place on Caresse's agenda was the art auction to be held in New York in October to raise funds for Fuller's geodesic dome. Robert Dowling, owner of the handsome East Side venue of the Parke-Bernet Gallery, promised Caresse that she might hold the auction there. Lorraine de Mun, acting as secretary to the art committee, was sending out letters from headquarters to prospective donors.

> World Man at this gateway between East and West [is] . . . a meeting place for the arts. . . . World artists are

spearheading this endeavor. Will you accept this invitation to participate by offering your work? . . .

William de Kooning and Isamu Noguchi gladly consented to
donate their works for the auction. Dali suggested that Caresse might
call upon some of the wealthy owners of his works to contribute. (He
still held tight to his dollars.)

Caresse next wrote to Picasso at his *atelier* in Vallauris in the South
of France:

> You once wrote, and I published in *Portfolio II*: "A
> painting is not an object to frame and hang upon the wall,
> it is rather a weapon with which to fight the enemy." Ever
> since that time, I have been dreaming that dream, that the
> artist must come into the arena from his ivory tower to
> save the world. . . .
>
> Now I am writing to ask you to help us with your genius
> in the fight to save the world from holocaust. . . . Could
> you donate one of your paintings for the auction, or do a
> special poster, an original Picasso, on the theme, "One
> World or None"?

Throughout the summer, Lorraine at headquarters kept in touch
with Caresse in Italy with a barrage of warm and affectionate letters:

> Darling Gran:
>
> I am absolutely thrilled that you are going to be in
> America on October 8 . . . in ten days I shall be seeing
> you! I spread the good news to Mrs. Rossides as soon as I
> got the letter, so Zenon and Mrs. Simpson will have been
> notified by now. I do love you, Gran. . . . My job is still
> going very well and as soon as the government grant comes
> through I shall be making a lot of money and shall be able
> to take you to *Quo Vadis* for lunch. I daren't ask you for
> dinner as I know you will have millions of beaux as soon as
> you set foot in New York.
>
> Oodles and oodles of World Love, Lorraine

In July, Caresse was involved with the contretemps that erupted
between Fuller and Rufus King, who suggested that World Man

should be confined to a smaller area of land. Fuller wrote to Rossides:

> Rufus King is an excellent lawyer but his astronomical hypothesis is incorrect. . . . There are no fixed points in space. . . . The World Man Center's 200 *donums* of land . . . is a spot on the surface of the 8,000-mile diameter spherical space-ship Earth. . . . It is obviously impossible to refer to "our airspace." There is no static space. There are no straight lines. There are only geodesic relationships.

In Fuller's view, laws made by human beings "do not give humans the power to substitute their futile hypotheses for the physical laws governing universal behavior. . . . The word 'sovereignty' was invented by weapons-wielding bullies who asserted and maintained with their swords and guns their claims to perpetual ownership over various lands of the spherical space-ship Earth. . . ."

If King's idea of reducing the ceded area to an infinitely small spot were acted upon, Fuller repeated, "there will be no need for a dome umbrella, and I will immediately withdraw. . . . Our joint acts of last summer can only prosper if we succeed in keeping the 200 *donums* utterly uncompromised for at least fifty years." He ended the letter to Rossides on a pessimistic note: "The chances of man's survival on the spherical space-ship Earth are in great jeopardy."

Bucky and his wife, Anne, went to the official opening of Expo '67 in Montreal that summer. He wrote to Caresse that they were "overjoyed by the reception of the Dome." Fuller's son-in-law, cinematographer Robert Snyder, described the Expo Dome as

> a three-quarter sphere, in which the walls start going away from you. [It] has the extraordinary psychological effect of releasing you, for you suddenly realize that the walls are not really there. . . . Something is keeping the rain away, like an umbrella, but you don't feel shut in, you feel protected.

In Fuller's view, the Dome demonstrated "the doing so much more with less for all humanity. . . . World Man will realize that his salvation on space-ship Earth is to be gained by such a design revolution and not by political revolution. . . ." The Dome was also a monument to Fuller's wife in the year of their 50th wedding anniversary. "I have brought about the production of our own Taj Majal as pure fall-out of my love for you [Anne]," Bucky wrote.

Caresse was distressed to hear news of the tragic accident that temporarily suspended Fuller's efforts on behalf of World Man. After the Fullers returned to New York, the airport taxi in which they were riding at high speed skidded on a rainy street, crashing against a bridge abutment and bouncing across the highway. Neither Fuller nor the taxi driver was hurt, but Anne suffered severe damage, including two brain hemorrhages. After a siege in intensive care when her life was in danger and an even longer hospital stay, Anne recovered. But it was another of the many cruel blows of fate that stalked Fuller throughout his life.

That summer, Caresse also invited Garry Davis to serve on the steering committee of the Cyprus project. The young man who surrendered his U.S. passport in Paris to become a Citizen of the World in the '40s was a delegate to the World Citizens' Committee meeting in Wolfach, Switzerland, when Caresse caught up with him to ask if he would be coming to Italy during the summer: "We must have a talk. I thought the letter you wrote to the *Herald Tribune* was very fine, and as you know, our beliefs are the same on that subject."

In September, Caresse requested a progress report on the WAAS from John McHale, now serving as executive director of Fuller's World Resources Inventory at Southern Illinois University. McHale replied that "I have no further information. . . . The WAAS has not . . . accepted trusteeship, but merely indicated that they may do so *when* the land is ceded *and* funds have been secured for the operation of the Center." In McHale's view, the Arab-Israeli conflict might influence the WAAS's cautionary stance—Cyprus seemed anxious to engage in the conflict just before it came to an end. The official attitude of the Cypriot government was incompatible with sympathy for World Man or peace.

Despite hovering war clouds, early in 1968 Caresse was in Beirut again, on a stopover en route to Cyprus. She wrote to Fuller that she had gotten the impression that "many English promoters already have their eye on Kyrenia;" Noel-Baker, one of the Parliamentarians for World Government, was anxious to know how to proceed in seeking the trusteeship. To Rossides, still in New York, she wrote:

Dear Zenon:
    I am waiting here in Beirut to join you in Cyprus
. . . impatiently, because I know that both the American

ambassador in Cyprus, Toby Belcher, and the British High Commissioner as well as the heads of the NATO College in Rome are anxious to hear more about the World Man Center and are very much in favor. . . . I am being written to from all parts of the world asking for information on World Man and I am anxious to get on with it. The interest shown by the Belgian group of promoters who might put money into real estate . . . is important. . . . It is my son-in-law who is interested in this group and hopes to meet me soon in Kyrenia. I gather that you do not want me to return to Nicosia without you—therefore I am flying to Jerusalem on Monday and will stay there until you are able to leave New York. . . .

She added that "Everyone in Athens was praising Makarios for his One World project."

On the return journey, she again stopped over in Beirut and wrote to Rossides: "What a pleasure to see you in Nicosia, and how delightful to have another visit with His Beatitude." She was giving considerable thought to the status of World Man:

If I understood you correctly, you think World Man should raise the necessary money before the land is transferred by the Cyprus Government. For my part, I think the land should be deeded to and accepted by the World Man Center, contingent upon our raising the money. This may seem like a minor difference to you, but it is a major difference to me. I would have much more difficulty getting the consent of artists and others to donate works to be auctioned if I did not have a document from the Government of Cyprus transferring a specific piece of land. I don't think that any artist—even my good friends—would contribute their work to be auctioned off without such a document.

She ended the letter prophetically, "I am impatient, there is so little time."

Caresse's host in Beirut, John Fistere, wrote to Philip Isely in Denver: "I am not sure exactly what I promised Caresse I would do in connection with the World Constitutional Convention, but whatever I said I would do, I will most certainly try to do. It is so easy to promise Caresse *anything*."

In May, she heard from John McHale in Carbondale:

> I have nothing to report from the WAAS. . . . My col-
> leagues in the World Academy have assumed that the
> project has been abandoned in view of the involvements of
> Cyprus in the present Middle East crisis. . . . I can appre-
> ciate your disappointment after the time and energy you
> have expended in this venture, but I am sure that the
> personal idealism which this reflects will find some
> equally worthwhile undertaking in our presently troubled
> world. . . .

Caresse was indeed relieved to keep the World Academy of Art
and Science out of the picture. "WAAS's interest, I believe, is not
wholly for One World led by artists, poets, and humanitarians of the
earth, but may have a complicated political bias." Michael Lekakis
supported her stand:

> I am not altogether convinced that something is there for
> artists—World Man seems to be a *peace* project. World
> Man artists can have a voice if organizable people will let
> them. The nature of creativity is against it. Lao Tze said the
> best government is possible when no-one wants to govern.
> Under present conditions, *everyone* wants to govern.

She proposed, as an alternative, representatives of other international organizations—the League for the Rights of Man, the Fellowship of World Citizens, the International Court of Justice at The
Hague, the Humanist Society, followers of Gandhi for non-violence,
the University Round Table, Parliamentarians for World Government, the Committee for a World Constitutional Convention, and
the Cypriot Development and Tourism Office—with Archbishop
Makarios and Rossides as over-all guardians of the project. Each of
these groups or units would be given part of the 68 *hectares* of land,
and leaders in each of the special fields would seek funds to construct
their own units, using Cypriot labor. "It is to be hoped that U Thant
could start a training school on Cyprus for a world police force,
which has always been envisaged by those planning for eventual
world government."

In a letter to Rossides, Caresse outlined her grandiose plan for an
art center, a world library, a world institute of research "to feed and
house the exploding population of the earth," and a "one-world

basilica for the religious and humanist expressions of man-kind . . . under Bucky's dome."

"Why not announce that *all* Cyprus will be ceded to World Man," she suggested, "giving to the artists and scientists of the world the opportunity to work out Man's destiny, free from the conflicting ideologies on Cyprus? President Makarios would go down in history as the greatest World Citizen of them all." (Lord Bertrand Russell, Mrs. Rajan Nehru, and Professor Linus Pauling were among the 13 world leaders who had signed up, at that date, with World Man.)

Meanwhile, the island continued to fulfill its historic destiny as a place of conflict, with the Greek Cypriot struggle taking place against the backdrop of the broader crisis in the Middle East, the civil war in Lebanon. At the United Nations Assembly, Cyprus was an active member of the Afro-Asian group (though there could be no one more European than the chief Cypriot delegate, Zenon Rossides). The Archbishop attended two summit conferences with the non-aligned countries, and developed a close relationship with President Nasser of the United Arab Republic. Makarios's policies were not popular with Turkey, Greece, or the United States, all of which supported NATO. But Caresse herself backed the Archbishop. "As President Makarios said to the press, the Center will help 'the inevitable trend toward One World accord.'"

She wrote to Rossides that "This World Man territory is to be protected by a United Nations police force and kept free from all *national* interference by NATO forces; *not* to be stationed on Cyprus." In her view, Cyprus would be a good testing ground for the disarmament agreements between the U.S. and the U.S.S.R. "It will undoubtedly have to be One World or none, and time grows short." Despite the problems in the Middle East, "I still want to try to establish the Center at Kyrenia."

In February, Caresse was en route to Beirut again with Robert Boone, the aide-de-camp. She wrote to Rossides: "on or about March 14 we plan to fly over to Cyprus to spend a day or two at the Ledra Palace . . . [then] Bob will drive me around the island. You know I have never been to Famagusta or to many other interesting towns, nor seen the home of the Marine Venus. I will be a tourist." While sightseeing on Cyprus, Caresse discovered an historic plaque attached to the wall of the Government Cottage near a small village in the Troödos mountains—all pine trees, bracken, and red earth:

Arthur Rimbaud, poète et génie français au mépris de sa rénomée contribua de ses propres mains à la construction de cette maison MDCCCLXXXI.

An early British High Commissioner had engaged Rimbaud, a self-described vagabond *aux semelles de vent*, to supervise construction of the summer cottage there. Rimbaud had starved in Paris, survived attempted murder by his friend Verlaine, grown rich in Africa, joined the French Army, and deserted to the West Indies to trade in gold, ivory, coffee, and spices. When he landed in Larnaca five months before the British troops, he was 24 and poor, glad to pick up 150 francs a month to take charge of Cypriot laborers quarrying stone near the village of Vorokline. What curious happenstance that Caresse's destiny led her to the young rebel who was Harry Crosby's idol, whose poetry Harry emulated.

After the week in Cyprus, Caresse stopped off at another place close to her heart. She described her visit to Madame Alexi Stephanou at the Greek Embassy on Cyprus:

> Our trip back via Delphi was most heartwarming. . . . All the blossoms on the almonds were in full bloom, a sea of white, on the crest of the hill where the Amphictyony used to meet in 470 B.C. [It] was radiant with promise for the world. I was given an ovation by the village—the Mayor and the Chief of Police said they wished me to become an honorary citizen of Delphi, so I was very happy. The four years of exile were worth the return.

Back in Rome, she discovered important new developments in the World Man project. Philip Isely had arranged to let the Center use its tax-exempt status. She wrote to Rossides:

> We can raise money for the school, the library and art gallery on land at Kyrenia, using the Association for Human Emergence, Inc. [of WCC] as our tax exemption claim, allowing them to declare their world government from the World Man Center under Bucky's dome at Kyrenia, with the assurance that a protective world police training school will function there also.

Max Habicht, who helped to draw up the Declaration for a World Government at the Wolfach Conference, offered to meet Caresse in

Rome to discuss ways and means of declaring the World Man Center extraterritorial if Caresse would provide a round-trip air ticket.

Another project for World Man was taking shape through the efforts of John Foster in London. Jacques Cousteau, the French oceanographer, was looking for a friendly government to cooperate in an exciting new venture. Foster proposed that Cyprus might offer its offshore shelf of the ocean to Cousteau. Doxiadis was already working on a plan for an undersea city.

> I have written to Bucky asking him if he can build under-water. . . . It would be a great coup if Cyprus could initiate the project. It would be a protection for Cyprus as well as a great step forward. The ocean bed can yield so many marvelous treasures and provide a source for feeding and protecting the world from atmospheric assault.

Caresse was again a woman ahead of her time in voicing environmental concerns.

On March 8, she wrote to the Archbishop, asking for "the honor of meeting with you again."

> The purpose of my visit would be a final discussion of a possible date later this year for an announcement that a plot of land is being given near Kyrenia for the establishment of a World Man Center. . . .

> Ever since the general agreement in 1966 between you, Ambassador Rossides, Dr. Fuller and myself to proceed over the Kyrenia project, I have been obtaining promises from artists all over the world to contribute their works to a fund-raising project for the World Man Center. What is needed is the signing of the deed for the property as evidence to the contributors that the project is going ahead. I hope that Your Beatitude will be able to give me that assurance and fix a date for the public signing of the deed.

Life and other mass-media publications requested advance notice of the meeting, to give "the whole Kyrenia project the attention . . . it deserves."

Caresse was welcomed by Makarios, "who was as polite and charming as ever." However, as she wrote to Lekakis, "he made it quite clear that he must see 'the color of my gold' before any signature was given to cede the property at Kyrenia to World Man." There were other unforeseen problems:

> I believe that since the land that Makarios offered belongs to the Church, and since Makarios is the Head of the Orthodox Church in Cyprus, it is possible for him to remove his sovereignty from the 68 acres—but is it actually enough to accept the Cypriot land as *World* land? I have always felt that it should be something that was *voted upon* and granted by the *Government* of Cyprus.

The Minister of Justice informed Caresse that the Cypriot Government, which includes the Turks and other minorities, would not by any means be willing to cede land. "I was, perhaps, too trusting," she wrote, "and that is possibly why the land I chose in the first place, and for which I paid half, was outside of Church property and therefore unacceptable to Makarios." Caresse was reminded of the debacle at Delphi. "I was judged by the [Greek] Supreme Court in plenum session and the verdict was that as a private citizen I might keep my land in Delphi, but not express any World or Socratic ideas there. . . . They judged me as a sovereign power and not as an individual. So, history repeats itself."

Rossides appeared to be subtly withdrawing his support of the Center. Caresse wrote:

> I think that perhaps the best solution, if you cannot accept my principles . . . is for the Archbishop to cede or assign to me as World Citizen the eight acres (for which I paid $2,000) within the 68 acres allotted on the outskirts of Belle Pais, which site you and I chose in 1965 and for which I hold President Makarios' cancelled check. On these eight acres I could offer the sovereignty to the League for the Rights of Man, Women Against War, or the youth movement of Citizens of the World, which embraces all creeds, colors, faiths and ideologies for peace versus violence. I must not be kept in the dark as to what is being done in the name of World Man Center, Inc., of which I am president.

*   *   *

She asked Mike Lekakis to call on Rossides to give her a candid report. Lekakis replied that "[Rossides] asked me to reassure you about World Man on Cyprus. It is *your idea*, and that will be respected beyond any question. He regrets that he was not present in Cyprus when you went there. The problem evidently is that Mr. Rossides has not been able to explain your position to the Archbishop."

Rossides mistakenly assumed that Caresse herself had great wealth and would be able to endow the Center with a substantial sum. "However I am sure that the Archbishop is not interested in 'the color of gold' as such, but in implementing the World Man Center." Lekakis wrote. An anonymous donor, a Cypriot woman, had given $200,000, but so far, no one else had come through.

With no precedent and no history, "[World Man] must be justified to the people of Cyprus, and that means Greek, Turks, Armenians, Jews, and many others. Mr. Rossides has been the catalyst and his performance has been remarkable thus far." If—in her view—Caresse had been put in an awkward position, the $2,000 would be returned with no strings attached.

> You still remain the one who inspired the World Man Center in Cyprus. You should not be discouraged by the indirectness with which these matters have been put together. It seems to me that under the circumstances, it cannot be otherwise. Somehow ideas take their own form, and going along with them, our experience and knowledge have the opportunity to give [them] the most noble form.

Rossides himself wrote later to Caresse that "World Man has all along been in my mind, and we are certainly *not* abandoning it." He reassured her that Archbishop Makarios was prepared to carry out his part of the agreement, as stated in the public announcement of July 1966. "Needless to say, if the project in Cyprus is achieved, you will have a preeminent position in it, and your recognition will be universal. The idea and the dedicated efforts over the years for the attainment of this goal are yours, my dear Caresse, and you certainly deserve all honor."

In September, Caresse heard from Fuller that "The Cyprus potential is too important now to be treated lightly." He had attended a luncheon meeting with Rossides, U Thant, both the Turkish and Greek ambassadors to the United Nations, the president of

Columbia University, and a half-dozen other important people interested in Cyprus. One of Fuller's primary concerns was the danger of leaving the World Man territory unprotected. "International gamblers with armed guards might move in and be extraordinarily difficult to dislodge." Rossides had proposed to U Thant a 50-year United Nations trusteeship, with the U.N. providing a small special guard for Cyprus, in addition to its regular armed forces.

Both the Greek and the Turkish ambassadors agreed that the World Man Center might pour oil on troubled waters and provide comfort to Cypriots divided by conflict. They also discussed the possibility of enlarging World Man territory to include all Cyprus, and "officially recognized" Caresse as the pioneer—together with Makarios—in initiating World Man. The donation of the critical matching fund of $200,000 eliminated the necessity of holding the art auction, but Fuller suggested that already-pledged artists' works might be displayed at the Center.

Fuller, who was invited to give the Nehru memorial lecture, had stopped off in India en route to Cyprus to discuss World Man with Prime Minister Gandhi. With the support of a major nation like India at the U.N., Fuller suggested, they might consider issuing a "World Man Territory" passport. He projected that "millions, if not billions, of young people around the world will apply for such passports and identify themselves as 'World Humans'."

> I think well of my fellow man. I admire all those who dedicate themselves to the elimination of wars, but I am personally convinced that . . . any special idea group operating within the framework of present . . . political structures can only add to the voices of all history that have decried destruction and injustice. I do not expect them to have much effect. *Nations must go . . . because their functions are rendered evolutionarily obsolete.*

Caresse viewed Fuller's use of the term "World Man" to replace "World Citizen" as a great ideological leap forward . . . "It is comprehensive and philosophical and could inspire the young more than any other term. . . . You have gone Socrates one better, for which I congratulate, admire, and love you," she wrote.

Several points in Fuller's letter puzzled her, especially the thought that the Center should be placed under the trusteeship of the United Nations. "I am *anti*-nationalist and I pray that the beautiful idea conceived for Cyprus with Zenon and Makarios in 1957 when His

Beatitude was still in exile in Athens will *not* now be taken over by a body of nations, with the largest nation, China, not even recognized. . . . I see only arguments and discord. . . ."

In her last letter to Rossides, Caresse was still carrying the torch. As if she had a premonition of her own passing from the scene, she asked: "Who will be carrying on the organizing, the coordinating, the deeding of the land?"

> I may have spoken too strongly about a United Nations armed force being caretakers of the Center, but I *feel* very strongly on this point. I suggest a triumvirate of: His Beatitude or you Zenon of Kitium, for Cyprus; U Thant, a United World of *people*, not nations; and Bucky the scientist and bookkeeper and prime coordinator, to be caretakers. . . . a directorate of five or seven individuals but not an unwieldy amount—the League for the Rights of Man, the Federalists, the World Citizens . . . would be represented.

At the time of her death, Caresse was still actively involved with promoting the World Man Center on Cyprus, though she must have known that her larger dream might never be realized:

> My alternative is that I accept the few acres that His Beatitude and I bought above Belle Pais and build myself a small house with a courtyard just big enough for a "*Soglia di Pace.*" . . . I do not want my $2,000 back, it must remain there in the spirit in which I gave it. I am sorry I did not turn out to be a millionairess, but I never was. . . . *faith and love and venture are the values I've built my life on.* I don't think they are going to fail on Cyprus.

Caresse never built the small house with a courtyard. The Soglia di Pace found a home in a 15th century castello, larger than even her most grandiose dreams.

*"There is nothing as strong as an idea
whose time has come, but it must be given
an eagle's nest from which to soar."*

—CARESSE

Chapter XV

THE PRINCIPESSA
OF ROCCASINIBALDA

On a picture postcard of Roccasinibalda, Caresse jotted this
message to Charles Olson:

> This is my latest abode. Just put on a new roof, guaranteed
> for 500 years. I have a 30-year Plan developing—Humanist
> and Utopian—come and help me—

"I knew that was where I had to live . . . It seemed to me it was just
the thing I had been waiting for all my life," she said of the "Grimm's
fairy-tale castle" topped by crenellated turrets where she was living
out her last years. Michelangelo's competitor, the great Baldasarre
Peruzzi, designed the dramatic eagle-shaped fortress palace, its walls
rising out of sheer slices of solid rock and "strategically impreg-
nable," Caresse said. "It may be the only spot that will survive atomic
war."

Some 30 years after she arrived on the scene, a *barone* with all the resources Caresse lacked restored the castle and the relics of its historic past—Cinquecento armor, carved armoires, and musical instruments—in the tradition of the original *castellani*. But in the '50s, when Caresse "religiously made a bid for [Roccasinibalda] every spring," the Vatican was using the shell of a castle and its grounds as a boys' camp. "I was unable to buy until it had almost fallen into ruins, and I had to replace not only the roof, but many of the battlements and floors as well." The 72 rooms were uninhabitable for some five or six months of the year, and in summer, the sun streamed through the paneless windows. The north wing was a regal succession of large, empty spaces with coffered ceilings and handsome fireplaces, its frescoes whitewashed over with arsenic to prevent the contagion of a 17th-century plague.

At the beak of the eagle a hanging garden lies on three levels with towering cypresses and a swimming pool. The V-shaped tail of the eagle, or *coda*, forms a covered terrace where Caresse and her guests used to gather at sunset for cocktails to view the spectacular panorama of the valley where the Turano encircles the mountain. In the quiet of the morning and at night, one can hear its rush.

The castle rises above the clouds, and in the early morning she awoke with a sense of being on a floating island. The bedroom that she chose for her own had one large window opening onto the valley to the west. It was connected by a narrow passage to the bathroom, where—in her time—a tub was attached to a primitive boiler, with water heated by a fire kindled from chunks of wood. (Each bath required fresh kindling.) Water was no problem. Rain from the battlements fell into a great cistern under the courtyard, and the water supply was carried in Etruscan-shaped jars balanced on the heads of village women. As Caresse wryly commented, "What a man could not carry in his hands was loaded onto the head of his wife or the back of his mule."

Her day began when she heard the bray of donkeys as the men of the village left for the fields. At sundown, she was tormented by the swooping and darting of bats around the four corners of her room—bats that strung themselves, heads down, on the canopy of her bed until midnight, when they disappeared as mysteriously as they had come. Caresse learned that, for her, eight to ten hours of sleep were no longer necessary; from midnight to sunrise was quite enough.

There was much to be done. In the bedroom during breakfast and while she was dressing, she confronted whatever conundrum the day might bring with Margharitta, the Italian housekeeper. Margharitta was tall, slender, dignified, and forever faithful to Caresse. She was extremely competent in running the day-to-day affairs of the castle, and was always at her side, "like the shadow of a medieval nun." Caresse admired Margharitta's simple country dignity. Margharitta's father, a "noble peasant," looked after the garden.

Caresse's idealistic dream was for the castle to be self-sufficient— to grow vegetables for the table, to harvest "fish from the river, snails from the vine, figs from the trees." Inspired by her father's Utopian community in Texas, she planned to make use of its natural resources, "to encourage flax-growing and the weaving of linen, to cultivate the vintner's art and wine-making, to start olive oil production from the trees in the valley. No man [or woman] should live well while his neighbor starves," she said, and as the new American neighbor, she set about practicing what she preached, to improve the quality of life for the villagers. Out of a population of some 500, there were 190 people on the dole of 400 *lire* a month (then roughly $1.75 a week). Every cent had to go for food and necessities, with very little left for "the trimmings of life." She wrote to Robert Meyer, chief of the CARE mission in Rome, asking his help under the Food Crusade program: "If packages could be directed here to me or to the Secretary of the *Commune* for distribution, they would have the greatest moral and physical effect. I am doing what I can on the spot, but my own funds are limited."

"Caresse Crosby was 'poor gentility' in so many ways," Desmond O'Grady, one of the young Irish poets who visited the castle, observed. "She was able to live like a *principessa* in Italy, but she did so in a modest way, with much more style than the equivalent 'lady' in England. Like many women of 'a certain age,' she lived frugally when alone, but she did her best for invited guests. She always put on 'high face' and 'high table,' even if there was little to eat. She could make a Renaissance meal out of a package of soup and a poetry reading."

Guests who could afford to, paid their own way. Those working or teaching in Rome, who came out on weekends and holidays to write or to paint, brought staples for the kitchen—boxes of pasta and rice, poultry, and cheap wine, with special treats for Caresse. "We ate well, the same as any Italian peasant down the hill," O'Grady remembered.

Soon she began to renovate the jail at the bottom of the hill—a dependency of the Castello—for use as a boy's club. With her usual flair, she had the cell-bars painted pink and the walls whitewashed, and let the boys exercise their creativity in decorating the walls with murals. She hoped to keep the young people out of the bars. The boys' club was a grand success, especially when the girls came around in the evening to dance, even though the doors closed at a respectable 11:00 p.m.

An article in the *Daily American*, Rome's newspaper for expatriates, noted that the fine arts and literature program was flourishing at Roccasinibalda. Robert Snyder, in Rome to film a documentary about the Vatican's Sistine Chapel, stopped by to pay homage to the Principessa, who was becoming a legend in her own time, surrounded by an international coterie. Snyder proposed to add Caresse and her Center to his series featuring Anaïs Nin, Henry Miller, and other contemporary artists.

Caresse was not a novice before the cameras, she told Snyder. After her youthful attempt to star as "Valerie Marno" for Myron Selznick, she appeared in Emlen Etting's surrealist epic, *Poème*, filmed in part on the lawn of her mother-in-law Henrietta's house, "The Apple Trees." Etting, who knew both Crosbys in Montparnasse in the '20s, chose as his theme the three faces of Eve: the sports-loving girl next door, the intellectual, and "passion plus," a role well suited to Caresse. "I was supposed to be a rather extraordinary woman," Caresse commented. "There were dahlias in the garden, and I was supposed to *eat* the dahlias." (She could not, at the time of the interview, remember what dahlias tasted like.)

Snyder's *Always Yes! Caresse* is a long string of reminiscences of the "passionate years" in Paris, New York, and Roccasinibalda. In the opening, Caresse explained how she first came to the castle with Bill Peabody. "My son, who was rather protective of me, thought it a crazy idea, and everybody else said, 'My, you have a lot of courage.' But I was in need of a place to help others and to express my ideas . . . and it seemed to me vast and empty and ready to be filled with activities. . . . I've never had enough empty rooms in my life."

Caresse said "Yes!" to the castle, with the idea of using the vast rooms to exhibit paintings and sculpture by resident artists. She took the Snyder camera crew on a tour, including "the room where we play chess . . . Marcel Duchamp says, and I believe, that one can fight one's battles across the chessboard without getting bullets and bombs to do it. The best man—the best idea—wins; that is the way the world should be."

Life at Roccasinibalda—as observed and reported by O'Grady, who came to the Castello from Rome on weekends with his family— was "Cistercian/Benedictine, not in a religious sense, but a spiritual and intellectual one." This comfortable monastery even accommodated offspring, though Caresse, like many older ladies not fond of small children, "tolerated them because she thought it was good for them." The accommodations were simple—country-style rooms with a bed, one chair, a table, bookshelves, and a bathroom down the hall. Another resident guest, Sy Kahn, remembers his turret room with a fine vista and an old wooden desk, over which Caresse thoughtfully hung a photograph of Dylan Thomas.

"What you did during the daytime was your own business, whether it was to think, to read, or to dream, but the common cause was to *create*," O'Grady recalled. There were no restrictions of any kind. Caresse only wanted those staying at the Castle to be engaged in creative work—and to hear about it at dinner. Old friends and visitors followed the same monastic routine as everybody else.

Caresse religiously observed the cocktail hour on the terrace at the *coda* of the eagle. "The cocktail hour was for banter, gossip, scandal, and 'scallywaggery,' and Caresse took the lead," according to O'Grady. "She could be sparkling, serious, sometimes silly during cocktail hour, but never ridiculous."

Dinner was the high mass of the day, when all gathered around the large refectory table, with Caresse or a distinguished guest at the head. Margharitta served, or oversaw the serving of the peasant who did the cooking. Dinner conversation was for artistic theory, criticism, evaluation, controversy. Caresse loved the high art talk, and always surrounded herself with poets and artists voicing conflicting opinions. She would contribute with anecdotes of Joyce or Pound or other significant literary lights in Paris in her day. Though she spoke less in her later years, she never missed a point.

"After dinner, we entertained each other over wine," O'Grady remembered. "We all drank our share. Caresse didn't approve of drunkenness, but enjoyed natural tipsiness and gaiety. She was Elizabethan rather than Puritanical about this." There was no radio or TV—not even a record player—at the castle. Guests read poetry and prose aloud in English, French, or Italian—*Finnegan's Wake* or Dylan Thomas or Pound or Lorca. "There was much story-telling, reminiscences, and literary criticism, opinionating. . . . Sometimes we dressed up and played charades."

Others O'Grady remembered at table were Robert Fitzgerald, poet and translator of the *Iliad* and the *Odyssey*, Eamon Grennan, and Patrick Kavanaugh—all young Irish poets. Kavanaugh could be difficult with people he did not like, but he got along famously with Caresse. When she told tales of Man Ray, Dali, and other creative spirits of her youth in Paris, Kavanaugh retorted, "My Dublin was never like that." The Spanish poet Rafael Alberti also partook of

Caresse's table, as did the English poet-translator Patrick Creagh and his wife, Ursula—D.H. Lawrence's granddaughter. One summer Peter O'Toole, in Europe after a film, visited Roccasinibalda and fell under the spell of the Principessa like everyone else.

During the castle years, Caresse began to feel a great need for an expression "beyond the actual excitement of the moment. I felt that the world was teetering, and that what we needed was a new vision . . . ." Her goal was

> To create a symbolic rallying point, . . . where no barriers to race, creed, color or nationalism exist . . . to be administered by Women of the World as a challenge against War and a symbol of the Four Freedoms: freedom from fear, from prejudice, from injustice and from want.

> Here the arts and crafts will be given full value as assets in a new order. . . . Here the matriarchal system of social welfare will be revised as an experiment in World Democracy, . . . a haven for civilized living.

Henry Miller commented from California: "Women will soon rule the world after man has destroyed it. He can't destroy the earth or kill the stars, thank God." Miller regretted that he could not be with Caresse at the "Center for Creative Arts and Humanist Living in the Abruzzi Hills . . . [where] people from all parts of the world wander in and out."

Anaïs Nin described Caresse at this time as "the chargée d'affaires of the heart of the world . . . Her short, softly waved hair is white, but her stance, her responsiveness is young. She has lively and gay blue eyes, a constant sparkling laughter, a short humorous nose, a warm manner which wins everyone and a gift for making friends. She never commands, but whatever she asks is immediately accomplished." If her grand scheme to found an Italian Yaddo Colony seems naïve, the fact remains that Caresse had an undeniable talent for acting as catalyst in the lives of young artists.

Irene Rice Pereira, a friend of long standing from New York, came to the castle with a reputation firmly established. She was deeply involved with some of the complex intellectual currents of the 20th century through her study of space, time, optics, and light. Caresse facetiously said, "We call her Miss Spacey, because she believes in the expanding universe. . . . She writes with great insight and vision of the future." Caresse planned to publish an introduction to Rice Pereira's works in a special "Castle Edition" of the Black Sun Press.

For her part, Rice Pereira thought that the impressive-looking castle left much to be desired. The plumbing was pure 15th century, and often when it rained, water poured into the bleak, sparsely furnished rooms. Rice Pereira soon fled to the relative comforts of Rome to prepare for an exhibit.

Fiona Dudley arrived from London to uncover and restore the valuable frescoes (attributed by some experts to the school of Raphael), and Professor Benalla came from the Uffizi Gallery in Rome to verify their origin. Caresse was searching for a foundation or a private patron of the arts to fund the fresco project. She wrote to Edward Bigelow, trustee of her estate at the State Street Bank in Boston:

> Dear Ned:
> The very welcome extra dividend arrived. I'm going to put it to use immediately in organizing a fresco class at the castle to uncover the many . . . Cinquecento frescoes that have been hidden from view for over 300 years. . . .I have never quite enough in the till to engage a professor from the Belle Arti to arrange for young artists to come out and do the work. I am sure Mrs. C. [Henrietta Crosby] would have been interested in the project. . . . Do let the word be known. There are so many exchange programs and art projects going on between here and there . . . that I hope this one will be a success.

At the time of the Snyder film, young talents of many nationalities were living and working at the castle. Jacques Gabriel, a Haitian, and his wife Sandra came to Caresse through Matta Echaurren. (Caresse discovered Matta, a young unknown, in Paris and later displayed his work at the Washington gallery.) Gabriel—another unknown—first designed surrealist collages that verged on pop art, but after his stay at the Center, created paintings that "had value far beyond anything [he had] done before." Raymond Panas, a sculptor-in-residence from Athens who worked in both metal and wood, decorated the hearth with "Angels of Peace" carved from logs found on the property. His angel with outspread wings salvaged from scraps of tin and bronze became the chandelier for the salon. Panas was so intent on his work that he didn't say much of anything one could under-stand, occasionally muttering a gutteral French patois. Wyatt

Osborne, who arrived via the circuitous route of Madrid and the Costa del Sol, was a native of Caresse's state, New York. He was inspired by Panas's "Angels" to invade the workshop and turn out metal figures of his own.

There were always young men in her retinue—a third generation of them. To the end of her life, Caresse was subtly and mildly flirtatious with men. In later years, those who knew her well insist that she was too urbane, too decorous, too much the lady, to act out her fantasies. But among the young, she continued to have a few slavish attendants.

Bill Barker first came to the castle in 1950, with Caresse's son. "He was looking, I think, for some interesting point-of-view, a life in Europe," Caresse said of Barker, just out of the army after World War II. He continued to keep in touch, wiring after the tragic death on January 25, 1955 of Caresse's beloved Billy:

—Stunned—frightful news—writing—I know this cannot help much, but please remember you have another son— Love

After the War, Billy followed his mother's footsteps to Paris, where he lived with his Brazilian-born wife Josette in an antiquated Left Bank apartment. One night a gas leak developed, and both lost consciousness. Josette had the telephone receiver cradled in her hand when the concierge and the gendarme arrived. They revived Josette, but were too late for Billy. The official coroner's report read "Death by Asphyxiation," but suicide was suspected. For some years, there had been signs of a troubled marriage. It was rumored that Bill had problems with his sexuality, that he could not satisfy Josette's fiery Latin temperament, that she had taken lovers.

Caresse was too fond of her daughter-in-law to listen to rumors. They remained friends throughout the years, even after the widowed Josette married Jacques Spiero. For a long time after Billy's death, Caresse might have asked herself, "Where did we go wrong, in those years on the rue de Lille?" After a prolonged period of mourning, she came back to life through the dark tunnel.

Billy's friend, Barker, was back again at Roccasinibalda, as chauffeur and confidant. In the mornings, Barker would often spend several private hours in Caresse's boudoir, planning the day's activities. But no one could misconstrue the relationship, particularly since Barker brought with him a beautiful young woman—tall, blonde, and given to "drifting like pale smoke through the stone corridors of the castle," Sy Kahn remembered. "Her gown, like a

scrim, did not hide, only blurred, her dazzling body." Sometimes she
would sunbathe nude on the battlements on a sunny afternoon, with
other members of the entourage, scarcely exchanging a word.

Barker had pretensions to poetry, reciting his "Adesso" for the
Snyder camera crew:

> Flame not for unthinking scissor fingers
> Mourn centimetres of Egyptian life in death,
> Nor curse the golden Unicorn which lingers
> Pacing the pane between that wind, this breath.

Caresse was fond of Barker, but not blind to the uneven quality of his
verse:

> The sophisticate today too often offers used currency as
> precious coin, which it is not . . . be it one line or an
> odyssey, a chemist he must be and not a trickster. But when
> the gold is there, glowing and rare, the poet alchemist can
> and does achieve his minted goal. In BB's work I find some
> verses contrived, some inscrutable, but also some poems
> that contain the rarest currency of all.

Robert Mann, another young weekend guest of limited means and
some talent who turned up at the castle, was invited by Caresse to
stay on as chief of staff. Mann wrote to La Principessa: "to express
the kind of special gratitude I feel with the phrase 'thank you for a
lovely time' seems not only inaccurate but a sort of profanation of a
sentiment at once broader and deeper." Caresse announced to her
friend Helen Simpson in New York that "Robert Mann is here to
help me administer the castle. He is a young and gifted composer. . . . up until last year, he was secretary-general of the international Society for Contemporary Music, sponsor of the festival in
Cologne." The friendship that began when Mann addressed a note to
"My dear Mrs. Crosby" after their first meeting ripened into a
lifelong attachment.

In a later letter to "Caresse, darling," Mann attempted to redefine
their relationship. His function might be to run a year-round office in
Rome, helping to choose the season's artists, answering correspondence, and file-keeping, but for this he would have to ask a
monthly salary. He could not promise to live at the castle in the

summer, because his job as a translator for Roman movie crews "kept body and soul together."

"Actually, the issue is a larger one," Mann wrote.

> . . . It hinges on the fact that a tranquil life of contempla-
> tion, tempered by friends, enhanced by books and art and
> brightened by laughter, seems to clash with your desires
> for a life of action. . . . Something of this kind must have
> struck you this summer, the day you had all to yourself
> lying in the garden, warmed by the sun. I remember your
> telling me about it as a special moment. . . . Because it
> was a moment I know well. . . . Bill [Barker] to the
> contrary. What is, in fact, his latest "act"-ivity? Aside
> from the flowing hair and drooping mustachios?

> . . . I know too well now, and we both have seen that my
> Trastevere isolation, my music . . . are demands so great
> that almost all other considerations crumble before them.
> You need a fuller share of someone's life, a larger embrace,
> a more complete devotion than my life, my arms, my heart
> are capable of.

"My original intention here was to write a letter of apology and explanation over the Helen-note," Mann added; "but I have preferred to reassert my love in a more constructive way." In closing, Mann offered his personal caveat:

> You can't on the one hand be a guardian angel (even if
> you are an angel) and on the other, the director of a starkly
> equipped country hotel. . . . *Give* everything free; you
> will have less headaches, and they greater inspiration (and
> devotion). And keep the number down . . . it's more fun
> that way. . . . Strike straight out for talent; true talent will
> never let you down.

Another penniless"true talent" who found his way to Roccasinibalda was Gregory Corso of the West Coast Beatniks, a shaggy, dark young man who boasted that he never combed his hair. In Caresse's view, "Bohemianism . . . has never meant five-o'clock shadow or untidy hair . . . but I like its indifference to dull formulas and its latitude for work and fun." She allowed Corso to stay on.

Stripped to the waist and looking quite like the god Pan, Corso posed for Roloff Beny with Caresse and Irene Rice Pereira in the courtyard.

Corso, who drank too much and was often high—on drugs as well as alcohol—was generally erratic and obnoxious. One evening, a guest remembered, Corso was making small talk about women and the inescapability of their being different from men. He reached out and cupped and grasped one of Caresse's ample breasts, to illustrate his point. She very quickly slapped his hand and, unruffled, continued on with the conversation.

After his departure, Corso wrote to Caresse from Venice:

> I loved my happy time with you—and good it was, too—
> for the last three years I was ill—and now I'm out of it—
> all's joy—and I hope I made you joyous—whatever, I'm
> with Bill [Barker] and he's an angel true. We meet in
> Venice and you be my girl friend—take me to the casino—
> I can win and we'll go haffy's—but you must put up the
> bread—if not, I call you a parsimonious un-lover—now
> how's that! I love angels like you—I can yell at you, and
> you take it like a lady.

One might wonder why she felt obliged to "take it like a lady"—to provide a haven for the unconventional, the unwashed. Perhaps it was because she suspected that behind every unimpressive exterior lurked genius, a latent Ezra Pound. Or, as one chronicler of the expatriates suggested: "What drove so many Americans to stay in Europe, to become patrons, setting up places to nest down their geniuses . . . [was that] the more they rebelled, the more they fled from Puritanism, somehow in the end they felt [it] their Christian duty. . . ."

After a short stay with Caresse in Venice, Allen Ginsberg, in his role as mother-hen of the Beatniks in Paris, wrote an update of their activities:

> I see Gregory [Corso,] Peter [Orlovsky,] and a few beat
> cats from the Bonaparte Café round corner from Deux
> Magots—hangout of foreign lowlife—some beautiful
> faces—a whole group of strange young (17-23) French
> boys with long hair, & their little dungareed French
> runaway girls. . . . when you get to America please look
> up On the Road by Kerouac, & Gregory Corso's book
> from City Lights SF Cal. . . . Gregory now all hung up on

Einstein, says he had epiphany other day, he was not walking around Paris but in Middle of Universe.

Expect I'll stay here half year at least. Sorry you didn't like the fragment of [William] Burroughs we left with you in Venice.—perhaps you thought him evil minded or being dirty for dirt's sake—not at all the case, . . . I won't go into huge explanations, please take it on trust the whole thing a vast insane masterpiece. Kerouac arrives and after that we all go off to the Far East beginning by way of Greece with knapsacks morphine needles bottles of California Tokay dreams extra socks long underwear & innumerable golden manuscripts. . . .

At least one unsavory character was suspected of involvement with the idealistic art colony at Rocca. Sydney E. Paulson, vice consul of the American Embassy in Rome, wrote to Caresse "to investigate the activities of one Jean Pierre LaFitte and his associates in Italy. We have reason to believe that you have had contacts with Mr. LaFitte." Caresse denied any knowledge of LaFitte or of his activities. She noted unequivocally in the margin of the file copy of that letter: "Saw the Consul . . . never heard of him."

One contemporary source who preferred to remain anonymous recorded a stark critique of the Center:

> . . . Here with Caresse's sour wine and goddam pasta our breath doesn't hold out, our livers ache, and even Caresse has forgotten her crystal chandelier background. Let's face it—here there are no folks around like Jo Davidson, Paul Valéry, Isadora Duncan, or John Reed—not here in Roccasinibalda. Her new crop of geniuses are mostly all phonies, freeloading fags and poets trying to make it on television.

Desmond O'Grady offered a kinder—if perhaps more rosy-hued—view of life at the castle. He remembered no orgies, no drunkenness. "It was all very civilized. . . . [not] a fight, an argument, or a breakdown." Caresse lived by the Greek "Golden Mean," O'Grady said, with everything in its place and nothing done to excess. The truth may lie somewhere between.

A long history of bronchial ailments forced Caresse to retreat to the well-heated drawing rooms of Washington when the winter chill set in. She began to cast about for a site in Rome where she might keep a closer eye on the Castello in the cold months. Roloff Beny, the young Canadian photographer-artist-writer whom Caresse befriended, came up with a solution. A Columbia University graduate, Beny won critical acclaim in New York for his one-man show at the Knoedler Gallery before going to Rome via Paris, where he lived for a year on a Guggenheim Fellowship. A native of the bleak, prairie village of Medicine Hat, Alberta, Beny realized his lifelong dream of living by the water on the Lungotevere Ripa, the bank of the Tiber.

In January 1960, Beny wrote to Caresse referring to her recent—not entirely successful—eye operation:

> What a joy to hear that both eyes are working again. . . . It is good to know you have survived your winter in Washington and all projects and activities as well, and I trust the princess will arrive in "fine fettle." Roma and Rocca already seem spiritually alerted for the head of the realm. My plans call for me to leave for NY the first week of March, which seems incredibly good timing.

He offered one wing of his penthouse apartment, with a new dining room and use of the main kitchen. A "charming arrangement" in the winter garden could be the setting for lunches or intimate suppers, with the services of Vittoria, the full-time maid.

> . . . Of course, Caresse, you must realize that I will have to charge at least enough to cover my expenses . . . in other words, 120,000 [lire] for a completely functioning house. In fact, 30,000 per week [less than $50 U.S. in 1960]. There will be a little heating to pay but that usually depends on the weather. I have had much more lucrative offers, but I would far prefer a tenant like La Principessa Roccasinibalda."

From Washington, Caresse wrote to Henry Miller in California about her forthcoming summer plans. The art gallery in one wing of the castle would open with a Black Sun Press retrospective exhibition: "The Giants of the Twenties, Thirties, and Forties." Miller would be represented in all three categories, and she hoped he could come. "There are gardens, mountains and streams all about, not as rugged as Big Sur," she urged, "but both soothing and exciting. . . . There are studios for artists and studies with turrets for

writers," (with space for Miller in either area). After Roccasinibalda,
John Brown arranged for the exhibit to go on a USIS-sponsored tour
of the Middle East. Caresse asked Miller to write the Foreword for
the BSP traveling exhibition catalog "as a final salvo."

Miller remained at Big Sur. When she thanked him for his
"exciting and challenging" introduction to the USIS catalog, she
wrote that Miller's pessimistic view of the world was unlike her own:

> . . . It is difficult for me to be despondent, but I do face
> the facts that the world is both grim and dangerous, more
> this year than last, more so today than yesterday, however I
> have completely come to believe in Humanism as opposed
> to the supernatural beliefs and theistic creeds. It seems the
> only true and hopeful outlook for humans.
>
> I am growing up while growing older. I long to stretch
> my brain as a [hand] stretches the fingers of a glove. . . .
> You are right when you say man has done nothing yet with
> his brain and skills and opportunity. Let's fervently hope
> that he is on the brink of a new and better day. . . . I saw
> Lindbergh land at LeBourget. . . . I was aware . . . when
> Gagarin was circling the earth . . . I rode in one of the very
> first "horseless carriages." What a century it is, and we are
> hardly more than halfway through. . . . who knows I may
> go to the moon! But for the moment, I'm perfectly willing
> to stay here, to carry on at Roccasinibalda.

Caresse continued her publishing activities that summer, using a
small printing press she discovered in the village of Rieti. The first of
the Castle Continental Editions was *Our Separate Darkness,* a small
volume of poetry by Sy Kahn.

Kahn, a professor of humanities at the University of the Pacific in
Stockton, discovered the collection of Black Sun Press papers and
memorabilia in a remote room of the Castello. He recognized their
value and rescued them from further damage—once from invading
flying termites, and again from water that came sluicing into the
room during a storm. Kahn helped Caresse to put the papers in order
and urged her to sell them to a library at a university where they
would be available to scholars.

When she began to search for a home for the papers, she thought
of Harry T. Moore, co-editor of *Portfolios* during the war years in
Washington. Moore also played an important role in bringing out
Caresse's autobiography. Many of the opening passages were written

during a Christmas visit to Moore and his bride Beatrice, then stationed at Craig Air Force Base. At the time, Moore described Caresse as "brilliantly successful as ever in conveying her magnetic geniality in Alabama."

He closeted the gregarious Caresse in his guest room to write her memoirs and even suggested an appropriate title, *The Passionate Years.* Caresse rose to the challenge and finished the book with characteristic optimism: "The answer to the challenge [of life] is always 'Yes.'"

She later wrote to Moore:

> I am full of gratitude for the belief you have in me and my memories—By now, you may have read the finished product . . . and I hope it is up to your expectations—I'd hate to fail you. . . . Tomorrow April 20th [Caresse's birthday] is publication day—but I couldn't wait and the world at Delphi couldn't wait, so I'm on my way there now. . . . If the book goes well, what wonderful things we can all accomplish.

After his discharge from the Army, Moore joined the faculty of Southern Illinois University at Carbondale. Caresse wrote again to Moore: "You may hear from Professor Sy Kahn, who . . . was interested in finding a university that might like to acquire the BSP collection."

In the early 1960s, with other civil rights advocates battling for desegregation, Caresse would not consider a library that denied access to black students. She expressed skepticism about SIU because of the "Southern" in its title. Moore reassured her that the campus was not segregated and that black students were allowed unlimited use of university facilities. Ralph McCoy, director of the Morris Library, was looking for valuable 20th century material for his Special Collections. The Black Sun Press limited editions and the Crosby papers—original manuscripts and letters from Joyce, Hemingway, Lawrence, Hart Crane, and Pound—were choice acquisitions to add to the SIU library's resources.

After discreet inquiries to other universities and more negotiations with Carbondale, Caresse announced her decision: "The [Southern Illinois] University sounds fine, directed by brilliant minds. Since receiving your letter, I have written to Dr. McCoy again asking him to please give me a definite answer. Your help there to supervise the use of the collection is a paramount reason for selling it to them."

Caresse also was selling the papers and manuscripts that Harry inherited from his cousin, Walter Berry, to SIU. When Moore replied that SIU was going ahead with the purchase, Caresse invited Olson to the castle, to advise and assist with a new project. "Memories of . . . cocktails on the *coda* are certainly made more glamorous by your being present," she wrote. "Several young poets were delighted that I had heard from you with such reckless energy in every line."

> I intended to write you before . . . to ask if this spring, just after or during Spoleto, you will meet with one or two poets to talk over and plan a prize in memory of Harry Crosby—a poetry prize of $5,000 which was paid me by SIU for letters and documents of Walter Berry, Harry's cousin. . . .

> Other judges besides yourself to be invited and provided with pasta, vino and lodging; from America, Ginsberg; from France, René Char and St. J. Perse; from Greece, Seferis; and from Italy, Montale, Ungheretti, and a number of others. The only conditions, that the poems must be submitted in English or in French . . . these are the only languages that Harry Crosby read or spoke . . . in his all-too-brief life. Have you any suggestions? Please give me your ideas and come over quickly.

It was obvious that Harry was the prevailing love of Caresse's life. A portrait of Harry in his World War I uniform hung on her bedroom wall at the castle, some 30 years after his death. Talk about Harry always brought a special look to Caresse's face as she seemed to conjure him in her mind's eye. In referring to Harry's infidelities, she once said, "Well, he was a poet—the most complete poet I have ever known—and being a poet, he acted as he had to."

"It isn't man's fate that I believe in, it is man's destiny . . . and destiny to me means a world united an at peace."

—CARESSE

Chapter XVI
A THRESHOLD FOR PEACE

The next winter, Harry and Beatrice Moore invited Caresse to the SIU campus again. She had visited them several times after their move to Southern Illinois, and once was persuaded to meet with Moore's class to discuss Fitzgerald, Hemingway, and the operation of a small publishing house in Paris in the '20s. On another visit, in October 1963, Caresse told Moore's students about her encounters with Joyce and Nora when Black Sun published a portion of Joyce's *Work in Progress [Finnegan's Wake]*. The proposed class was interrupted by an event that canceled everything for the rest of that day and for several days thereafter throughout the country—the assassination of John F. Kennedy. It was a traumatic time, when people needed to be together. The Moores and Caresse gathered at Buckminster Fuller's dymaxion house on the Carbondale campus, a building that stood out in stark relief among the conventional Grant Wood/Midwest Gothic structures.

Caresse wrote the Moores regretting that she would not be with them again, since "traveling alone is more and more difficult for me on account of advancing years, which if I sit still and let them advance

198

on me, are wonderful but to meet them even halfway takes every ounce of energy I can muster."

In May, Moore wrote from the Gresham Hotel in Dublin—the first stop in his sabbatical year abroad—that he was dedicating his most recent work, *Clifftower*, to Caresse. She dashed off a note of appreciation, including a counter-offer: "Why not Rome and Rocca? Here we are beautifully remote. . . . I'll send in the car. . . . Do try to come."

Moore postponed his visit to the castle, but at the end of another busy summer, Caresse wrote that "Sy Kahn has been here, and now he and Nancy are off to Poland. Bucky [Fuller] has been here, Gregory Corso has been here, and of course Robert Mann a lot. I saw Ezra [Pound] last week in Venice when I visited Peggy Guggenheim— Summer [has] flown."

Recently released from St. Elizabeth's Hospital in Washington, Pound had returned to Italy with Olga Rudge. Caresse invited him to visit her at Roccasinibalda. Unlike the rambunctious, combative youth she had danced with in Paris, Pound at 72 was a tired old man with listless eyes and a shock of white hair. Having spent the last quarter of his life in confinement, he regarded his years at St. Elizabeth's as martyrdom.

The castle was cold and damp that summer, and Pound never could find a room warm enough to suit him, though he spent long sunny hours in the courtyard. Caresse wrote to Sam Rosenberg, another friend from the Washington years, that there were some days when "he [Pound] doesn't say a word, and hardly whispers 'yes' or 'no' in answer to direct questions. . . . His mind is alert, and I am sure he has a lot to say, but it would be better if he could write instead of speak. His mood swings were dramatic. By turns he was alert and energetic, despondent and apathetic."

Frances Steloff also was dismayed to see Pound's deteriorating condition when they met at Roccasinibalda that summer. She had known both Pound and Caresse for many years, as owner of the venerable Gotham Book Mart, home of the James Joyce Society and gathering place of the New York literati for two-thirds of a century.

Steloff often told an anecdote that epitomizes Caresse's generosity and genuine affection for female friends. This late in life, Caresse could not afford Paris designer dresses, but she was always well turned out in self-designed "costumes." When Steloff admired the gown she was wearing, Caresse exclaimed, "But you must have it! I'm sure we wear the same size."

"Oh, no," Steloff protested. "It is so becoming to you, dear Caresse."

Later that evening, without saying a word to Steloff, Caresse took "the dress off her back" and tucked it into the suitcase, where Steloff discovered it after she returned to New York.

Caresse was aware that her days at the Castello were "dwindling down to a precious few." She began to search for a philanthropist or institution to buy the castle and continue with her One World concept after she was gone. She again turned to Harry Moore to ask if Southern Illinois University might be interested.

"I am waiting with some impatience for the advent of [President] Delyte Morris," she wrote, "for it is very necessary that I make some arrangement about the castle before next season, and now castles in Italy seem to be at a premium. I see that Mr. Getty has just bought a lovely ruin not far from Rome. Anyway, I am in the market for an exciting university to share my beautiful Castello di Roccasinibalda."

Morris, who was planning to be in Europe that summer, promised to stop at the castle to report on the condition of the property. Caresse met him in Rome in her chauffeur-driven car. As they arrived at the gate, members of the household staff came down to meet them with the special sedan chair Bucky Fuller designed to carry the Principessa up the steep hill to the entrance. Doctors warned her not to climb even a short distance up the hill with the weakened condition of her heart.

By the time of Morris's visit, Caresse had doubled the asking price for the castle, so negotiations with SIU ended permanently. She reported to Moore:

> I was terribly put off by SIU's decision not to take the castle. . . . I had expected to be "in the chips" in 1967, and instead I find myself quite deep in bedrock and must start all over again to try to find a buyer for this year. . . .
>
> I find that during the time I waited for the answer from SIU, one of the art colleges who wanted to look it over last summer has landed elsewhere—but I know that I can make it work, once I get going again.

Despite her disappointment at the failure of the negotiations with SIU, she led an active and peripatetic life with many friends in New York that winter. Throughout the '60s, Caresse stayed with Helen

Simpson in a gracious old brownstone on the Upper East Side at 109 East 91st Street. She was never a paying guest, but there was an informal arrangement with Helen that whenever Caresse cabled she was coming, there was a room ready for her. Caresse would appear for extended stays with a case of wine or some other hostess treat. Simpson was, in those years, almost totally deaf, but her many friends communicated on a large notepad, and she enjoyed any number of guests at her bountiful table.

In October, Simpson wrote to ask Caresse "When will you and Robert appear? I suggest any day after Sunday, November 7, because Kerensky will have flown back to California where he is giving seminars at Stanford University, and the fifth floor 'Kerensky rooms' will suit Robert. . . ."

Among those who came to dinner at Simpson's and stayed on for months or even years was Alexander Kerensky, who succeeded Prince Lvov in 1917 as premier of Russia's provisional government before the Bolshevik Revolution exiled him. In February 1927—the tenth anniversary of the Revolution—Kerensky and his first wife Olga had arrived in New York Harbor on the S.S. *Olympic*, to be welcomed by Helen and her husband, Kenneth F. Simpson, then Republican candidate for New York's 17th Congressional District and Assistant U.S. Attorney. The Simpsons installed the Kerenskys in their home until they could cope on their own.

The friendship persisted throughout Kerensky's exile, with Helen long after Simpson's untimely death in 1941. For a number of years, Kerensky lived in a dacha on the New York-Connecticut border, then visited Australia with his second wife, Nell. When he returned to New York after Nell's death, he was only too happy to accept the everlastingly kind Helen's offer of accommodation in her fifth-floor apartment, where he would remain for the next two decades. An *éminence grise* of amorphous features topped by a crew-cut, Kerensky could be seen leaving a side entrance of the brownstone with "the quick, nervous step of a caged lion," disappearing inconspicuously among the passers-by on Madison Avenue. Caresse always enjoyed his "debonaire, monocled wit" when they met at table.

She wrote to Moore about other activities that winter. "I am lunching tomorrow with John Gordon, head of the Berg Collection of the NY Public Library—do you know him or it?" Bucky Fuller and Mike Lekakis were coming to dinner, "knitting up the loose ends of the Cyprus project." Kay Boyle would be in town on the 12th, but Caresse would miss her because she expected to fly back to Rome via London and Paris, with a stopover in Madrid to visit Polleen and

Lorraine before returning to Roloff Beny's flat on the Tiber. In May she would be in Roccasinibalda again.

Caresse continued to search for a prospective buyer for the Castello. "I have spent several legacies on living well and with excitement—now I still live well and with exciting ideas but there are no more legacies in view and I do not have money to carry on any plans for 'One World' here or elsewhere," she observed. Perhaps she was grasping at straws when she wrote to Dr. Boris Pregel, whom she met casually at Simpson's:

> You told me on our first meeting . . . that you could sell the castle for me and that you know more about me than I know myself. Therefore, among other things you must know that I have vast ideas and no wealth. I intend to live another 20 years and during that time I must find means to live as I plan to. One way would be to find a foundation that would back me with the intention to set up a school of restoring here in the castle . . . To set up and conduct such a school . . . I need 100,000 dollars a year. The castle I own, . . . and on my death the place could become the property of the donor or the school. . . . Lacking the school idea I would like to sell to some institution for 40,000 dollars a year for fifteen years. At the end of that time or on my death it would become the property of the institution (you must know my age too). The World Academy of Art and Science, which at present has no headquarters might be such an institution. . . .
>
> My own five-room apartment in one of the wings with private entrance I would keep for myself during my lifetime. . . . On my death, this too would revert to the institution or foundation that buys. It is well worth the 600,000 dollar investment. Can you sell it for me? . . . "The days dwindle down."

The World Academy of Art and Science was her next target. She wrote to its president, Dr. Boyko, asking if a date was set for a meeting to decide on the trusteeship of Roccasinibalda and ways to maintain it as a One World Center. If the Italian government granted the Castello extraterritoriality, the WAAS could proclaim its World Constitution from a pilot plot of earth in the center courtyard.

> Until the Castle becomes the seat of The World Acad-
> emy of Art and Science with the necessary steps taken

vis-à-vis the Italian Government I will continue to use and run it and pay the taxes, but once WAAS takes over I will expect taxes and maintenance to be the obligation of the Academy, leaving me one wing for tenure during my lifetime. . . . The property is ideally situated and its value is increasing yearly. It can be used for rather large conferences as well as giving ample living space to a resident body of from 20 to 30 fellows of the Academy. . . . For ten years the castle has flown the World Flag and the mondial ideas for which it stands have gained wide respect and acceptance. Please let me hear soon what you have decided. . . .

(Caresse closed all official letters at this time with: "Hopefully, faithfully.")

The next spring, Caresse's travel plans changed dramatically. She advised Harry Moore that she would not fly off to Europe on May 23 as intended. "I have been getting steadily worse in the heart department since last summer," she wrote. She had been to see the experts at the Mayo Clinic in Rochester, and after a three-day check-up, they advised that they were willing to operate with a new, experimental technique "if I care to take a chance." Again, she said "Yes!" to life. "I am very excited," she told Moore, "this could give me a new and *active* lease on life which I truly want. . . . now I am given this chance to feel fit to climb Mt. Parnassus again."

As a postscript she added, "Maybe I'll stop off for a few days' breather in your garden guest room on my way East from Minnesota." Her courageous spirit never considered—or refused to admit—that she might not return after the difficult, and at that time experimental, "open heart" surgery.

En route to Europe on the S.S. *Italia* after the operation, the irrepressible Caresse wrote to Moore from Gibraltar: "I am fine but have grown enormous—at least two inches 'round the waist, four 'round the chest! It's being able to breathe that's done it—I'm furious!!!" Surgical intervention increased Caresse's awareness of the passing of time—that her Thirty-Year-Plan was no nearer to completion. "I don't know enough, not anything really. 'Tis maddening to feel so ill-equipped to meet whatever time is left, and there is so little time for me." She drafted an agenda for a meeting of Humanists to discuss "the evolution of the individual in relation to the infinitude of the Cosmos, which summons him, and the earth, from which he has come. . . ." She posed other difficult metaphysical questions:

Where is man going and why? Will he find within his own nature a center of gravity to withstand the forces of an expanding universe? How can a finite mind deal with the infinite? What is the power within man that evolves his own consciousness? Where should man place himself . . . as a catalyst between a continuous eternity and never-ending force? as a force to withstand an expanding universe and to mobilize humanity as the perfect anchorage within time and space?

Despite the obscure language, there was no doubt about Caresse's seriousness of purpose when she invited an eclectic group of Humanists, including Julian Huxley, Lewis Mumford, Bertrand Russell, Arthur Toynbee, Robert Oppenheimer, Roger Baldwin, Norman Thomas, and Jean-Paul Sartre. (She did not forget her friends of long standing, Henry Miller, Kay Boyle, Anaïs Nin, and Charles Olson.)

Her recuperative powers were remarkable. Early the next year, she wrote to Foster Parmalee of the World Constitutional Convention:

> Your interesting and really flattering communication of February 28 reached me in Rome only a few days ago. I have been traveling around the Middle East, touching bases in Lebanon, Cyprus, Turkey and Greece, always with the One World idea in view.
>
> I am putting my mind and heart into your suggestion that I draw up a list of 100 persons of the world who might serve suitably in a top group for the World Government movement. I feel the young people are the ones that should back this development, and since there are so many who believe in it, it is through them, backed by "elder statesmen," that it can come about. I hope that by the 2nd session of the world convention in 1970 we can have an important list to present.
>
> Sorry I have been so out of touch but in the countries where I have been traveling the mail just did not go as fast as I did!

"Blessings on you and my affection for you is real," Parmalee replied in a handwritten message. . . .

> "The young people" are the goal of a new project in NYC, the National Teach-In for World Community, developed by the WCC, a local group stimulated by the Interlachen-Wolfach meeting last summer. Columbia

University in October is the first program. Clark has sponsored it, and another 50 professors have promised their sponsorship.

About Norman Cousins . . . he was president of UWF [United World Federalists] and is also President of the World Association of World Federalists. WAWF now has the able services of Andrew Clark, executive director. He *was* head of Canadian WF and works out of Canada with European office moved from The Hague to Copenhagen, where the Parliament is almost solid for W.G. Be sure you become a member and receive "The World Federalist" monthly or bimonthly. . . . Norman is *for* the *top group.*

Among other "top" people, Caresse wrote to Pope Paul VI in appreciation of his journey around the world in the cause of peace, expressing her own beliefs:

Your Holiness,
. . . I call myself a Christian Atheist believing in love as Christ did when He said, "Love Thy Neighbour as Thyself", and in St. Paul's appeal, "I come to you from all the world"; and I believe that the journeys Your Holiness has taken to Jerusalem and India have truly expressed a love for all mankind and a willingness to consider the value of other doctrines as well as the Roman Catholic faith.

I have never been able to accept the divinity of a *personal* God, which I believe man through vain desire and self-righteousness has framed in his own likeness. . . .

I do completely and objectively believe that Jesus Christ lived, and died the most perfect life ever known and I believe it is right to raise Mary, the Mother of Christ, to beatify and sanctify the Church. Mary was human and Jesus her Son was human, but by whose knowledge has God the Father ever existed? That is why I am a Christian Atheist and a Humanist as well. . . .

I . . . believe that the Humanities, and Humanism . . . may one day save the world through understanding and love, understanding of the mysteries and complex laws of the Cosmos and love of one's fellow men.

Helen Simpson reported to Caresse after the Pope's visit to New York that "even the weather rejoiced . . . a beautiful clear early autumn day, although rather windy. It was a great event. He should receive letters of thanks (such as you wrote) from all Catholics, Protestants, and Atheists. I only hope he gets back safely . . . there are so many crackpots who might take a shot at him."

During that winter, Caresse began to plan for a Threshold for Peace ceremony to be held in the courtyard of the Castello. First on her guest list were poets, no doubt inspired by the memory of Harry Crosby—Robert Lowell, Pablo Neruda, and the Italian poets Ungheretti, Montale, and Murillo. She originally planned to time the event to coincide with the opening of the Gian-Carlo Menotti Festival of Two Worlds at Spoleto on July 1, which would draw world press attention and outstanding artists and writers. In the end, she decided on a later date when the eyes of the world might focus solely on Roccasinibalda.

A galaxy of stars of the literary world gathered at Spoleto that summer—Pablo Neruda, Stephen Spender, Allen Tate, Ted Hughes, Lawrence Ferlinghetti, John Ashberry, Rafael Alberti, and the Russian exile, Yevtushenko. Fuller, who designed the "Spoletosphere" for theater and dance, appeared with Isamu Noguchi. O'Grady was there to organize the poetry reading for Menotti. Pound, who emerged from his self-imposed silence to give the first public reading since his return to Italy, inscribed a volume of poetry to Bucky: "Friend of the universe, bringer of happiness, liberator." Olson came with Caresse, folding his huge frame into the only transportation available, a Volkswagen "bug." (Together, Caresse and Olson were an odd couple; it appeared that Olson could hold the petite Caresse in the palm of one hand.) She lunched or dined almost daily with the Spoleto artists—at her happy, vibrant best in the company of creative minds.

Plans for the Threshold for Peace continued throughout the summer. The date was finally set, and invitations were dispatched to friends and colleagues around the world to rally at the castle.

CARESSE CROSBY
Citizen of the World
invites

to the inauguration of a "Threshold for Peace" at the Castle of Roccasinibalda, Province of Rieti, Italy. This mondial step will be symbolized by the placing of a marble plaque in the earth of the courtyard of the castle, inscribed with the words, LOVE, TRUTH, BEAUTY, JUSTICE, CHOICE. This round of earth, a man's span, will be ceded out of present ownership to the youth of the world, in the belief that man's future lies in the acceptance of a cosmos without frontiers and a globe freed from waste and from want, without barriers to individual expression or opportunity. This round of earth is to be safeguarded by the mondial rights of man, and bequeathed in perpetuity to humanity by humanity as a symbol of ONE WORLD.

Sunday, October 6, 1968.
3-7 P.M.

In Caresse's invitation to Fuller, she asked his help in petitioning the Italian government to make the castle plot extraterritorial. "You said you know who we might approach," she reminded.

She also asked Max Habicht of the WAAS to help with the legal work in setting up an autonomous territory. She regretted that she could not attend the Convention for World Government in Interlachen with Boyko, and concluded that

> for me, it is best to stay firm on my own land and hope that, as a gesture for world accord, Italy will give this territory autonomy, held in trust for the youth of the world. . . . There is nothing as strong as an idea whose time has come, but it must be given legs to walk with, and a base from which to expand. In fact, an eagle's nest from which to soar.

Roger Baldwin, president of the League for the Rights of Man, replied:

> Dear Caresse Crosby—Thanks for thinking of me with your invitation to a ceremony I will assist with my spirit. The world will catch up with you some day, unless we all perish from our follies first.

Responses arrived from many friends in far places. Irene Rice Pereira wrote from New York:

Caressima. . . . . dear Caressima;

I was so happy to get word; and, exultantly so; and Bless You, you are still on the path of the eternal. MAY THE ROUND OF EARTH TO BE DEDICATED ON OCTO- BER 6th 1968 POLARIZE THE EARTH WITH THE STARS —THE COSMIC REASON—AND MAGNI- TIZE [sic] ONE WORLD OF LOVE, TRUTH, BEAUTY, JUSTICE, CHOICE WITH THE ETERNAL AND UNDYING CONTINUITY OF MANKIND TOWARD HIS TRUE DESTINY OF EVER-EVOLVING GREATER, GRANDER AND MORE MAGNIFICENT FORMS OF HIMSELF. I SALUTE YOU MY DARLING CARESSE. YOU HAVE GONE FULL CIRCLE. And, your handwriting! I was so happy to see it—firm, fluid and as sure as Forever. Bless You Again.

Allen Ginsberg, representing the Beatniks, sent his regrets:

With you in word in spirit in Rieti but body gotta stay here and milk cow and goats on Upstate New York farm with Peter Orlovsky and poet friends. Gregory Corso was here a few weeks—sort of a poetry ashram small, in fact tiny, scale. Your idea of the meek young inheriting planet is happy. Good Chance, Bon luck with love, truth, beauty justice and choice also hare krishna, hare krishna, krishna, krishna, hare rama, hare rama, hare hare. You're always such a lovely idealist it's good cheer to hear your vibra- tions from wherever you are.

The Threshold for Peace ceremony took place as scheduled on a bright Sunday in early fall. The Castello flag—white with a blue circle indicating peace, with One World in the center—flew high above the "beak" of the Eagle, a signal that the Principessa was in residence. Many of the world figures she invited sent their regrets, but this did not diminish the high point of Caresse's eventful life, surrounded by friends in the central courtyard around a marble disc set in concrete, a permanent symbol of her efforts for peace—at least in this time and place. If the eyes of the world did not focus solely on Roccasinibalda, press coverage was widespread and favorable.

Among the critics of Caresse's activities, this citizen of Rieti took a skeptical view: "I acknowledge your ideas about peace in the world, that are perfectly like mine ones [sic] but I acknowledge also you are considered a good writer, but a quite funny person, and [your] ideas of impossible realization." Many others agreed with Sally Tate of New York, who wrote Caresse "how wonderful I thought all went on Sunday . . . how beautiful and happy you looked . . . and I feel sure that all went away rather more inspired than when they came."

"Time yapping at our heels."

—CARESSE

Chapter XVII
ALWAYS YES! CARESSE

In spring 1969, Caresse wrote to Helen Simpson from Rome that she had spent four and a half weeks in the Salvator Mundi International Hospital because "[the] doctors couldn't cure me of a devastating asthmatic bronchial condition."

Caresse already had outlived many friends of her youth, including Cole Porter. Of the creative people whose lives she had touched, she had lost Joyce, Lawrence, Hemingway, Cummings, Eero Saarinen, Marcel Duchamp, Jean Cocteau, William Carlos Williams, Tristan Tzara (Dada), Giacometti, Brancusi, and Grosz. Yet her sense of humor prevailed when she wrote to Matt Shermer in New York: "Don't worry about me any more. I am alive and kicking at the idea that I may not live to 2000 A.D., since the papers say today that by 2000 we will be practically immortal and lovemaking will go on forever."

Simpson reported the news from New York, that she was planning to be in Italy in the middle of July if convenient. She held "a sort of castle reunion" on 91st Street the night before. Bill Barker and George Stillwaggon ("with a whole bush of hair") were there, and both expected to visit the Castello that summer. George would be an art student at Positano, and Bill was "always a bit unpredictable." Lorraine de Mun was "looking *very* beautiful." She liked her new job at the Park Avenue branch of National City Bank with "big pay, she says," and was sharing an apartment on East 76th Street now with an English girl friend.

Kerensky was not entirely happy in his last years, as he found his increasing infirmities demeaning and was nearly blind. He had moved to an air-conditioned sublet on East End Avenue, and Elena Ivanoff, a former research assistant at Stanford, was "his eyes and ears, his nurse, his pride and his most devoted servant." (Robert Payne, Kerensky's biographer, called it an intricate and spiritual relationship.)

That summer in Roccasinibalda, Robert Mann was living down the hill in the former jail that had been converted first to a youth club and then to Mann's living quarters. He remained a loyal retainer and Caresse's contact with the villagers, as he spoke perfect Italian and could summon the men to do repairs, to lend a hand in times of practical problems or crises. Ruth and Steve Orkin, young teachers from the University of Nairobi, were "castle-keepers" that summer. (When the Orkins left, they wrote back nostalgically that "French and psychology are old hat, we hope to change our majors to castle-keeping.")

In the fall, Caresse returned to Beny's apartment on the banks of the Tiber. She urged Mann to join her, but he offered a counter-proposal. To avoid another winter in Rome, Caresse should take a comfortable flat in London to use as off-Rocca headquarters. She had many friends, her daughter and granddaughter were there, and

> the pace of life seems to me the only one for civilized people with any range of social and cultural appetites. God knows the weather there is no dream, but sunny climes and stimulating milieus don't seem very often to coincide. As I remember, you got through December last year without any undue twisting of the bronchial tubes. . . . Why don't you give it serious thought?

He ended the letter:

> How astonishing and touching to find quoted . . . a line from a poem I wrote to you years ago! It suddenly gave a kind of "permanence" (I hesitate to say

immortality) . . . one is struck by the patina which has aged in beauty, yet turned into something else, removed from the grasp of their creator forever.

Caresse agreed to spend a traditional Christmas in London with Polleen and her youngest granddaughter, Serena North. After taking all "Firsts" at Oxford, Serena was pursuing a medical degree. Charles Olson was invited to join them:

> Other members of the clan will be there.—Robert Mann and I have taken this splendid flat for one month, i.e. until Jan. 2 and are seeing all we can of London in thirty days. Robert has a flat in the village of Roccasinibalda and is a very tried and true friend. . . . I hear that your book has made a great name for you in England and as I am so beautifully presented to the reading public with Ezra [Pound] beside me I can't thank you enough for paying such a lovely tribute. I see a lot of Desmond O'Grady and we speak about you.

In her youth, she was as adept at expressing her finely-tuned emotions on the page as in the privacy of the bedroom. She took up her pen again to compose a verse for O'Grady on her 77th birthday:

> . . . give us time
> O Overlord of this your bestiary, our mating place
> give us time to work it out . . .
> A man with woman interlaced
> the WE.
>
> time was when time there was
> but not today
> We die a pressured death
> Between the first emitted squeal
> and final breath.
>
> And as we strain for latest news
> and circumvole [sic] the Globe a thousand ways
> between this morning and the next
>
> How can we touch our hands in quest?

Time yapping at our heels.

In reply, O'Grady wrote a moving tribute to his benefactor:

> Like me, you covet your every habit: the morning
> scribbling in bed, the fixed speed of the car, the ritual
> change for dinner—all those daily reassurances that mat-
> ter more than luxury or dull money. But one grand habit I
> admire and envy over all.
>
> For years now, watching you—taking the stairs, easy on
> my arm, toasting with the first glass at dinner, helping you
> into your coat after an evening out—I never cease to
> marvel and admire the sheer vitality of your interest in all
> people and in all things, your persistent refusal to be
> bored. Your heart has not grown old. . . .
>
> And when, like tonight, home again from the town, you
> have news in the mail of a friend's death in another
> country—a new addition to a sadly long list—the light in
> your eyes pauses in remembrance, and in reverence, and
> then you get on with being all that you have always been
> and are: most dignified, most youthful, and most gay.

Caresse again invited friends and colleagues to a "BE-IN" at the
Castle of Roccasinibalda during the first week of September 1969,

> in the central courtyard of this monumental stronghold,
> as a meeting place for Younger Citizens of the World,
> regardless of race, creed, colour, religion or ethnic dif-
> ference. You are invited to express new approaches to
> peace and your ideas to achieve One-World before it is No
> World. . . . We need the young in heart and limb, the
> strong in mind and spirit to give us guidelines, to turn the
> dreamers from their apathy, the greedy from their spoils,
> the mad from their wars.

"That last season together, we made serious plans," O'Grady
remembered. "I calculated possible courses and professors, on
working/writing holidays, who could teach at the Castle." Polleen
was mentioned often. Quite clearly Caresse wanted her daughter to
carry on the Creative Center after her death. It was extremely
important to her, but apparently Polleen wasn't interested.

*　*　*

At Christmas, as always, Caresse heard from absent friends throughout the world. Gerard, Lord Lymington, her devoted lover from rue de Lille days, communicated from Kenya:

> I am writing this last Christmas card from the farms up here. They are all being bought out by the Government in the New Year, and nearly 22 years of work, planning and building plus some achievement will be over. . . . I shall think wistfully that you have never seen these lovely hills and valleys. It is all rather melancholy, especially as the garden is looking so beautiful and the farms are fruitful and flourishing, and the cattle . . . the finest herd in Kenya. . . . I am trying to be objective. *"Les lauriers sont coupés nous n'irons plus aux bois."*

> I shall still be in Nairobi when with luck you can come and visit me. In the meantime, there is nobody I would rather write to in what should be a time of peace and good will toward men. You are one of the rare people who possess it. . . . I will be coming via Italy to see you in the summer. Keep well my darling wench. I loved you all the years and love you just as much now. God bless you.

She was making plans for the New Year with her usual enthusiasm, following up a number of projects, not the least of which was the grand plan for the World Man Center on Cyprus. She wrote to Zenon Rossides that she planned to leave for Beirut at the end of January. But on January 16, when Volume III of Anais's just-published *Diary* arrived on her doorstep, she wrote to her:

> I was terribly pleased with the way you treated me, with amaze and gaiety—a will-o'-the-wispish quality. . . . I envy you your ability to put your fingertip on the very nerve that controls a secret zone of the other's self. . . . You use words like golden needles of the Chinese acupuncturists . . . you heal or hurt by remote control.

She added prophetically: "I have such little stamina these days that I can't write more than a line or two without feeling exhausted." The possibility of the anticipated trip to Beirut actually happening seemed remote.

A Parisian fortune-teller once told Caresse that some day she would live in a castle and die at age 77. Both prophecies would come true. "She was aging more rapidly than any of us were aware," O'Grady remembered. "She was so joyful up to that last week. We had dinner together in Rome, and then the next day or so, suddenly she was in the hospital."

With a bronchial condition, complicated by the strain on an already weakened heart, Caresse lived with the constant threat of pneumonia. Even in the comparative comfort of Roloff Beny's apartment in winter, she had difficulty breathing. On a chill evening in mid-January, despite Robert Mann's admonishments, Caresse insisted on making an entrance in a thin cocktail gown. She was taken to Salvator Mundi that night, where she remained the following week with a tube of oxygen in her nose, making it difficult for her to speak. Mann suspected that by the end of the week she was too tired, too tired of living, to care.

Polleen was called to her mother's bedside, but did not arrive in time. "I was there. She sent for me," wrote O'Grady. "She died well. I must have looked sad. She smiled her big Caresse smile, then she went to sleep." Death came quietly during the night on January 24, 1970, when the tired heart simply stopped.

A wake was held in Rome at Roloff Beny's apartment, where Caresse haunted friends with her symbolic presence. She was toasted in pink champagne, her favorite libation. Peggy Guggenheim, who, like Caresse, "whirled through life in a kind of dream . . . [and] never quite realized what was happening," sat in a corner with a gloomy face, perhaps foreseeing her own death a year later.

During one of Caresse's earlier prolonged stays at Salvator Mundi, a Jewish psychologist suggested that they make tape recordings of her life story, so that he could better understand her psyche. She loved to be the center of attention, even at the end, and was quite amused by it all. When Malcolm Cowley edited the autobiography, he asked Caresse to "dig deeper into the motives and purposes of your actions." She replied with true understanding of her own character: "As for the ideas underlying the actions, . . I haven't the foggiest notion. . . . I am not introspective, nor do I ever judge motives, only actions. . . . I am 100 percent extrovert. . . . I can't describe . . ideas, only what we *did*."

"Vitally alive and interested, curious and aware to her last gasp, never bored in any company," O'Grady remembered Caresse in her last years. "She was a shrewd *giver*—she held nothing back if she had to give, asked nothing for herself except *dignity*. Caresse delighted in all forms of freedom, all demonstrations of love. She was a loving and lovable woman, a whole human being. She was trusting of humanity, anti-war and anti-apartheid—hers was the vibrancy of Humanism."

Harry Moore wrote an admiring obituary for the London Times, praising Caresse Crosby's many positive contributions to world peace and to the lives of artists and writers of her time. Back in New York, her friends gathered with Frances Steloff at the Gotham Book Mart for a memorial service on February 18, 1970. Buckminster Fuller was master of ceremonies. Steloff praised Caresse's joy in life, her gaiety and charm, for which she will be remembered, as well as her positive achievements. Kay Boyle, Henry Miller, and Anaïs Nin, who could not be present, sent tape recordings from California. Robert Snyder showed the evocative film of Roccasinibalda, with flashbacks of Caresse in other places with other companions from Salvador Dali to Bob Hope. "Always 'Yes!' Caresse"—the perfect epitaph.

NOTES

Prologue

i   "a pollen carrier": Nin, Diary III, p. 39.
ii   "*Caresse Crosby a l'invente le soutien-gorge*": PY, p. 294.
iv   "charge d'affaires of the heart of the world": Nin, *Diary VI*, p. 144.

Chapter I: The Passionate Years
(All quotations not attributed to other sources in this chapter are from PY.)

1   [Richard Peabody] drinking himself to oblivion: PY, p. 91-92; *see also* Eleanor Early, *Boston Globe*, SIU 140/62-6.
2   "a love affair should be as delicate and as swift as a modern pursuit plane": HC, "Aerodynamics of Flight," *Aphrodite in Flight* (Paris: Black Sun Press, 1930).
2   "metamorphose from boy into man": HC to Henrietta Crosby (Nov. 22, 1917), SIU 140/46-10.
2   "Most people die of a sort of creeping common sense": HC/SOS, SIU 140/40-1 (quoted from Oscar Wilde, *The Picture of Dorian Gray*, p. 385).
2   BUNNY CAN'T STAND ANOTHER DAY . . .: HC to CC (Aug. 30, 1922), SIU 140/42-10.
3   escapists from Puritan backgrounds: *see* Putnam, *Paris Was Our Mistress*; Cowley, *Exile's Return*.
3   Les Desenchantes . . . "Am I?": HC/SOS (Sept. 21, 1922), SIU 140/40-1.
4   "blessed and burdened by eccentric, wildly self-indulgent parents": PPD memoir, pp. 1-3.
5   "Good for the breasts": PY, p. 116; *See* Rogers, *Ladies Bountiful*, p. 6.
5   "*Over the top with Polly!!*": HC, loose pages from a diary, SIU 140/41-2; *see* Wolff, BS, p. 77.
7   "very comfortable, but not grand or grandiose": Wolff, interview with MacLeish, quoted in BS, p. 146.
7   "Upstairs, Downstairs" way of life: *see* PPD memoir, pp. 12-19.
7   one might meet Andr Gide: Wolff interview with Gerard Lymington, BS, p. 166.
7   "*Paris* is a bitch": McAlmon, *Being Geniuses Together*, p. 125.
8   "I assume that the idea of your writing poetry as a life's work is a *joke*. . . .": HC/SOS (Aug. 27, 1924), SIU 140/40-1.
8   "Perhaps it is: 'we intend . . .'": HC to Stephen Crosby, SIU 140/44-3.
8   "You must choose the art . . .": Proust to Walter Berry, quoted in PY, pp. 117-18.
9   "I'm so glad you chucked the Bank!": Berry to HC (Nov. 25, 1923), SIU 140/32-4.
9   "Uncle Jack is as *un*stimulating . . .": HC to Henrietta Crosby (Oct. 19, 1927), SIU 140/46-10.
9   to "put aside daily hours for work . . .": HC/SOS (Apr. 19, 1925), SIU 140/40-1.
10   "square, like a cube of Domino sugar": CC, "How It Began," introduction to *Bibliography of BSP* (Minkoff), p. ii.
10   "You and me at Etretat. . . .": HC to CC (1928), *see* Wolff, BS, photo facing p. 81.
10   "Mary . . . looking very pretty and younger than ever. Everyone adores her . . . I most of all": HC to Henrietta Crosby (Dec. 20, 1924), SIU 140/46-10.
10   "The next week we spent composing sonnets . . .": CC, "How It Began," p. ii.

Chapter II: Black Sun Press
(All quotations not attributed to other sources in this chapter are from PY.)

13   "It's like undressing in public": Mrs. Elizabeth Beal, p. 145.
13   "One Way Like the Path of a Star": CC, *Crosses of Gold*.
13   . . . a book that shows none of the pretentious gravity of the minor poet: *Poetry* (London, Sept. 1926), SIU 140/2-3.

13 "I shouldn't change a word . . .": Walter Berry, p. 222.
14 "I've never seen the distaste . . .": *see* Ford, *Published in Paris*, p. 183.
14 For you remember that the voyage . . .: CC, *Painted Shores*.
14 "I am very touched by your kind thought. . . .": Antonine Bourdelle to CC [tr. from the French] (Jan. 7, 1925), SIU 140/34-4.
14 Everything you write has . . .: Boyle to CC (Apr. 11, 1930), SIU 140/33-6.
15 "madder than hatters . . .": Boyle, "The Crosbys: An Afterword," *ICarbS*, III, 2, p. 119.
15 That very early morning . . .: *Ibid.*
15 "It was a litmus paper of his life, past and present": Ford, *Published in Paris*, p. 173.
16 . . . more of a means of blacking out . . .: Boyle, "The Crosbys: An Afterword," p. 123.
16 "Writing is not a game . . .": HC to Henrietta Crosby (Nov. 15, 1923), SIU 140/46-10.
16 "that small woman with the fierce courage of a hummingbird . . .": Boyle, *Stories* (Paris: Black Sun Press, 1929).
16 "Harry used to dart in . . .": Beach, *Shakespeare and Company*, p. 134-35.
17 "You're dumb as an oyster . . .": *see* McAlmon, *Being Geniuses Together*, p. 248.
17 "pranced about as the spirit of the jazz age . . .": McAlmon, p. 122.
18 The Black Sun Press writers . . .: CC, "How It Began," p. i.
18 "like a Delta dog . . .": HC to Henrietta Crosby (Jan. 7, 1927), SIU 140/46-10.
18 dining with the trend-setting Crosbys on American cuisine . . .: PPD memoir, p. 13.
19 "Val-Kulla": an etching by the Swedish artist Anders Zorn.
19 "Our One-ness is the color of a glass of red wine": HC/SOS (June 1929).
19 "Mama's Gypsy Lover": PPD memoir, p. 8.
19 "Caresse believes that woman . . .": HC/SOS (Apr. 15, 1928), SIU 140/40-1.
20 "anything she herself wanted . . .": Boyle, interview by Wolff, BS, p. 22.
20 I have been feeling very physical. . . .: HC to CC (June 25, 1929), SIU 140/43-1.
20 a Boston friend was shocked . . .: Wolff, BS, p. 146.
21 "At one o'clock, it was WILD . . .": *see* Wolff, BS, pp. 167-70, for description of the Quatre Arts Ball.
21 Polleen "came to know the servants well": PPD memoir, pp. 14-19.
23 "drink this, my Wretched Rat . . .": PPD memoir, pp. 12-13.
23 . . . stepfather's flirtations . . .: *Ibid.*
23 One evening, I was dressed . . .: PPD memoir, p. 3.
24 "He wrote the most beautiful love letters . . .": PPD memoir, p. 3.
24 "*plus emancipe*, plus independente . . .": Headmistress of Chalet Marie Jose to CC (Feb. 28, 1927), SIU 140/62-1.
25 "If I get to Paris . . .": Lindbergh, *see* Wiser, *The Crazy Years*, p. 187.
25 "My ears, which are unusually keen . . ."; "he looked boyish . . .": For CC's reportage of the Lindbergh arrival, *see* PY, p. 152.

Chapter III: Moulin du Soleil
(All quotations not attributed to other sources in this chapter are from PY.)

27 "Right now?" Armand asked: This story is apocryphal. For the facts behind the legend, *see* Wolff, BS, pp. 226-27. According to Wolff, the Crosbys rented the mill for 5,000 fr. (U.S. 200) *a year on a 20-year contract.*
27 "Our swimming pool was no larger than two postage stamps . . .": PPD memoir, pp. 22-23.
28 "to die at the right time": HC/SOS (July 6, 1928), SIU 140/40-1.
28 "Hart Crane here, and much drinking . . .": HC/SOS, SIU 140/40-1.
29 "M. Henri liked to eat snails . . .": PPD memoir, pp. 24-25.
29 "Hart, what thunder and fire . . .": HC to Crane (Mar. 1, 1929), SIU 140/36-5; *see also* Unterecker, *Voyager*, p. 586.
29 "the most inspiring novel . . .": HC/SOS (Feb. 10, 1928), SIU 140/40-1.
30 "My wife went to Florence . . .": Lawrence to HC (May 26, 1928), SIU 140/55-6.
30 "He is direct, I am indirect . . .": HC/SOS (Mar. 15, 1929), SIU 140/40-1.
30 "a glimpse of chaos . . .": Lawrence, intro. to *Chariot of the Sun* (Paris: Black Sun Press, 1931), pp. ii-iii.
30 "Harry was really so well . . .": see Moore, *Priest of Love*, p. 490.
31 "It's all so vivid to me . . .": Frieda Lawrence to CC, quoted in Moore, p. 469.

31   . . . weekend at the Mill . . .: PPD memoir, pp. 23-25.
31   "the new atrocities": see Unterecker, *Voyager*, p. 581.
31   "Mobs for luncheon . . .": HC/SOS (Feb. 3, 1929), SIU 140/40-1; *see also* Wolff, BS, p. 255.
31   "The top floor of the Mill . . .": PPD memoir, p. 25.
32   Opium was his drug of choice . . .: HC/SOS (Nov. 22, 1925), SIU 140/40-1.
32   ". . . a fairly 'normal' way of life . . .": PPD memoir, p. 25.
32   "A mixture of Surrealists . . .": Dali, quoted by Wolff, BS, p. 228.
32   Caresse collected titles . . .: *see* PPD memoir, p. 26; Wolff, p. 229.

Chapter IV: Lit de Mort

(All quotations not attributed to other sources in this chapter are from PY.)

33   ". . . married seven years . . .": HC/SOS, quoted in PY, p. 253.
33   "An *aeroplane*? Is Harry *really* tired of life?": Lawrence to CC (Nov. 1, 1929), SIU 140/55-6.
33   "The most simple Sun-death . . .": HC/SOS, SIU 140/40-1.
33   In the fall of 1929 . . .: see Wiser, *The Crazy Years*, pp. 227-28.
34   . . . another Princess cabled "Impatient!": Josephine Rotch Bigelow to HC (Nov. 19, 1929), SIU 140; see Wolff, BS, p. 10.
34   "I have invited our little seamstress . . .": HC, *Sleeping Together* (Paris: Black Sun Press, 1929).
35   "You will adore this room": CC to HC (Nov. 25, 1929), SIU 140/43-1.
35   "One is not in love . . .": HC, unpublished notebook, SIU 140; see also flyleaf of SOS, "*si ma dame mourroit je mourrois avec elle.*"
35   "I ponder death . . .": HC, unpublished notebook, SIU 140/41-3.
35   "I promise with the absolute Faith . . .": HC to CC (Dec. 25, 1921), SIU 140/42-9.
36   "pick a card": Malcolm Cowley interview, in Wolff, BS, p. 8. (CC preserved the ace of hearts, SIU 140/46-6.)
36   Fire Princess was known locally as a "strange wild girl who delighted in saying things to shock people": see Wolff, BS, p. 282.
38   "she was too uncertain of herself . . .": Boyle to Wolff (Jan. 23, 1973), quoted in BS, p. 299.
36   "It was madness, like cats in the night . . .": HC, unpublished notebook, SIU 140/41-3.
37   "This is the letter Josephine brought Harry . . .": see SIU 140/42-8 (also the two unpublished poems by Bigelow).
37   They discovered Harry Crosby . . .: *see* Wolff, BS, p. 9.
37   "I shall die within my Lady's arms . . .": HC, *Red Skeletons* (Paris: Black Sun Press, 1927).
38   "2 Boston/Dolls . . .": e.e. cummings, *Poems*, IX (1923-34).
38   "SUICIDE PACT EVIDENT . . .": Boston *Post* (Dec. 12, 1929). "CROSBY POEMS CLEW . . .": New York *Daily News* (Dec. 12, 1929).
38   "in spite of Harry's crazy ways . . .": PPD memoir, pp. 4-5.
39   "Harry Crosby willed himself to die . . .": CC to Olson (Jan. 20, 1950), SIU 140/61-1.
39   "Those of us who knew Harry . . .": MacLeish to Henrietta Crosby (Dec. 12, 1929), SIU 140/46-7.

Chapter V: Born to Myself

(This chapter is based on PY, corroborated by interviews and correspondence with Polly Peabody Drysdale and surviving members of the Jacob family and friends. Page numbers refer to PY.)

40   The name Jacob . . .: p. 18.
41   "Poor father never liked being a businessman": p. 69.
41   distinguished ancestors: p. 20.
41   "[mother's] belligerent and caustic spirit . . .": p. 21.
41   "I was the first child . . .": p. 14.
42   [East Island] cottage . . .: p. 15.
42   "Into my ears the waters poured . . .":

43   their first literary venture: pp. 44-46.
44   Cole Porter: p. 53.
44   Richard Peabody, p. 63.
45   "Idealists are all crackpots . . ." [father's death]: p. 69.
46   brassiere invented by CC: pp. 71-74.
47   marriage to Peabody: p. 75.
48   birth of son, Billy: p. 75.
48   at Peabody home in Mass.: p. 88.
49   birth of daughter, Polleen: p. 77.
49   army wife in South Carolina: pp. 84-87.

Chapter VI: Life After Harry

(All quotations not attributed to other sources in this chapter are from PY.)

53   "I was at boarding school when Harry died": PPD memoir, p. 3.
53   "I presumed she meant . . . Harry would have seduced me": PPD memoir, p. 4.
54   "You are meant to heartbreak people . . .": Crane to CC, SIU 140/36-5.
54   "Mama draped herself . . .": PPD memoir, p. 6.
55   "a death from excess vitality . . .": Pound, "Notes" to *The Torchbearer* (Paris: Black Sun Press, 1931), p. i.
55   [Pound] "In his loud checked trousers . . .": PPD memoir, p. 1.
55   "the list of Mama's lovers grew . . .": PPD memoir, p. 8.
56   "Will you be in Paris . . .": Lymington to CC (May 23, 1930), SIU 140/56-9.
56   "With my dearest love . . .": Lymington to CC (Dec. 1969), SIU 140/56-9.
56   "I don't know why he loved my mother . . .": PPD memoir, p. 9.
57   ". . . It's three o'clock . . .": Porel to CC (Aug. 3, 1930), SIU 140/64-3.
58   "the only place where you can see life and death . . .": see Cowley, *Think Back On Us*, p. 221.
59   "They say they have a big demand . . .": CC to Pound (Aug. 28, 1931), YaleU.
59   "Your wonderful and enthusiastic letter about bucking Tauchnitz . . .": CC to Pound (Sept. 20, 1931), YaleU.
59   "get hold of a public": see Ford, *Published in Paris*, p. 223.
60   "Do you remember that torrential day . . .": CC to Hemingway, PY, pp. 298-99.
60   "Yes, I was wise in leaving . . .": Porel to CC (1930), SIU 140/64-3.
61   "You have been a dear . . .": Porel to CC (Oct. 1930), SIU 140/64-3.
61   "She died without a bob": author interview with PPD, London, 1985.
61   "Caresse, you don't understand me . . .": Porel to CC (Oct. 1930), SIU 140/64-3.
62   "I have already written . . .": Porel to CC (Feb. 2, 1931), SIU 140/64-3.
62   "Just one week . . .": Porel to CC (Feb. 9, 1931), SIU 140/64-3.
63   [Jacques was] ". . . a *pic-assiette* . . .": PPD memoir, p. 11.
63   "*dans sa langue maternelle*": Porel to CC (Oct. 28, 1931), SIU 140/64-3.
63   "I have one more word to say . . .": Porel to CC (Nov. 1931), SIU 140/64-3.
64   "So your doctor says . . .": Porel to CC (1931), SIU 140/64-3.
64   "Consider how many years . . .": Boyle to CC, SIU 140/33-6; *see also* Ford, *Published in Paris*, p. 227.
64   "I find it discouraging . . .": CC to Boyle, SIU 140/33-6.
64   "had not one cent of working capital": *Ibid.*
65   "About CCE . . .": CC to Pound (1931), YaleU.
65   "Caresse Crosby, alone, is carrying on . . .": Leeds (London: UWS, April 1931).
66   "Mama's chauffeurs . . . often rebelled . . .": PPD memoir, p. 15.

Chapter VII: Hampton Manor

(All quotations not attributed to other sources in this chapter are from PY.)

69   "Green Hat Tree": refers to Michael Arlen's popular novel, *The Green Hat*, a thinly disguised portrait of Nancy Cunard.
69   some 433 shares of common stock: document dated Sept. 30, 1936, SIU 140/27-3.
70   "Bert dearest: You went away again . . .": CC to Young (1937), SIU 140/72-2.
70   A license had been applied for in September 1936: document in SIU 140/27-3.
71   Polleen never forgave her mother: see PPD memoir, p. 4.

71 "a very unpleasant scene . . .": PPD to CC, SIU 140/62-1.
71 "the wheat dust flew around her . . .": Nin, *Diary III*, p. 38.
71 "Henry Miller, originally of Brooklyn . . .": page from guest book, Hampton Manor (1937), SIU 140.
72 "Henry came to my Black Sun Press . . .": CC, narration of "Always Yes! Caresse" (Snyder film). For the true story of their meeting (at Crosby's East 53rd St. pied—terre in NY), *see* Nin, *Diary II*, pp. 54-56.
72 "he looked for all the world like a rosy-skinned Buddhist monk . . .": Nin, *Diary I*, p. 8.
72 [Dudley,] "penniless and nowhere to go": Nin, *Diary III*, p. 40.
72 (According to Henry, he was "gestating"): Miller, "Letter to Lafayette," *The Aircondi-tioned Nightmare*, p. 44.
73 "I am counting on you . . .": CC to Dali, SIU 140/46-13.
73 "Maybe with your help . . .": CC from Doubleday editor, SIU 140/46-13.
73 "Dali used to come down to the Mill . . .": CC, "Always Yes! Caresse."
73 a "Dream Ball": *see PY*, pp. 330-32, 382; "Always Yes! Caresse."
74 "that nut Dali": Miller to CC (July 27, 1968), SIU 140/58-5.
74 "We were not allowed to enter . . .": Nin, *Diary III*, p. 40.
74 [of Dali's moustache] — "I have a bigger one . . .": "Dali Reapproached, *The New Yorker* (Feb. 1963).
74 "He was so full of inventions . . .": Nin, *Diary III*, p. 40.
74 "with all of us sitting around her table . . .": Nin, *Diary III*, p. 39.
75 "Dear Caress: As when all things . . .": Young to CC, SIU 140/72-2.
76 "I'm on my way without you . . .": CC to Young (Aug. 13, 1940), SIU 140/72-2.
77 "Dear Caress: You were wrong . . .": Young to CC, SIU 140/72-2.
77 the meals were deadlocked by undercurrents of hostility: Nin, *Diary III*, p. 4.
77 "He has no need of wine . . .": Nin, *Diary I*, p. 8.
77 "When [Dali] finished working . . .": Miller, "Letter to Lafayette," p. 43.
77 "So far everything is fine . . .": Miller to CC (July 20, 1940), SIU 140/58-5.
78 ". . . distant roads looked wet . . .": Nin, *Diary III*, p. 42.
79 "At noon the next day . . .": Miller, "Letter to Lafayette," p. 43.
79 "I'm still tremendously afraid of grasshoppers . . .": "Dali Reapproached," *The New Yorker* (Feb. 1963).
79 "Bert arrived in the middle of the night . . .": Miller to CC (Sept. 1940), SIU 140/58-3.
80 The *Young v. Young* divorce was granted on grounds of "incompatibility": document in SIU 140/27-1.
80 [Dali's] "photo opportunity": *Life* (Apr. 7, 1941).

Chapter VIII: Wartime Washington
(All quotations not attributed to other sources in this chapter are from *WIW* I, III, IV, IX (SIU 140/5-1).)

87 Mary Jacob Crosby [Caresse] signed the lease: document (Jan. 1943), SIU 140/7-7.
88 "Dear Baby: I wish you had been here . . .": Porter to CC, SIU 140/64-5.
88 Lazzari delighted in telling people: author interview with Evelyn Lazzari (Washington), Oct. 1985.
89 Porter contributed . . .: author interview with Porter (Wainscott, NY), Aug. 1985.
89 "We want to bring the Museum of Modern Art's . . .": open letter from "The Directors," 1943, SIU 140/7-7.
90 "De Chirico's work is immortal . . .": program note to exhibit, Nov. 1943.
90 "Yesterday was a social and artistic triumph . . .": Porter to CC (Dec. 1943), SIU 140/64-5.
90 "In private life, Mrs. John Latham . . .": Washington *Times Herald* (Apr. 29, 1944).
91 "Till human voices wake us and we drown": Eliot, "The Love Song of J. Alfred Prufrock," *Collected Poems*, p. 7.
91 "Washington is in for . . .": *Art Digest* (Nov. 11, 1943), p. 15.
91 "Dear Baby: New York dealers . . .": Porter to CC, SIU 140/64-5.
92 "Dear Snooks: *Life* wants photos . . .": *Ibid.*
92 "Canada Lee came down . . .": Rodman, unpublished diary (Feb. 1, 1944).
93 "The motive-force . . .": Romare Bearden, program note to "The Passion of Christ" exhibit, May 1945.

93 Porter defrauded one of Crosby's black artists: Rodman, unpublished diary (July 7, 1945).

93 "This is to confirm our verbal agreement . . .": CC to Porter, SIU 140/64-5.

95 "I was very disturbed . . .": Wallace to Sam Rosenberg, in letter to author (Jan. 26, 1986).

95 According to one of her guests: author interview with Evelyn Lazzari (Washington), Oct. 1985.

96 Born Lionel Cornelius Canegata: *see Dictionary of American Negro Biography* (NY: Norton, 1982).

97 "I first heard his warm voice . . .": Nin, *Diary III*, p. 269.

98 Dearest my sweet: Everything in the world . . .": Lee to CC (Feb. 1941), SIU 140/56-2.

98 "Last week was one of our biggest . . .": Lee to CC, SIU 140/56-2.

98 "I just got your letter . . .": Lee to CC, SIU 140/56-2.

99 "Every day I say . . .": Lee to CC (Mar. 19, 1941), SIU 140/56-2.

99 "The quality of life . . .": *New York Times* (Dec. 26, 1943).

99 "an immensely touching and kind and gentle man . . .": *Zorina*, p. 296.

99 "warm, orange-toned voice . . .": Nin, *Diary III*, p. 106.

100 "Fortunately, I can write . . .": Lee to CC (July 11, 1946), SIU 140/56-2.

100 an "insult to the Catholic Church": see Chris Mathisen, *Washington Star* (Oct. 11, 1946).

101 "a man like St. Anthony . . .": Tanning, *Newsweek* (Sept. 30, 1946).

101 "You haven't seen such creatures . . .": Charles Yarbrough, *Washington Post* (Oct. 11, 1946).

101 "The silence for a poet . . .": David Rennick, "Pound: The Voice and the Silence," *Washington Post* (Oct. 30, 1985).

101 On a typical day . . . Eliot and Pound: *Ibid.*

102 "his eyes worried . . .": Charles Olson, quoted in Tytell, *Ezra Pound*, p. 292.

102 The exhibition notes for "The Private and Public Life of the Animals": privately printed, 1944.

103 "an opening door to a more enlightened, saner world . . .": press release (1945), SIU 140/7-6.

103 "I am putting wheels in motion . . .": open letter (June 15, 1945), SIU 140/7-6.

Chapter IX: Portfolio
(All quotations not attributed to other sources in this chapter are from *WIW* VI and VII (SIU 140/5-1).)

111 "Phoenix-like, the world emerges from the ashes": CC, "Full Armor of Light," Foreword to P-I.

111 "Caresse Crosby called me . . .": Rodman, unpublished diary (July 3, 1945).

112 "It is wonderful to hear . . .": Miller to CC (1945), SIU 140/58-3.

113 "In a wild crowd . . .": Harry T. Moore, "The Later Caresse Crosby," *D.C. Magazines*, p. 13.

114 "I have talked with Mrs. Shipley . . .": CC to MacLeish (May 21, 1945), SIU 140/7-2.

117 "The going is difficult . . .": CC to Moore (Oct. 10, 1945), SIU 140/59-2.

117 "I wrote you airmail . . .": Moore to CC (Oct. 3, 1945), SIU 140/59-2.

117 "Delighted to hear . . .": CC to Moore (Oct. 1945), SIU 140/59-2.

118 "You indicate that a trend-review . . .": Moore to CC (Oct. 16, 1945), SIU 140/59-2.

119 *Portfolio* was received in Paris. . .: CC to Miller (Jan. 14, 1946), SIU 140/58-3.

119 "I liked *Portfolio I* better . . .": Miller to CC, SIU 140/58-3.

120 "Please don't forget . . .": CC to Davenport, SIU 140/8-2.

120 "it expresses exactly how I feel . . .": *see* HC/SOS, SIU 140/40-1; paraphrase of Whitman's "Whoever You Are Holding Me Now in Hand," from *Leaves of Grass*, Library of America, p. 270.

121 "Last fall, Selden Rodman . . .": Rexroth to CC (May 22, 1946), SIU 140/66-2.

122 "The Rexroth business . . .": CC to Moore, SIU 140/59-2.

122 "Everything seems to have happened today . . .": Paccasi to CC, SIU 140/8-3.

124 *Mademoiselle* feature (Jan. 1947): SIU 140/8-4.

124 "Back again full of Italian news . . .": CC to Moore (Aug. 16, 1946), SIU 140/59-2.

124 "I am enclosing my check . . .": CC to Giovanelli, SIU 140/8-5.
125 "Dear Romie: We are sending you . . .": CC to Bearden (Oct. 19, 1946), SIU 140/31-9.
126 "Miller said, 'Prison is not the worst place . . . to write . . .'": Miller to CC, SIU 140/58-3.
126 "Remember Caresse? . . .": *Toledo Blade* (n.d. 1947), SIU 140/8-5.

Chapter X: Sun and Shadow
(All quotations not attributed to other sources in this chapter are from *WIW* VIII and XXVII (SIU 140/5-1).)

127 "In going to Greece . . .": "Modern Muse," a profile by Carley Dawson, SIU 140/8-6.
127 *Boston Herald* review: Lawrence Dame, SIU 140/8-6.
128 [Calamaris,] a "beautiful" young Greek poet: PY, p. 292.
130 "spiritual collaboration" with scientists: Robert Reinhold, *The New York Times* (Dec. 31, 1968), SIU 140/8-6.
131 Vlachos interview, *Kathimerini* (Athens: May 24, 1947), SIU 140/8-6.
133 "not only by his acknowledged eminence . . .": CC to members of the Stockholm Academy, SIU 140/67-9.
133 "Dear Aleko: After trials and tribulations . . .": CC to Alexander Xydis (Jan. 24, 1948), SIU 140/8-6.
134 "I am using the Greek translation . . .": CC to Derek Patmore (Jan. 15, 1948), SIU 140/8-6.
134 "Herewith is a copy of *Portfolio VI* . . .": CC to Bruce Blevin (Feb. 25, 1948), SIU 140/8-6.
135 "I have great confidence . . .": CC to Wagman (June 1946), SIU 140/8-6.
135 "After trials and tribulations *Portfolio VI* . . .": CC to Miller (Jan. 24, 1948), SIU 140/8-6.
135 "Never has so much . . .": CC to Wagman (June 1946), SIU 140/8-6.
135 "Whoever has worked with his hands . . .": "Modern Muse," a profile by Carley Dawson, SIU 140/8-6.
136 "I'm in a jam myself . . .": CC to Olson (Nov. 1946), UConn.
136 "Here are proofs of the text . . .": CC to Olson, UConn.
136 "I return the proofs . . .": Olson to CC (May 7, 1946), SIU 140/61-1.
136 "I regret to say *Portfolio* . . .": CC, form letter in reply to inquiries (Nov. 14, 1956), SIU 140/8-6.

Chapter XI: A Citizen of the World
(All quotations not attributed to other sources in this chapter are from *WIW* X and XIII (SIU 140/5-1).)

138 "dreamed of . . . a better world . . .": PY, p. 69.
138 "We have just survived a cycle . . .": J.C. and R.G. King, *Manifesto*, pp. 9-10.
139 "No one really understood . . .": Davis, *My Country*, pp. 17-19.
140 "Are you Garry Davis? . . .": Davis, p. 38.
140 "I am now official printer . . .": CC to Olson (Apr. 10, 1948), UConn.
141 "Norman Cousins . . . praised the World Citizens movement: *see* CC, "World Citizens," p. 2, SIU 140/10-2.
141 *Conseil de Solidarit*: *see* Davis, pp. 46-47.
141 the world press began to swing in Davis's favor: quotations from *Life, Harper's Magazine, The New Yorker; see* Davis, p. 49.
142 *Citta del Mondo*: Declaration of June 10, 1950, SIU 140/10-4.
142 "During the past two months . . .": CC to "Ella" [unknown], Washington (July 19, 1950), SIU 140/10-4.
142 "these men and women . . . I have visited . . .": open letter to "Dear Readers" (June 1950), SIU 140/10-4.

Chapter XII: Women Against War

144 "We who have known war . . .": HC/SOS (Feb. 1, 1925), SIU 140/40-1.
144 Roosevelt speech: April 1945.
145 "WE PRAY THAT THE NEW . . . BOMB . . .": CC to President Truman (1950), SIU 140/10-4.
145 "Now it's up to the *women*": address by Eleanor Roosevelt (1933).
145 "Until I reached fifty . . .": PY, p. 325.
145 "Stop, stop, for God's sake, stop! . . . The collision is just around the bend . . .": CC statement (Sept. 1950), SIU 140/10-4.
145 "In dreams begin responsibility. . . .": *The Poems of W.B. Yeats* (New York: Macmillan, 1983), p. 100.
146 "I think I have hit upon . . .": CC to Olson (July 1950), UConn.
146 "God help us, you're right. Love is the law . . .": Olson to CC (Aug. 4, 1950), UConn.
146 "I propose to form a World Association . . .": CC to Boyd-Orr, SIU 140/10-5.
147 "WOMEN OF AMERICA: Join me in my endeavor . . .": chain letter (Mar. 1950), SIU 140/10-4.
147 "I have chosen your name . . .": CC to Rozhneva, SIU 140/10-4.
148 "Your Majesty: You rejoiced the hearts . . .": CC to Queen Elizabeth II, SIU 140/10-4.
148 "Eleven Points for World Peace": draft of letter to Women of the World (July 1950), SIU 140/10-4.
148 . . . registered to lobby . . .: CC, "World Citizens," p. 3, SIU 140/10-2.
148 "Women neither need nor want protective legislation . . .": St. George, from *Washington Post* (1953), quoted in obituary (May 6, 1983).
149 "That's a grand idea . . ." (Bolton); "Anything I can do for Peace . . ." (Rogers): comments on the Peace Bond Bill, SIU 140/10-4.
149 "I appeal to you, Women of America . . .": CC, open letter (Jan. 2, 1950), SIU 140/10-4.
150 "The story of the Phoenix . . .": CC, handwritten statement (1951), SIU 140/10-6.
150 "Our representation in *our* government . . .": *Ibid.*
151 "Now we must succeed . . .": CC, Bulletin, World Center of Women's Organizations (Paris 1951), SIU 140/10-6.
151 women "in every walk of life . . .": CC, handwritten statement (1951), SIU 140/10-6.
151 height of '50s fashion: photo in *Rome Daily American* (ca. Feb. 1951), SIU 140/10-6.
152 "I have traveled to India . . .": CC to Dean Acheson (Dec. 1, 1951), SIU 140/11-1.

Chapter XIII: Dedication at Delphi

153 "I shall never forget my first sunrise at Delphi . . .": *WIW*, Prologue, SIU 140/5-1.
154 "No good, that land . . .": see Nin, *Diary VI*, p. 141.
154 She planned to build a marble Thesaurus: CC, press release (June 13, 1952), SIU 140/11-5.
155 "A new dawn is breaking! . . .": CC, open letter from Delphi (July 1952), SIU 140/11-6.
155 Telegrams . . . to the Big Four (draft on Gran' Bretagne letterhead): SIU 140/11-6.
155 "I plug away and cry 'shame' . . .": CC to Olson (Feb. 14, 1952), UConn.
156 "I have been working . . .": CC to Barr (Jan. 2, 1952), SIU 140/11-5.
156 "a lack of funds . . .": CC to Schonfield (Jan. 28, 1953), SIU 140/12-2.
157 "Are you going ahead with it, Mrs. Crosby?": see Nin, *Diary VI*, p. 142.
158 "We Citizens of the World . . .": CC, draft of address (May 24, 1953), SIU 140/12-2.
159 "I have a right to peaceful assembly . . .": see Nin, *Diary VI*, p. 143.
159 "You have requested this office to inform you of any decision . . .": Berge to CC (July 3, 1953), SIU 140/12-3.
159 "I firmly believe that the interference . . .": CC to Prokopiou (Nov. 10, 1953), SIU 140/12-3.
160 "This organization works for international peace . . .": English translation of *Eleptheros Logos* article (Dec. 1953), SIU 140/12-3.
161 "I will not be in Greece . . .": CC to Wadsworth (May 12, 1954), SIU 140/12-6.

Chapter XIV: World Man Center, Cyprus

162 "The world . . . stands on the brink . . .": CC to Makarios (Dec. 27, 1963), SIU 140/18-5.

162 In recent history: *see* Luke, *Cyprus.*

163 "The Archbishop would be known . . .": CC to Makarios (Dec. 27, 1963), SIU 140/18-5.

163 2,000 from her personal account: *see* CC to Rossides (July 8, 1969), SIU 140/18-5

164 "Very dear Caresse: This letter confirms . . .": Fuller to CC (Feb. 14, 1966), SIU 140/49-4.

165 a large, geodesic structure: Fuller to Rossides (June 1, 1966), SIU 140/49-4.

165 "Mr. Lekakis called me . . .": Fuller to CC (June 17, 1966), SIU 140/49-4.

166 "terribly distressed . . . about the abusive report . . .": CC to Fuller (June 23, 1966), SIU 140/49-4.

167 "I know that you have enthusiastic friends . . .": CC to Makarios (Apr. 22, 1966), SIU 140/18-5.

167 "I can't play at secret diplomacy . . .": CC to Fuller (June 23, 1966), SIU 140/49-4.

167 statement in the name of Makarios (July 7, 1966): SIU 140/18-5.

168 "You will guess that I am not completely happy . . .": CC to Fuller (Aug. 16, 1966), SIU 140/49-4.

168 "I have not heard from you since Beirut . . .": CC to Fuller (Aug. 30, 1966), SIU 140/49-4.

168 "I am confident that everything is in good shape . . .": Fuller to CC (Sept. 24, 1966), SUI 140/49-4.

169 "I actually own some land on Cyprus . . .": CC to Isely (Jan. 20,1967), SIU 140/17-1.

169 "Cyprus Plan of Action" (Jan. 20, 1967): SIU 140/17-1.

169 "World Man at this gateway . . .": form letter to artists on World Man Center letterhead (1967), SIU 140/17-1.

170 "Dear Picasso: You once wrote . . .": CC to Picasso (Mar. 29, 1967), SIU 140/17-1.

170 "Darling Gran: I am absolutely thrilled . . .": Lorraine de Mun to CC (Sept. 28, 1967), SIU 140/59-12.

171 "Rufus King is an excellent lawyer . . .": Fuller to Rossides (July 20, 1967), SIU 140/49-4.

171 "overjoyed by the reception of the Dome": Fuller to Gene Fowler (June 6, 1967), SIU 140/49-4.

171 "a three-quarter sphere . . .": Snyder, ed., *Buckminster Fuller*, p. 169.

172 "I have brought about the production of our own Taj Majal . . .": Fuller to Anne Fuller, quoted in Fowler letter (June 6, 1967).

172 "We must have a talk . . .": CC to Davis (Feb. 14, 1967), SIU 140/18-2.

172 "I have no further information . . .": McHale to CC (Sept. 28, 1967), SIU 140/17-2.

172 "many English promoters already have their eye on Kyrenia": CC to Fuller (Feb. 2, 1967) SIU 140/49-4.

172 "I am waiting here in Beirut . . .": CC to Rossides (Feb. 3, 1967), SIU 140/18-1.

173 "If I understood you correctly . . .": CC to Rossides (Feb. 23, 1967), SIU 140/18-1.

173 "I am not sure exactly what I promised . . .": Fistere to Isley (Mar. 24, 1967), SIU .140/17-1.

174 "I have nothing to report . . .": McHale to CC (May 9, 1967), SIU 140/17-5.

174 "WAAS's interest . . .": CC to Lekakis, SIU 140/56-3.

174 "I am not altogether convinced . . .": Lekakis to CC, SIU 140/56-3.

175 "Why not announce that *all* Cyprus . . .": CC to Rossides (Jan. 6, 1969), SIU 140/18-1.

175 the Greek Cypriot struggle: *see* Stephens, *Cyprus,* for overview.

175 "This World Man territory . . .": CC to Rossides, SIU 140/18-1.

175 "I still want to try . . . Kyrenia": CC to Fuller, SIU 140/49-3.

175 "On or about March 14 . . .": CC to Rossides (Feb. 19, 1969), SIU 140/18-2.

176 "Arthur Rimbaud, pote et gnie . . .": *see* Luke, *Cyprus,* pp. 171-72.

176 "Our trip back via Delphi . . .": CC to Mme. Stephanou, SIU 140/17-1.

176 "We can raise money . . .": CC to Rossides (Feb. 19, 1969), SIU 140/18-5.

177 "I have written to Bucky . . .": *Ibid.*

177 "The purpose of my visit . . .": CC to Makarios (May 8, 1969), SIU 140/18-5.

178 [Makarios was] "as polite and charming . . .": CC to Lekakis (Apr. 18, 1969), SIU 140/56-3.

178 "I think that perhaps the best solution . . .": CC to Rossides (July 8, 1969), SIU 140/18-5.
179 "[Rossides] asked me to reassure you . . .": Lekakis to CC (May 2, 1969), SIU 140/56-3.
179 "World Man has . . . been in my mind . . .": Rossides to CC (Sept. 27, 1969), SIU 140/18-5.
179 "The Cyprus potential is too important . . .": Fuller to CC (Sept. 19, 1969), SIU 140/49-4.
180 "It is comprehensive and philosophical . . .": CC to Fuller (Oct. 30, 1969), SIU 140/49-4.
181 "I may have spoken too strongly . . .": CC to Rossides (Jan. 7, 1970), SIU 140/18-5.
181 "My alternative is that I accept the few acres . . .": *Ibid.*

Chapter XV: The Principessa de Roccasinibalda
(All quotations not attributed to other sources in this chapter are from *WIW*, XIII (SIU 140/5-1).)

182 "This is my latest abode . . .": CC to Olson (Aug. 25, 1959), UConn.
182 "I knew that was where I had to live . . .": CC, narration to "Always Yes! Caresse" (Snyder, 1963).
182 Michelangelo's competitor, the great Baldasarre Peruzzi: for a history of the Castello, *see Cronologia Storica*, or Gualdi, *Il Castello*. . . .
183 "religiously made a bid for [Roccasinibalda] . . .": CC to Snyder (Aug. 1963), SIU 140/67-15. (The purchase price was 10 million lire, US *16,000 in 1959*.)
184 "like the shadow of a medieval nun": O'Grady to author (Jan. 5, 1989).
184 people on the dole: CC to "Ella" [unknown], Washington (July 19, 1950), SIU 140/10-5.
184 "If . . . packages could be directed here . . .": CC to Meyer, SIU 140/15-6.
184 "Crosby was 'poor gentility' . . .": O'Grady to author (Jan. 5, 1989).
185 An article in the *Daily American*: see Meyer to CC (Aug. 2, 1961), SIU 140/15-6.
185 "Valerie Marno": for CC's brief career and film test with Selznick, *see PY*, pp. 100-04.
185 Emlen Etting's surrealist epic: *see PY*, pp. 312-13.
185 Life at Roccasinibalda . . . "Cistercian/Benedictine . . .": O'Grady to author (Jan. 5, 1989).
186 Sy Kahn remembers: "A Personal Note," Devour the Fire, p. xxxiii.
187 "Women will soon rule the world . . .": Miller to CC (June 1960), SIU 140/58-3.
187 "charge d'affaires of the heart of the world . . .": Nin, Diary VI, p. 144.
188 Rice Pereira . . . came to the castle: see Hill and Brown, Pereira's Library, p. 16.
188 "Dear Ned: The very welcome extra dividend . . .": CC to Bigelow (Apr. 23, 1968), SIU 140/17-4.
189 [Bill Barker] "was looking . . .": CC, "Always Yes! Caresse."
189 "Stunned — frightful news . . .": Barker telegram to CC (Jan. 1955), SIU 140/31-5.
189 "Death by Asphyxiation": English translation of coroner's report (Paris), SIU 140/62-10; interview with Josette Spiero, New York, Oct. 1985.
189 blonde, and given to "drifting like pale smoke": Kahn to author (Jan. 16, 1989).
190 "The sophisticate today . . .": CC critique (Sept. 1963), SIU 140/31-5.
190 "to express the kind of special gratitude . . .": Mann to CC (Aug. 19, 1959), SIU 140/57-8.
190 "Robert Mann is here . . .": CC to Simpson (May 1960), SIU 140/67-12.
191 "It hinges on the fact that a tranquil life . . .": Mann to CC (May 17, 1960), SIU 140/57-8.
192 Corso, who drank too much: Kahn to author (Jan. 16, 1989).
192 "I loved my happy time with you . . .": Corso to CC (1960), SIU 140/34-10.
192 "What drove so many Americans . . .": *see* Longstreet, *We All Went to Paris*, p. 285.
192 "I see Gregory [Corso,] Peter [Orlovsky,] and . . .": Ginsberg to CC, SIU 140/49-12.
193 "to investigate the activities of one Jean Pierre LaFitte . . .": Paulson to CC (Aug. 18, 1961), SIU 140/15-7.
193 "Here with Caresse's sour wine . . .": *see* Longstreet, *We All Went to Paris*, p. 285.
193 "It was all very civilized . . .": O'Grady to author (Jan. 5, 1989).
194 "What a joy to hear . . .": Beny to CC (Jan. 18, 1960), SIU 140/32-2.
194 "There are gardens . . .": CC to Miller (Jan. 6, 1961), SIU 140/58-3.

195 "It is difficult for me to be despondent . . .": CC to Miller (May 1, 1961), SIU 140/58-3.
195 Black Sun Press papers: see Kahn, "A Personal Note," *Devour the Fire*, p. xxxii.
196 "brilliantly successful . . .": Moore, "The Later Caresse Crosby," *D.C. Magazines*, p. 14.
196 "I am full of gratitude . . .": CC to Moore (Apr. 19, 1953), Beatrice Moore collection, Carbondale, IL.
196 "You may hear from Professor Sy Kahn . . .": CC to Moore (Nov. 1963), Beatrice Moore collection.
196 skepticism about SIU: see Moore, "The Later Caresse Crosby," *D.C. Magazines*, p. 14.
196 "The [Southern Illinois] University . . .": CC to Moore (Aug. 5, 1963), Beatrice Moore collection.
197 "I intended to write you . . .": CC to Olson, UConn.
197 "Well, he was a poet . . .": CC, quoted by Sy Kahn to author (Jan. 16, 1989).

Chapter XVI: A Threshold for Peace
(CC/Harry T. Moore correspondence is from the private collection of Beatrice Moore.)

198 October 1963 visit to Carbondale: see Moore, "The Later Caresse Crosby," *D.C. Magazines*, p. 14.
198 "traveling alone is more and more difficult . . .": CC to Moore (Mar. 27, 1963).
199 "Why not Rome and Rocca? . . .": CC to Moore (May 3, 1963).
199 "Sy Kahn has been here . . .": CC to Moore (Sept. 12, 1963).
199 "he [Pound] doesn't say a word . . .": CC to Rosenberg (Sept. 12, 1963), SIU 140/66-8.
199 Steloff anecdote: author interview (New York, Oct. 1984).
200 "I am waiting with some impatience . . .": CC to Moore (Mar. 28, 1966).
200 "I was put off by SIU's decision . . .": CC to Moore (Jan. 1, 1967).
201 Helen Simpson's brownstone: interview with Helen-Louise Simpson Seggerman (New York, Oct. 1987).
201 "When will you and Robert appear?": Simpson to CC (Oct. 4, 1965), SIU 140/67-12.
201 Kerensky at Simpson's: see Abraham, *Alexander Kerensky*, ch. 18.
201 "I am lunching tomorrow . . .": CC to Moore (Nov. 4, 1966).
202 "You told me on our first meeting . . .": CC to Pregel (July 15, 1968), SIU 140/17-5.
202 "Until the Castle becomes . . .": CC to Boyko (Feb. 15, 1969), SIU 140/18-2.
203 "I have been getting steadily worse . . .": CC to Moore (May 16, 1965).
203 "I am fine but have grown enormous . . .": CC to Moore (Sept. 14, 1965).
203 "I don't know enough . . .": CC to Moore (n.d.).
203 "agenda for a meeting of Humanists . . .": CC, handwritten memo, SIU 140/15-5.
204 "Your interesting and really flattering communication . . .": CC to Parmalee (Apr. 16, 1969), SIU 140/18-2.
204 "Blessings on you . . .": Parmalee to CC (May 18, 1969), SIU 140/18-2.
205 "Your Holiness, . . . I call myself . . .": CC to Pope Paul VI (Apr. 26, 1965), SIU 140/16-5.
206 "even the weather rejoiced . . .": Simpson to CC (Oct. 4, 1965), SIU 140/67-12.
206 "Threshold for Peace": typescript of "Organizational Program," SIU 140/17-4.
206 A galaxy of stars . . . at Spoleto: O'Grady letter to author (Jan. 5, 1989); author interview with Priscilla Morgan (New York, Nov. 1988).
206 Pound emerged from his self-imposed silence: see Snyder, ed., *Buckminster Fuller*, p. 167.
206 "CARESSE CROSBY, Citizen of the World" (invitation to Threshold for Peace ceremony), SIU 140/7-6.
207 "You said you know . . .": CC to Fuller (Aug. 30, 1968), SIU 140/49-4.
207 "Dear Caresse Crosby, — . . . The world will catch up with you . . .": Baldwin to CC (Sept. 19, 1968), SIU 140/17-6.
208 "Caressima . . . . . dear Caressima; I was so happy . . .": Rice Pereira to CC (Sept. 12, 1968), SIU 140/17-6.
208 "With you in word . . .": Ginsberg to CC (Sept. 24, 1968), SIU 140/49-12.
208 "I acknowledge your ideas . . .": Dott. Tristano Cabrini to CC (Oct. 15, 1968), SIU 140/17-6.

209 "how wonderful I thought all went on Sunday . . .": Tate to CC (Oct. 1968), SIU 140/17-6.

Chapter XVII: Always Yes! Caresse

210 "[the] doctors couldn't cure me . . .": CC to Simpson (June 21, 1969), SIU 140/67-12.
210 "a sort of castle reunion . . .": Simpson to CC (July 11, 1969), SIU 140/67-12.
211 Kerensky's last years: see Abraham, *Alexander Kerensky*, p. 381.
211 "French and psychology are old hat . . .": Ruth and Steve Orkin to CC (Sept. 10, 1969), SIU 140/18-2.
212 "the pace of life . . .": Mann to CC, SIU 140/57-8.
212 "Other members of the clan . . .": CC to Olson (Dec. 6, 1968), UConn.
212 "give us time/O Overlord . . .": unpublished poem by CC (Apr. 20, 1968), SIU 140/60-12.
213 "Like me, you covet your every habit . . .": O'Grady to CC (May 18, 1969), SIU 140/60-12.
213 Invitation to BE-IN (June 9, 1969): SIU 140/18-2.
213 "That last season together . . .": O'Grady to author (Jan. 5, 1989).
214 "I am writing this last Christmas card . . .": Lymington to CC (Dec. 15, 1969), SIU 140/56-9.
214 "I was terribly pleased . . .": CC to Nin (Jan. 15, 1970), NYPL, Berg.
215 A Parisian fortune-teller: Kahn, "A Personal Note," p. xxxii.
215 "She was aging more rapidly than any of us were aware . . .": O'Grady to author (Jan. 5, 1989).
215 "entrance" in a thin cocktail gown: author interview with Mann (Rome, July 1985).
215 "I was there . . .": O'Grady to author (Jan. 5, 1989).
215 A wake was held in Rome at Roloff Beny's apartment: author interview with Brian Swann (Bennington, VT, July 1988).
215 a Jewish psychologist: author interview with Mann (Rome, July 1985).
215 "dig deeper into the motives . . .": Cowley to CC (Dec. 14, 1949), SIU 140/36-4.
215 "As for the ideas underlying the actions . . .": CC to Cowley (Nov. 19, 1949), SIU 140/36-4.
215 "Vitally alive . . .": O'Grady to author (Jan. 5, 1989).
216 Caresse Crosby obituary, Harry T. Moore, *The Times* (London), Jan. 24, 1970.
216 Memorial service at Gotham Book Mart: interview with Steloff (New York, Oct. 1985); see also Moore, "The Later Caresse Crosby," *D.C. Magazines*, p. 14.

BIBLIOGRAPHY

The Caresse Crosby Collection in the Morris Library, Southern Illinois University at Carbondale (SIU 140) has the largest body of material relating to both Crosbys (72 boxes, 172 freestanding volumes, and seven packages). It includes the personal correspondence and assorted memorabilia, the Crosbys' efforts at poetry and prose, plus a large collection of prints, drawings, and photographs, as noted, "generally in excellent condition despite several trans-Atlantic crossings, storage in an Italian castle, and numerous exhibitions." In addition, the Caresse Crosby Collection includes a preliminary draft of an unpublished sequel to the autobiography, the correspondence, and press releases relating to Crosby's role as political activist from 1948 to her death in 1970.

Primary Sources:
  Poetry by Caresse Crosby:
Crosses of Gold (Paris, Albert Messein, 1925).
Graven Images (Boston, Houghton Mifflin, 1926).
Painted Shores (Paris, Editions Narcisse, 1927).

Impossible Melodies (Paris, Editions Narcisse, 1928).
Poems for Harry Crosby (Paris, Black Sun Press, 1931).

  Portfolio:
P-I (Washington, Black Sun Press, August 1945).
P-II (Paris, Black Sun Press, December 1945).
P-III (Washington, Black Sun Press, Spring 1946).
P-IV (Rome, Black Sun Press, 1946).
P-V (Paris, Black Sun Press, Spring 1947).
P-VI (Washington, Black Sun Press, Spring 1948).

Other primary sources, with their abbreviations:

PY	Crosby, Caresse. *The Passionate Years*. New York: Dial, 1953, reprint ed., Ecco Press, 1979.
WIW	Crosby, Caresse. *Who in the World?* (unpublished sequel to PY), SIU 140/5-1.
HC/SOS	Crosby, Harry. *Shadows of the Sun*. Paris, Black Sun Press, 1928.
PPD	Drysdale, Polleen Peabody, unpublished memoir. (Collection of the author.)

BBSP   Minkoff, George Robert. A *Bibliography of the Black Sun Press*, with an introduction by Caresse Crosby, "How It Began." Great Neck, NY: printed by Minkoff, 1970.

AYC   Snyder, Robert, ed. Always Yes! Caresse, narration to documentary film of CC at Roccasinibalda. Pacific Palisades, CA: Masters and Masterworks, 1963.

Also of primary importance, a biography:

BS   Wolff, Geoffrey, *Black Sun: The Brief Transit and Violent Eclipse of Harry Crosby.* New York: Random House, 1976.

Other library resources:

UConn   University of Connecticut, Storrs (correspondence of Charles Olson with CC).

YaleU   Beinecke Library, Yale University, New Haven, Conn. (correspondence of Ezra Pound with CC).

NYPL   Berg Collection, New York Public Library.

BU   John Hay Library, Brown University (Harris Collection). (Catalog of the Black Sun Press, ed. Millicent Bell.)

Secondary sources:

Abraham, Richard. *Alexander Kerensky: First Love of the Revolution.* New York: Columbia University Press, 1987.

Arlen, Michael J. *The Green Hat.* New York: Doran, 1924.

Beach, Sylvia. *Shakespeare and Company.* New York: Harcourt, Brace and World, 1959.

Benstock, Shari. *Women of the Left Bank: Paris, 1900-1940.* Austin: University of Texas Press, 1986.

Boyle, Kay. *My Next Bride.* New York: Harcourt, Brace & Co., 1934.

Breton, Andre. *Mad Love,* tr. Mary Ann Caws. Lincoln, NE: University of Nebraska Press, 1987.

Carpenter, Humphrey. *Geniuses Together: American Writers in Paris in the 1920s.* New York: Houghton Mifflin, 1988.

————. *A Serious Character: The Life of Ezra Pound.* New York: Houghton Mifflin, 1988.

Chisholm, Anne. *Nancy Cunard.* New York: Alfred A. Knopf, 1979.

Cowley, Malcolm. *Exiles Return.* New York: Viking, 1956.

————. *A Second Flowering: Works and Days of the Lost Generation.* New York: Viking, 1973.

————. *Think Back On Us: A Contemporary Chronicle of the 1930s.* Carbondale, IL: Southern Illinois University Press, 1967.

Crane, Hart. *The Bridge, A Poem.* (limited ed.) Paris: Black Sun Press, 1930.

Davis, Garry. *My Country Is the World*. Washington, D.C.: published by the author, 1961.

Donnelly, Honoria Murphy, with Richard N. Billings. *Sara and Gerald: Villa America and After*. New York: Times Books, 1982.

Durrell, Lawrence. *Bitter Lemons*. New York: E.P. Dutton, 1959.

Fitch, Noel Riley. *Sylvia Beach and the Lost Generation: A Literary History of Paris in the Twenties and Thirties*. New York: W.W. Norton, 1983.

Ford, Hugh, ed. *Published in Paris: American and British Writers, Printers, and Publishers in Paris, 1920-1939*. New York: Macmillan, 1975.

————. *Four Lives in Paris*. San Francisco: North Point Press, 1987. (Kay Boyle, pp. 137-225.)

Givner, Joan. *Katharine Anne Porter: A Life*. New York: Simon and Schuster, 1982.

Hardwick, Elizabeth. *Seduction and Betrayal*. New York: Random House, 1974.

Hill, Martha, and John L. Brown. *Irene Rice Pereira's Library: A Metaphysical Journey*. Washington, D.C.: National Museum of Women in the Arts, 1988.

Kahn, Sy M. *Devour the Fire: Selected Poems of Harry Crosby*. Berkeley, CA: Two Windows Press, 1983.

Kenner, Hugh, *Bucky*. New York: William Morrow, 1973.

Kert, Bernice, *The Hemingway Women*. New York: W.W. Norton, 1983.

King, J.C. and R.G. *Manifesto for Individual Secession Into a World Community*. Paris: Black Sun Press, 1948.

Kromer, Tom. *Waiting for Nothing and Other Writings*, ed. by Arthur D. Casciato and James L. West II. Augusta, GA: University of Georgia Press, 1986.

Longstreet, Stephen. *We All Went to Paris: Americans in the City of Light, 1776-1971*. New York: Macmillan, 1972.

Luke, Sir Harry. *Cyprus: A Portrait and Appreciation*. 2nd rev. ed. London: George G. Harrap, 1964.

McAlmon, Robert. *Being Geniuses Together, 1920-1930*. Rev. ed., with supplementary chapters by Kay Boyle. New York: Doubleday, 1968.

McMillan, Dougald. *Transition: The History of a Literary Era*. New York: George Braziller, 1976.

Mellow, James R. *Charmed Circle: Gertrude Stein and Company*. New York: Avon Books, 1974.

Miller, Henry. *The Airconditioned Nightmare*. New York: New Directions, 1970.

Moore, Harry T. *The Priest of Love: A Life of D.H. Lawrence*. Carbondale, IL: Southern Illinois University Press, 1974.

Nin, Anaïs. *The Diary of Anaïs Nin*, ed. with an introduction by Gunther Stuhlmann. [Vol. I (1931-34); Vol. II (1934-39), Vol. III, 1939-1944); Vol. VI (1955-66).] New York: Harcourt, Brace, Jovanovich.

Olson, Charles. *The Maximus Poems*, ed. by George F. Butterick. Berkeley, CA: University of California Press, 1983.

Putnam, Samuel. *Paris Was Our Mistress: Memoirs of a Lost and Found Generation.* New York: Viking, 1947.

Rogers, W.G. Ladies Bountiful: A Colorful Gallery of Patrons of the Arts. New York: Harcourt, Brace, Jovanovich, 1968.

Secrest, Meryle. *Salvador Dali, A Biography.* New York: E.P. Dutton, 1986.

Shinkman, Elizabeth Benn, ed. *So Little Disillusion: An American Correspondent in Paris and London.* Washington, D.C.: EPM, 1983.

Snyder, Robert, ed. *Buckminster Fuller: Autobiographical Monologue/Scenario.* New York: St. Martin's, 1980.

Spanier, Sandra W. *Kay Boyle: Artist and Activist.* Carbondale, IL: Southern Illinois University Press, 1986.

Stephens, Robert. *Cyprus: A Place of Arms.* New York: Praeger, 1966.

Tompkins, Calvin. *Living Well Is the Best Revenge.* New York: Viking, 1971.

Tytell, John. *Ezra Pound: The Solitary Volcano.* New York: Doubleday, 1987.

Unterecker, John. *Voyager: A Life of Hart Crane.* New York: Farrar, Straus & Giroux, 1969.

Weld, Jacqueline Bograd. *Peggy, the Wayward Guggenheim.* New York: E.P. Dutton, 1986.

Wescott, Glenway. *Goodbye, Wisconsin.* New York: Harper & Brothers, 1928.

Wilson, Edmund. *The Twenties,* with an introduction by Leon Edel. New York: Farrar, Straus & Giroux, 1975.

Wiser, William. *The Crazy Years: Paris in the Twenties.* New York: Atheneum, 1983.

Zorina, Vera. *Zorina.* New York: Farrar, Straus & Giroux, 1986.

Journals, Magazines, and Newspapers

Bell, Millicent, ed. *Black Sun Press, 1927-Present,* a catalog. Providence, R.I.: Brown University, 1961.

Boyle, Kay. "The Crosbys: An Afterword." *ICarbS**, Vol. III, No. 2 (Spring-Summer 1977).

Black Sun Press, a catalog prepared by Shelley Cox. Carbondale, IL: Friends of the Morris Library, Southern Illinois University. Supplement to ICarbS, Vol. III, No. 2.

Cronologica Storica del Castello e Feudo di Rocca Sinibalda. Introduzione per il Visitatore. Rieti, Italy, 1983.

Cohen, Jean Lawlor. "The Old Guard: Washington Artists in the 1940s." *Museum and Arts.* Washington, May-June 1988.

"Dali Reapproached." In "Talk of the Town," *The New Yorker.* 1963.

Germain, Edward B. "Harry Crosby, His Death, His Diaries." *ICarbS,* Vol. III, No. 2.

"Gotham Book Mart." Introduction by Kathleen Morgan in Special Issue of *Journal of Modern Literature,* Vol. IV, No. 4. Philadelphia: Temple University, April 1975.

Gualdi, Luigi (Ispettore Onorario dei Monumenti). *Il Castello di Roccasinibalda*. Rome, Italy: no date.

Hill, Martha, and John L. Brown. *Irene Rice Pereira's Library: A Metaphysical Journey*. Washington, D.C.: National Museum of Women in the Arts, 1988.

Kahn, Sy M. "Hart Crane and Harry Crosby: A Transit of Poets." *Journal of Modern Literature*, Vol. I. Philadelphia: Temple University, 1970.

Leeds, William. "Profile of Caresse Crosby." Paris, France: UWS, 1931.

"Life Calls on Salvador Dali." *Life* magazine, April 7, 1941.

Moore, Harry T. "The Later Caresse Crosby: Her Answer Remained 'Yes!'" D.C. *Magazines: A Literary Retrospective*, ed. Richard Peabody. Washington, D.C.: Paycock Press, 1982.

Rouse, William. "Hampton Manor." *Virginia Gazette* (Richmond), April 1941.

Stuhlmann, Gunther, ed. "Years of Friendship: Correspondence With Caresse Crosby, 1941-1970." *Anas Nin: An International Journal*, Vol. II, 1984.

*(National Union Catalog symbol for the Morris Library, SIU).

INDEX